K

Books of Merit

VIRTUAL CLEARCUT

OR, THE WAY THINGS ARE IN MY HOMETOWN

OR, THE WAY THINGS ARE

IN MY HOMETOWN

VIRTUAL
CLEARCUT

BRIAN
FAWCETT

Thomas Allen Publishers
Toronto

National Library of Canada Cataloguing in Publication

Fawcett, Brian, 1944–
Virtual clearcut : or the way things are in my hometown / Brian Fawcett.

ISBN 0-88762-122-8

1. Prince George (B.C.)—Social conditions.
2. Prince George (B.C.)—Economic conditions.
3. Globalization—Social aspects—British Columbia—Prince George.
4. Quality of life—British Columbia—Prince George.
5. Globalization—Social aspects—Case studies.
6. Clearcutting—British Columbia—Bowron River Valley.
7. Prince George (B.C.)—History.
I. Title.

HN110.P74F38 2003   971.1'82   C2003-900117-2

Editor: Patrick Crean/Michael Holmes
Jacket and text design: Gordon Robertson

Published by Thomas Allen Publishers,
a division of Thomas Allen & Son Limited,
145 Front Street East, Suite 209,
Toronto, Ontario M5A 1E3 Canada

www.thomas-allen.com

At Thomas Allen Publishers we are working with suppliers and
printers to reduce our use of paper produced from ancient forests.
This book is one step towards that goal. It has been printed on 100%
ancient forest–free paper (100% post-consumer recycled), processed
chlorine- and acid-free and supplied by New Leaf Paper; it has been
printed with vegetable-based inks by Friesens.

ONTARIO ARTS COUNCIL
CONSEIL DES ARTS DE L'ONTARIO

The publisher gratefully acknowledges the support of
the Ontario Arts Council for its publishing program.

We acknowledge the Government of Ontario through the
Ontario Media Development Corporation's Ontario Book Initiative.

07 06 05 04 03   1 2 3 4 5

Printed and bound in Canada

To the memory of Bill Morris (1926–2001)
citizen, friend,
connoisseur of life's slapstick

All trees of noblest kind for sight, smell, taste
And all amid them stood the Tree of Life,
High, eminent, blooming ambrosial fruit
Of vegetable gold. And next to life
Our death, the Tree of Knowledge, grew fast by,
Knowledge of good bought dear by knowing ill.

—JOHN MILTON, *Paradise Lost*, Book IV, 144–149

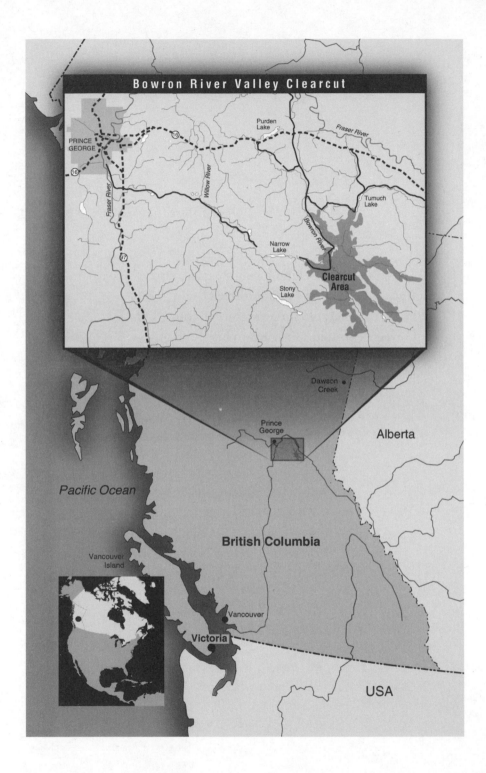

Bowron River Valley Clearcut

CONTENTS

xiii   *Acknowledgements*

xv   *Preface*

1   Paradise, 1990

77   Alexander Mackenzie's Supermarket, 1993

157   The Buddy System, 1996

215   Elm Trees, 2001

ACKNOWLEDGEMENTS

Too many people have provided help to name on a single page, so I'll confine it to those who provided information or read parts of the manuscript at various stages. In Prince George, Ken Bernsohn, Bev Christensen, John Harris, Vivien Lougheed, Barry McKinnon, Kent Sedgwick, Paul Strickland, Bill Walsh. Elsewhere, Leanna Crouch, Slobodan Drakulic, Max Fawcett, Rolf Maurer, Stan Persky, and Don White.

The other indispensables came from Graziano Marchese of Dooneys Café in Toronto (for the good coffee and the office space); Patrick Crean and Michael Holmes for their editorial acumen; and Hartlea Fawcett for the sheer fun she's brought to my life.

I have tried my damndest to secure the facts in this book. Doing so has served to convince me that there is no such thing as non-fiction, but that the effort to reach it is among the sacred projects of human intelligence.

PREFACE

In the Bowron River valley of northern British Columbia there is a clearcut so large that in the early 1980s, orbiting astronauts were able to see it during the daylight hours. Foresters in Northern B.C. claimed that, along with the Great Wall of China, it was the only human alteration of the planet that could be distinguished. What they saw was the 20th century's largest contiguous forestry clearcut, larger than any in the Amazon or the former Soviet Union.

I first heard about this clearcut from smiling officials of the B.C. Forest Service in their Prince George offices. It was five years after the cutting ended and shortly after tree-planters finished setting millions of tiny spruce and lodgepole pine seedlings in the gravelly soil of the valley. Prince George, a city that calls itself the hub of North Central British Columbia when it isn't crowing about being the Western White Spruce Capital of the World, sits about 60 kilometres northwest of the clearcut at the juncture of the Fraser and Nechako rivers.

The Forest Service officials who told me the story were proud professionals, and *very* proud that this clearcut was in their jurisdiction. That they'd helped to create something so large and unique was, to them, a profound accomplishment. In their calculation of large and unique clearcuts, the Forest Service officials weren't counting the clearcuts we now call North Africa and the Tigris-Euphrates basin of Iran and Iraq—but never mind that. By the time I left their office that day, this book had become inevitable. I'd been given a glimpse of the way things are, and I knew that, sooner or later, I'd have to try to understand why a clearcut as large as theirs could be invisible to everyone except astronauts and a few local forestry bureaucrats whose impossible job was to flatten and protect the forests of British Columbia all at once. What I didn't recognize that day was that I was staring down the newly minted version of the Global Village, a phenomenon that has alternately fascinated and disturbed me since I first encountered Marshall McLuhan's blue-eyed enthusiasms while I was in university in the late 1960s.

Not *every* effect of the Global Village has turned out to be pernicious. From the promised enhancement of communications, we've gotten the Internet, which may, one day, offer more than cheap pornography and a rebirth of mail-order shopping. It has already provided me with the luxury of being able to see the view from City Hall in Prince George any time of the day or night. I can go home now any time I wish, at least electronically. The WebCam overlooks what was once one of the city's two prime commercial thoroughfares. Today it is tree-lined, sort of, and generally deserted. (The Web site address, if you're curious, is www.city.pg.bc.ca/pages/webcam.html)

But most of the things the Global Village promised us have not been delivered. Along with all those irritating hand-held personal communications devices—cell phones, pagers, and Palm Pilots—that enable us to supervise one another and our money better while we're smashing up our cars and filling our brains with magnetic-field tumours, we got the unpredicted atomization of television. The generically scripted, one-way flow of information from a handful of powerful and remote networks 25 years ago has become a flood of generically scripted and looped programming from hundreds of channels—almost wholly controlled by a handful of powerful media conglomerates that dwarf the old networks in size, influence, and remoteness. Most of the new programming invites viewers to register opinions about their favourite programs, but meaningful interactivity—the kind that doesn't involve calling a 1-800 number and giving them your credit card number—remains as distant as the far side of the moon.

The improvements to participatory democracy McLuhan predicted haven't had much more positive substance than the changes to television. They've been made fatuous as governments give up their powers to multilateral trade agreements designed to ensure corporations full access to our smallest markets and political processes on terms more favourable to the corporate bottom line than to individual citizens. Canada can no longer protect either its culture or its business community if it means restricting the privileges of corporate CEOs and their shareholders based in New York City, or Paris, or Tokyo—or the far side of the moon. And places like Prince George get less protection than most.

The Global Village's recent shift in focus from culture and communications toward economics and the marketplace as the governing medium for human interaction has fostered the emergence of a darker identity that has come to be called globalization. "The central fact of globalization," as defined by American philosopher Richard Rorty, "is that the economic situation of the citizens of a nation state has passed beyond the control of the laws of that state. . . . We now have a global overclass which makes all the major economic decisions, and makes them in entire independence of the legislatures, and . . . of the will of the voters, of any given country." That phenomenon, and what it has done to Prince George, is the underlying subtext of this book.

As with most hinterland communities, the inventory of Prince George's recent cultural exports isn't a very long one. Along with its trees—shipped out mostly in the form of 2x4 structure wood and wood pulp for making paper—a few gory murders have gotten into television's burgeoning tabloid apparatus, and a 4-foot-11 pornography princess named Marilyn Star became an international story when one of her stockbroker boyfriends got charged with insider trading because he was feeding her stock tips for sexual favours. More recently, a foot-in-mouth federal cabinet minister claimed that the Prince George chapter of the Ku Klux Klan was burning crosses on people's lawns. The city doesn't have a Ku Klux Klan chapter, just a slightly larger-than-normal load of bigots, social opportunists, and loudmouths, none of whom burn crosses. The cabinet minister eventually lost her job when an onslaught of convincing evidence made it clear that she'd had her head in the clouds—or in a rather less lofty location.

Readers have the right to know who I am, and what gives me the licence to write a book about something no one but astronauts could see. I was born in Prince George. I was raised and received my elementary and high school education there. To this day, when people ask me where I'm from, I say, without hesitation, that I'm from Prince George, B.C. It has never occurred to me to tie my identity or my fate to any other place even though I've lived elsewhere for 35 years. Every book I've written has been informed by Prince George, and most have been written in direct or indirect defence of it, if not of the human behaviours and technological practices that have made it the city it has become.

I have a couple of additional qualifications. I spent most of two years in the B.C. Forest Service while I was in my early twenties, and I was an urban planner in Greater Vancouver for more than a decade after that. Thus, I could begin with a fundamental if antiquated grasp of forestry, and some understanding about how governments make (or don't make) decisions.

While I was trying to do urban planning I learned the value of researching issues and ideas without letting ideology screw up my selection of what is factual and true and what isn't—which is to say, I learned to do more than merely find the answers to the ostensible questions being asked. I learned to uncover what official paths of inquiry characteristically ignore or misrepresent. Planning also gave me my first glimpses of the stinking underbelly of the information revolution, where the sleek engines of hyper-management inflate production and improve managerial control and comfort without improving the quality of life. I learned how more and "better" data has made contemporary life more stupid and chicken-hearted than is safe, and that its well-propagandized positive effects we can somehow never quite feel in our bones or take to the bank.

Despite all this—or maybe because of it—I don't have a conventional right–left ideological mission to fulfill, and no political prejudices I need to impose. Readers who prefer devotional views on the treatment of forests can easily obtain them. In British Columbia, corporate-funded agencies provide abundant propaganda to convince us that all is well and that everyone can keep doing what has been done for the past century, except with more profits for remotely head-quartered corporations and fewer employed workers.

If you're devoted to the environmentalist view, that'll be slightly harder to locate, but not by much. Most environmentalists in British Columbia have their hearts in the right place—insofar as they're not operating from personal self-interest and are trying to address basic questions about how people ought to live and how we ought to treat the planet we're living on. Unfortunately, in their enforced need to respond to the demands of corporate-owned media addicted to pictorial novelty, they're too often engaged in trying to save some spectacularly moss-enfurled morsel of old-growth forest that just happens to be within a helicopter ride of Vancouver's major television stations. They find it hard to get to places as remote as the Bowron River valley. Over the years I've noticed that both the corporations and the environmentalists tend to engage in offering answers to questions nobody has really asked, like, "Shall we log it all?" or "Should we stop all logging?"

I won't attempt an exhaustive quantification of the effects the clearcut has had on the natural communities that surround it, nor will I statisfy the clearcut's effect on the human communities nearby. Either task will quickly become mired in ideologically tainted facts. What I can and will do is offer one person's story about what happened to a city in the great, green forests of the Canadian north. I will definitely have some comments to make about current forestry practice and about the specifics of clearcutting, but my primary concern will be with the fracturing of home and other earnable values that is among the little-publicized effects of globalization. In this book, I am most interested in—and concerned about the fate of—the people who live and work in and around the forests. They're the people I was raised among, and I like and respect them. They don't have many slick answers, and they have far too few questions about why things have gone wrong, maybe because they're trying to hold onto their jobs and otherwise keep their faces out of the financial muck.

If I'm partisan against globalization and its negative effects, it isn't merely because I grew up in Prince George and canoed in the Bowron River valley. It is because I can't see how globalization serves local interests there or other places like it, and because globalization has made it impossible for either the town or the river valley to get fair treatment—or even the time of day—from governments and their regulators, much less corporations and their shareholders. Such places don't do much better with the environmentalists and urbanists whose societal role is to oppose the indifference of governments and the belligerent single-mindedness of corporations.

This is also, accidentally but unapologetically, a book about men. I have tried to depict what they think and how they act in the world, as boys, friends, husbands, and as workers, bosses, technologists, or as critics and apologists of globalization—even, occasionally, as reasonable adults and citizens. Again, I take no recognizably partisan stance except to assume that men are human individuals and capable of goodwill when they are provided with adequate information and the means to act responsibly. One of my findings is that globalization is making these essentials to the practice of just humanity very hard for any individual, of any gender, to achieve.

Readers may notice that I have made no effort to speak to politicians as part of my research, and have spoken only rarely to their bureaucrats. As a former bureaucrat, I have come to believe that our political representatives almost never understand the way things are, and that their paid officials have the job of keeping them—and often themselves—as carefully ignorant as possible. The few politicians who, while in power, do catch a glimpse of how things are being done, and why, are never willing to be candid about it, even in their memoirs. Thus I have gone directly to the ground level, even though the ground in the Bowron River valley was destroyed before I arrived, and the ground in Prince George was experiencing, and continues to experience, something worse than mere destruction.

It took 12 years to write this. For most of the first five or six years, I thought I was after a single story: the right—or true—facts that would expose the contingent manipulations of public understanding, along with the self-deceptions by which people see themselves and their lives, not just in the relative backwater I was focused on, but more generally. But to impose a polemical narrative would have been a fool's errand, one that would merely pit my hysterical word and my anecdotal evidence against that of a thousand other partisans, all likewise convinced of the absolute virtue of their world view. That led me to present four portraits of ground level set in 1990, 1993, 1996, and 2001, each with a fallible narrator trying to uncloak the way things are in his or her cynical, oppressed, and dynamically joyful complexity.

Just one narrative value remained stable from start to finish: my determination to make this book understandable to two distinct and often different audiences. One audience is the citizens of North Central British Columbia, the people I grew up among, people I was determined not to misrepresent or to humiliate. The other audience is that larger but less tangible one, national and international, of unaffiliated readers and citizens of goodwill. I believe many of these readers have an instinct similar to the one I have: that the cultural and economic changes brought about by globalization, always presented as inevitable and inexorable, might be something quite different—the stupid trajectory of ill-conceived theoretical mechanisms that will degrade the quality of life for the overwhelming majority of those whose lives fall under their influence.

VIRTUAL CLEARCUT

OR, THE WAY THINGS ARE IN MY HOMETOWN

PARADISE, 1990

1

The boundary of paradise appears suddenly, 70 kilometres from Prince George, British Columbia. It is the summer of 1990. A hot, August mid-afternoon haze mirages bears and moose onto the shimmering pavement, and I'm behind the wheel of a steel-grey, 10-year-old Mazda 626 heading west on the Yellowhead Highway. A blond 11-year-old boy named Max perches on the passenger seat next to me, humming some popular tune that's stuck in his head. He's my son.

To be precise, the boundary marker is a freshly logged forest. This isn't a shock to my senses—or to my sensibilities. But the logging I've seen in recent years has been on television: ominous panoramas of steep coastal mountainsides cleared of trees down to the water's edge. Panorama clearcuts make good television clips, but they're typical of the medium's preference for spectacle over detail. They offer none of the gory specifics of what has been taken or what remains when masses of trees are cut down and removed to make lumber or wood chips for pulp mills. The television spectacles anger some people enough that they send a cheque to Greenpeace, but they render most of us too numb and helpless to do anything except go with the flow, which translates into supporting the job-giving corporations—and consuming more wood-based product because there don't seem to be any reasonable alternatives.

Another thing. It isn't until I'm well into the clearcut that I realize I've been repressing the recognition that nearly all the surrounding hills along this highway have been logged. Every 5 or 10 kilometres, green Forest Service billboards have announced that this isn't really the after-effect of logging. These are "New Forests." The billboards even provide the year that replanting was completed and the forests became new: 1973, 1975, 1979. But they aren't quite the splendid moments in the general renovation of the world the Forest Service advertises. Nearly all of the logging along this road preceded the building of the highway. If it hadn't, there'd be a narrow strip of uncut trees between the road and the clearcuts, and you'd be looking at what would appear to be virgin forests, wall-to-wall and unsullied by the hand of commerce.

In case you're still not quite onto how unusual this is, let me explain. It is rare to find clearcutting that comes right down to the edges of major B.C. highways. Even on Highway 97, the north–south highway into Prince George, you have to peer into the distance to see logging, even though pretty well all the usable timber in a 30-kilometre radius of the highway has been taken. For decades now, the common practice has been to leave strips of trees to obscure the extent of the cutting. For aesthetic reasons, so to speak.

I've always understood, sort of, the logic behind this, and so do most people who live in the B.C. interior. It involves a weird grade of Lenny Bruce common sense, and it goes something like this: First, if you're screwing around, it's never smart to flaunt it. Ergo, you screen the cut areas from view, and even insiders will forget what you've done, and no one else will notice what you're up to just now. Second, when you're caught red-handed while doing something loathsome, you can sometimes get yourself out of it by claiming that what you're really doing is wholesome and public-spirited. That's what King Gilgamesh did 5,000 years ago in what is now treeless Iraq when he claimed that he and his friend Enkidu killed the monster Humbaba to protect the people of Uruk. What they were *really* doing was logging the cedars of the sacred groves because they wanted to build a bigger palace for themselves.

Only recently have the deeper implications of these industrial aesthetics begun to register—like, for instance, what they imply about our governments' understanding of their responsibility to tell citizens the truth. A cynic would suggest that aesthetics are designed to deceive people. But cynicism doesn't look far enough on this one. Life has changed so profoundly in northern B.C. over the past 30 years that no one is clear who the "people" are any more. If you're on the money-making side of the forest industry, it's usually a derisory term for anyone who isn't smart enough to take a profit from the forests. These days, that's most of us—and in particular, the people who live and work in Prince George, B.C.

Now, logging isn't pretty, not ever. But if something isn't being crammed down my throat, I'm like most people—prepared to spare myself the gory details. And why not? A clearcut is ugly from near or far. Worse than that, it is dull. There's nothing to see or hear inside it because the trees have been removed, and that makes the sightlines a monotone of nothingness, even up close. The wildlife has fled, and the game fish have either suffocated or moved elsewhere because the waterways are fouled with logging debris or gill-clogging runoff. About the only thing that doesn't disappear from a clearcut are the mosquitoes and blackflies. And they're not much fun to spend an afternoon with.

This clearcut is very fresh. Judging from the green of the debris and the yellow-orange of the shattered scrubs and stumps, the fallers couldn't have finished their work more than 10 days ago. And from the fresh rubble along the gravel haul-road, the trucks are still taking out trees.

"Have you seen logging this close up?" I ask Max, who has stopped humming and is gazing out at the passing desolation with a look on his face halfway between bemusement and horror.

"Oh sure," he answers. Then he stops and corrects himself. "No. Just on television. This," he admits, "is realer. It's pretty gross."

I pull the car over to the side of the road and wonder aloud if this might be part of the big clearcut in the Bowron River valley I'd been hearing about.

"Where's the Bowering River?" he asks.

"Bowron," I correct. "It's up ahead a ways. It used to be a very beautiful valley, full of trees and fish and wild game."

I launch into the story about how a couple of Forest Service cruising crews I'd been part of in the early 1960s tried to canoe the Bowron. The trip, I tell him, was a failure, and a nearly lethal disaster: we'd started with four canoes, eight young guys, but within the first few kilometres a submerged snag had drummed a huge hole in the bottom of one canoe, and a second had broken apart while we were trying to cross a log-jam a few more kilometres downstream. We'd been about to quit when we found a badly scraped but perfectly sound third canoe on the far side of that same jam. We took this piece of good luck as an omen, and struggled on through another 25 kilometres of river over the next two days. We should have quit while we were ahead. When we did, the three canoes that remained were so battered they'd never be usable on a white-water river again.

We'd chosen the Bowron to canoe because we'd heard it was wild, supposedly the wildest river in the northern interior of B.C. outside of James Creek and the McGregor River over on the north side of the Fraser. I'd seen the lower reaches of the McGregor in person and had sensibly advised we take a pass on it. I was also familiar with a bit of history associated with it. A few miles upstream on James Creek, the waterway was so rough that it nearly put an end to Alexander Mackenzie when he came through from the Arctic Divide in 1793. Since I wasn't an explorer and it wasn't the late 18th century, I had, along with my Forest Service friends, the option of choosing which river to run, and of chickening out when the going got too rough.

That's what we'd done when the Bowron got too nasty, and there was no shame attached to it. We were Forest Service, and we knew that fools in the bush die. We weren't fools, but we had made a serious mistake: the three-year-old air photos we used to plan the trip had proved useless because the log-jams and riffles moved and changed with every flood season. The Bowron, we conceded, was like those rivers to the north: *too* wild. Still, we were glad we'd made the attempt. The Bowron was as pretty a river as any of us had been on, and I wasn't surprised when, a few years later, the government turned its headwaters into a major provincial park.

After 10 days on the road with me, Max is rolling his eyes by the time I finish the story.

"Never mind about the olden days," he says, not quite joking. "What do you know about this stuff here?"

Max is my main reason for making this trip to Prince George. He's on the doorstep of childhood's glory year—still open-minded and fresh-eyed, but as capable physically as an adult. We're on his summer holiday, and mine, too. We've been on the road just long enough to have developed routines—and one or two irritabilities.

We've already made stops in the Okanagan to visit his grandparents, and after that, my older brother Ron in Kamloops. From there we'd driven up to Edmonton through the Yellowhead Pass to visit friends before heading west again for the part of the trip I've been looking forward to: Prince George. It's my chance to show him where I lived when I was his age, and a little of how I lived. In the next year or two, adolescence is going to capture him, and to him I'll become an adult and in many ways The Enemy. It could be 20 years before he'll listen to anything else I tell him.

I'm not looking forward to it, but I'm not about to kid myself. It's the way things are. Childhood's sunny openness evaporates, and from behind it, the fogs of adolescence roll in, supplanting sweet certainty and security with unlocated desires, peer pressure, and cynicism. About the only thing that helps a kid navigate the fog is being able to read what's etched on the pillars that hold up the sky while he—or she—is a child. As Max's father I am, whether either of us wants it that way, one of the pillars.

A generation ago, my own father had been monumentally imposing. But from where I stood, he didn't rest on any part of the earth—except my toes—that I understood or wanted to inhabit. As I saw it then, he was an old-fashioned don't-give-me-any-crap authoritarian whose rigid life-philosophy always seemed to be talked up so far in front of his actions that idea and action rarely connected. By the time I reached adolescence and was awash in the cloudy hostilities of my hormones, I'd decided that the separation between his ideas and his actions was his—and his entire generation's—shield against The Truth, which was a substance to which I quite naturally thought I had an exclusive grasp. I wasn't about to have anything to do with my father's philosophies or his practicalities. And my father, busy making his fortune, had no time to explain himself. He was a busy man who believed sons were meant to listen and obey, and he simply couldn't understand why I wouldn't do either.

I was deep into my thirties before I was able to look closely enough at his ways of thinking and acting to understand that they were different and much more complicated than I'd thought, and that, for the world he'd had to face, they'd constituted a workable and decently intelligent response.

He made his life from a consuming ambition to get rich, but his ambition didn't dim a paternalistic protectiveness toward his family —which is to say, he wanted wealth for the right reasons. In retrospect, I can see that he possessed a common sense lodged in a strong understanding of the mechanical details of getting things done, and was hamstrung by a private xenophobia that sometimes looked like bigotry but usually went generously benign when he got to know people. It wasn't until he was 78, when I spent two weeks exploring his childhood haunts with him, that I finally understood enough about him to recognize that his life had deep and specific roots, and that he was a human being with forgivable failings and strengths I wasn't mindlessly obliged to disagree with or compete against. We'd wasted 20 years fighting over things that weren't convertible on either side.

I don't want history to repeat itself. When it comes time for Max to make his private judgment about who and what I am, I want him to have some better data to work with, something other than the Oedipal trap that mandates sons to fight their fathers and deny their works. I'm hoping that what Max learns on this trip will give him a base that isn't just father-versus-son, and dogs pissing on fire hydrants. That way, maybe his decisions about how to assert his identity will be wiser and more generous than mine have been.

I have another, more selfish motive. I've been hoping that if I see my hometown through the eyes of my son, it will reduce the muddiness of my own memories, rid them of a few of the rancid sentimentalities that a quarter century of absence has annealed to them. For too many years, I've lived with contradictory views of North Central British Columbia. It is time to reconcile them.

The view I'm most attached to is of the spare beauty and vigour of the boreal landscape: a country of rivers and mountains without end; of chilly, dappled lakes and streams filled with trout and salmon; of abundant moose, bear, and wolves gracing pristine forest meadows; of tall skies, beneath which the hillsides are choked with wild lupines, daisies, and Indian paintbrush. Surrounding and infusing all of this are the dense forests local people call, with a deliberate lack of poetry, "the bush."

Calling the boreal forest "the bush" is an acknowledgement that the things you become intimate with in a northern forest aren't centuries-old tree-giants looming over bunny-festooned carpets of green moss, with trout-filled brooks ambling gently by as if it were some dope-smoker's sentimental greeting card. The northern forests are pine and spruce and balsam firs, none of them very large or picturesque. The forest flora runs from alder to thickets of Russian willow to spine-laden devil's club that grows two metres or more high. And don't forget the clouds of blood-sucking bugs, because they won't forget about you. Only crazy people and loggers willingly enter the northern boreal forest. Sensible people live on the margins, in the clearings, along the streams, rivers, and lakes. They screen their porches and windows when they can afford to, and they buy insect repellent in gallon jugs whether they can afford it or not.

The other view is of Prince George, where I was born and spent the first 22 years of my life. When I packed up and left town for good I was like most young men leaving home: terrified of the larger world that beckoned even though I'd been seduced by its promises. A part of me wanted to stay home. I knew everybody, I understood the city's unique—if often violent—rule book, and even if I'd never felt entirely at ease there I sensed I'd never feel like I belonged anywhere else. In leaving Prince George I felt I was betraying a trust—not quite a sacred trust, but at least a bond of loyalty created by familiarity and comfort. I was also doing what everyone else did, and that bothered me.

Prince George hasn't ever been the sort of place that makes it easy for people to get and stay comfortable, particularly not if they were intent, as I was, on having a thoughtful life. The city was and remains a town where most people are merely passing through, and those who stay sneer at what little it has retained of its past. It has been, then and now, more interested in the commercial opportunities it enables for aggressive individuals than in tradition, history, and civility. In that respect, Prince George is a microcosm of what has occurred in Canada, which is a country with a sparse history, particularly along its north and western edges, and one that is largely indifferent to the history it does have, unless it involves sending men off to foreign wars. Along the country's west and northern margins, indifference lives a short distance from hostile contempt.

I'm not sure what it was about Prince George that made me leave. Small-town intolerance? Sure. Lack of appreciable beauty and opportunities for culture? Don't make me laugh. Or was it Oedipal—my father's overbearing will that I needed to get away from? Yes, of course. I understood that my character bore similarities to his, and that in the physical sense, I was my father's most obvious offspring. But I had been brought up properly, which is to say, I didn't feel compelled to want to *be* my father. The portion of his common sense I inherited enabled me to see the always-changing world in front of me clearly enough to recognize how foolish it would be to make myself into a junior version of him. I was therefore free to be whomever I might turn out to be, and in a world that would be vastly different from his.

It was no single thing that made me leave, then. Yet taken together—the small-town intolerance, the family politics, and the lack of any cultural devices able to look beyond the obvious and immediate added up to an oppressive private destiny I could feel bearing down on me. Only the two-year stint I did in the Forest Service allowed me a respite. There, the trees, the rivers and lakes and streams commanded my attention. I watched my contemporaries leave town, most of them hooting with delight as they cleared the city limits. I didn't leave that way, even when it was time to go. I took it that leaving was the way things were, and I went with mixed emotions and no whooping at all.

Now I'm coming back home, as I have since I left with a regularity that startles everyone who knows me. This time, I have my own son in tow, a boy who hides his thoughtful nature behind the same air of distraction I once used to mask a nature I hoped could become thoughtful.

I reach across the seat and nudge him.

"Prince George coming up," I say. "You'll be able to smell it soon."

From inside reveries of his own, Max merely grunts, "Sure thing, Dad," and tunes out again.

2

At the end of the Second World War there were 4,000 people living in Prince George, including my family. My father, a travelling salesman for a meat-packing company and a man who'd never taken well to supervision, moved my mother and my three older siblings there from Edmonton at the end of 1942. In his mind, Prince George offered freedom from head office in a land of seemingly endless financial opportunity. He'd be able to branch out on his own and make his fortune.

When wartime rationing forced him to cool his entrepreneurial heels, he took some time off and built the house on Hemlock Street that I grew up in. He'd hire contractors to start different parts of the building, ones willing to let him work with them. Once he understood enough to finish the job himself, he fired them. Somewhat accidentally, about this time he also did his part to engineer my entrance into the world.

The main travel route in and out of Prince George in the 1940s was still the Grand Trunk Pacific Railway (by now owned by the CNR) that crossed the Rocky Mountains through Yellowhead Pass from Edmonton and on west to Prince Rupert after passing through Prince George and the Coast Range. There was no highway east from Prince George, nothing north beyond McLeod's Lake and the Rockies, and the road south to Vancouver was a gravel track that snaked precipitously through the river canyons on flimsy roads that followed the pack-horse trails used during the 1858 Cariboo Gold Rush. The roads west weren't quite highways, but they were passable in winter, and only became unreliable during spring breakup. The biggest road hazards seemed to be wild game. My father chased down and ran over several timber wolves with his 1941 Chevrolet, an automobile that eventually met its demise in another collision, with a bull moose.

In 1952 the Pacific Great Eastern Railway (today named B.C. Rail, and now, as then, half epic and half farce) arrived from the south, the same year the completion of the Kenny Dam to the west ended the floods on the Nechako River forever, along with much of what was left of the salmon runs.

In the years that followed, the roads improved, more newcomers arrived, and by B.C.'s centennial year of 1958 the population of Prince George had grown to about 14,000. That year the city fathers adopted a civic mascot to run with Centennial Sam, the provincial government's mascot, who himself bore a close resemblance to the cartoon figure Yosemite Sam and had the same sort of cosmopolitan personality. The city's mascot was named Mr. PeeGee, and he had no personality at all. He was 4 metres tall, made out of spruce logs, sported a hard hat, and stood guard over the Chamber of Commerce's new tourist information building near the train station, as stiff and humourless as the Chamber itself. Folks were proud of Mr. PeeGee despite his lack of charm, and also he served as target for 30 years of high-school pranksters.

Around the same time, City Council, on the advice of the Chamber of Commerce, declared Prince George the Western White Spruce Capital of the World. I suppose the designation was accurate enough, but its limited claim filled my head with irritable cogitations. Shouldn't it be the *Spruce Capital of the World*, or forget about it? Claiming that you're the Western White Spruce Capital of the World was a little like saying that the Fraser River was the *Largest Fraser River in the World*. If some other town challenged us for the designation, would the Chamber of Commerce retreat and declare that, truly, Prince George was merely the *Spindly Black-Barked Swamp Spruce Capital of the World*, or would it admit that it had only wanted the white spruce bragging rights to help the local lumbermen sell 2x4s, and really didn't give a tinker's damn about civic pride?

The 1956 Sloan Commission report on the condition of forestry in British Columbia counted 604 mills in the Prince George Forest District, nearly all of them locally owned and operated—a condition that won't seem remarkable until it is compared with how few independent mills remain today. For sure, the economy in the late 1950s was strong, every business in town was talking unlimited expansion, and most of the businessmen were plugging their profits back into the local economy. Plans were afoot to build a huge power dam on the Peace River that would create a lake 800 kilometres long and provide cheap power for any industry that wanted to move north. Cautious thinkers suggested that Prince George might have 100,000 residents by the 1980s, while optimists believed it could have half a million—or why not a million?—by the year 2000. The resource seemed infinite and self-renewing, and the only limits visible were those of human imagination and commercial confidence.

These wild predictions of future wealth made for an atmosphere of glorious opportunity for anyone focused on making their fortune, but for the children growing up in its "let-'er-rip" currents, it wasn't much fun. The schools were constantly overcrowded and filled with bewildered strangers—teachers and students alike; neighbourhood tree forts and vacant lots disappeared to make room for new houses and streets; the old river sloughs that had served as playgrounds— and parents' safety nightmares—were filled in and developed one after another. By the time I was in my teens, Prince George bore only a faint and fading resemblance to the town of my early childhood.

It pissed me off. With my hormones blowing hot, I directed my hostility not at my parents but at the changing city—and at change itself. So did most of my friends. We seemed to be the only ones who noticed that something worthwhile was being lost. We broke a few windows and a lot of streetlights, we set fire to a few lumber piles, and we ran amok in more than one half-built house. No one recognized that these were acts of protest, and when the newspaper wrote us up as vandals it made us more furious still.

Around us, the pace of development continued to accelerate. After 1958, it was fuelled by the hysteria surrounding Swedish millionaire Axel Wenner-Gren's logistically ludicrous announcement that he was going to build a monorail from Vancouver to Prince George. The first fast-food franchises, Dairy Queen and A&W, arrived and quickly began to kill off the locally owned drive-in cafés and restaurants. Supermarket chains just as easily decimated the local grocers, and before long the same kinds of changes were affecting local manufacturers and suppliers. No one seemed to think there might be a downside, even though most of the locally owned businesses being bought up were closed, and the goods they once manufactured were being trucked in from Vancouver and points east.

Within the forest industry itself, the independents were also selling out, cashing in, and moving on. When they didn't, they found that their timber rights were being overbid, and their option of leaving town wealthy was being taken away. By the early 1960s, three Kraft pulp mills were under construction, and the engine of change had altered its character. That the merchants, manufacturers, and mill operators of Prince George weren't in the driver's seat any longer was masked by the heady perfume in the air. Everyone was drinking it in, and most found it irresistible and intoxicating.

With my disaffection growing, I decided that it—all of it—stunk. I won't go so far as to say I foresaw the future, just that I'd gotten a prescient whiff of how it was going to smell. Everyone else found out when the pulp mills opened and the prevailing winds didn't blow the perfume upriver the way the experts had assured the few who'd worried about it, instead draping over the town like a fetid blanket that rarely lifted for more than a few days at a time. When some poor soul complained to Phil Gagliardi, the Bible-thumping provincial minister of highways, Gagliardi laughed long and hard. "Why, that's the smell of money," he boomed.

For most, that explanation was good enough. In those days there literally *was* a job for everyone who wanted to work, and the wages were good. Mill workers owned their own homes and could afford to fill their carports with Ski-Doos and boats and RVs. Better yet, the surviving local mill owners and manufacturers were getting rich on the increased forestry harvest or the expansion of commercial services it fuelled. Still more of them were getting rich from the proceeds of selling their businesses to the bigger companies now flooding into town. My father was typical. He got squeezed out of his ice cream and frozen foods business, then sold the soft drink plant and moved south to the Okanagan Valley. By 1968 no one in my family was left in Prince George. Most of my parents' generation eventually did what he'd done: they took the money and ran. You can't fight progress, they said.

I was never convinced, and I'm still not. So I'll ask the question straight up: Is it possible to fight progress? Or better, Is fighting progress occasionally a necessary and sensible thing to do?

Once upon a time, I thought I had the answers to cosmic questions like this one. But in 1990, on this highway outside Prince George, surrounded by desolation on both sides, the question is only one of many I've lost my stuff on. It's also pointless to try to explain to Max that I'm having a 30-year-old argument with myself, and I don't try. When I spot a roadside clearing, I pull into it, shut off the car motor, and get out. Prince George can wait.

Max literally bounces from his seat. Once out, he's quickly subdued by what's there. Or at least he is until the blackflies discover us and begin ripping chunks of flesh from wherever they find exposed skin.

"What a mess," he says, gesturing at the shattered trees while he swats a buzzing fly from his forehead. "How big do you think it is?"

Off in the near distance, I can hear another buzzing sound, this one less evenly modulated than the whine of the flies. "Hard to say, exactly." I answer, motioning toward a low rise on the south side of the road. "Let's climb that hill over there and have a look."

He groans. "Do we have to? These flies are all over the place."

"No," I answer, "We don't have to do anything. But we're taking this trip so we can see new things, aren't we? This looks pretty new to me."

"I suppose," he says.

I rescue an aerosol can of mosquito dope from the trunk, and a few minutes later we've scrambled up the rise and are standing atop two hefty stumps, dodging blackflies who aren't deterred by the river of repellent I've sprayed across our arms and necks.

A ragged line of trees at the top of a distant rise indicates that the clearcut isn't infinite. Still, it is large enough. A Caterpillar—it looks like a D-7—is working a few hundred metres down from us, pushing slash into piles for burning.

Max catches my eye and shrugs. "What do you think of this?" I ask.

"It's awful," he answers after a moment's pause. "Why did they do this?"

"For money. It's called logging. That's what people do around here."

"Well," he says very decisively, "this is wrong."

I have to test him on this one, so it'll stay in his memory. "How do you mean, 'wrong'?"

His decisiveness crumbles. "Well, I don't know *exactly* what I mean, Dad. Maybe just that things like this shouldn't be happening."

"People have to make a living, kiddo," I answer without thinking.

He puts a barb much older than he is right between my ribs. "That's what adults always say when they want to keep on doing something that's crappy and bad."

3

As the last kilometres of Highway 16 slip by, I feel the sort of excitement I used to feel coming home after a long trip. But as the particulars of today's Prince George loom, impinge, and pervade, other emotions crowd in. They're as childish as the excitement, but they have a sour edge to them. There's disappointment that the old approaches to town are gone, and that this new highway takes me through so little that is familiar. When I remember that most of the old landmarks have disappeared anyway—torn down or renovated beyond recognition —my spirits sink further.

The old, childish anger returns, but the target is different. I'm not even in town and the ersatz is everywhere: houses that began as tarpaper shacks and have evolved into half-assed space age aluminum-and-plastic slum dwellings; the broad ditches along the new highway, already silvered with dumped petroleum leachate and garbage. Beyond that, the denuded hillsides, ubiquitous. Everything gets logged here, and everyone is a logger, right down to the homesteaders on their two-acre parcels.

It's an anger that rarely sinks far beneath the surface when I'm in or near Prince George. But now that I'm an adult, its edge is blunted by understanding most of the reasons—or excuses—for that willingness to log everything. The weird pragmatisms of northern B.C., boiled down to their essentials, come out something like this: 1) When it's 30 below zero and your fingers are freezing along with your ass, you toss out the fine details and do whatever is needed to keep yourself warm and dry; 2) You don't expect a string quartet to be playing Mozart while you're cranking up the chainsaws.

But is this what I'm up to, here? Have I come all this way just to convince my son that the loony jamboree of entrepreneurial capitalism that now fills the airwaves and sometimes the air itself has a dark side that can be seen here better than elsewhere? I suppose it's a good enough motive, and my targeting is accurate. Prince George has been the northern headquarters for the "let 'er rip" crowd for 50 years. Anyone who spends half an hour walking around this town gets a clear look at capital-P Progress in the long, drawn-out process of collapsing on people who have sung its anthems as loudly and uncritically as anywhere on the planet.

Because the rips and tears here are so visible, it makes the partisan condemnations and defences alike ring hollow. Maybe that will make it easier for Max to see that the too-orderly world he gets shoved down his throat at school and on television isn't quite real. And believe me, I want him to see Prince George as it really is, with its warts and its remaining beauty spots. I want him to see the good things I had growing up here—and a considerable portion is left over, even if I'm reluctant to admit it. No easy task I've set myself, in other words.

I glance at Max. He's gazing at a derelict homestead coming into view, whistling distractedly to himself, wondering what led the owners to leave it.

From time to time people like me have to remind ourselves that just because we lived in the North while there were still woolly mammoths running around, it doesn't make us elephant trainers. This isn't a mere litany of sentimental childhood memories.

I think Prince George is a special case. The overwriting and the overhauling and the bulldozing and the redeveloping and sometimes the just-for-the-hell-of-it demolitions of its natural, built, and human resources have occurred with a mix of headlong abandon and myopia that is transparent enough to reveal things about our collective condition, things that can't be seen elsewhere. No town or small city anywhere in North America has been more screwed up by irrelevant, misguided, or downright stupid planning and development practices than this one.

Some of the destruction is the result of standard 20th-century urban planning idiocy—ill-conceived traffic management schemes; using the building code as a guide to aesthetics when its real purpose is to make buildings safe for habitation; thinking that uniform setbacks and other zoning standards prevent squalor when all they really

No, wait a minute. That's the sort of thing *I'd* have been doing. Max's curiosities about the world are as different from mine as mine were from my parent's, and so I don't know what's going through his head.

"Whatcha thinking about?" I ask.

He gives me a fish-eye stare. "I'm looking out the window," he answers. "I'm not thinking."

The original street layout of Prince George was created by the Grand Trunk Pacific Railway around 1911 in preparation for the arrival of the rail line from the east. Two other small communities that were vying to host the railroad—South Fort George, a mile to the south on the banks of the Fraser, and Central Fort George, not quite a mile to the northwest on the Nechako, were already the focus of ferocious land speculation, but neither had the flat land needed for rail yards. The third and least populated of the three locations, Fort George, was little more than a few decrepit shacks huddled around the Hudson's Bay trading post. In 1911 it was low-lying river delta intercut by dozens of volatile backwaters and sloughs, and most of it belonged to the local Carrier Indian band. But those were small impediments to a company that was used to moving mountains. The Indian land was flat, and it would come cheap. The sloughs and backwaters could be backfilled or dyked against flooding.

---

do is tone down visual disorder for real estate sales people. But the damage penetrates deeper here, and it runs closer to the century's darkest nerve tracks. Some of it is easy to see, like the denuded hillsides and the polluted rivers and creeks. Other elements are now so integrated with the urban fabric of the city that their stupidity is masked by habituation, like building pulp mills within sight of downtown and then letting urban sprawl surround them. But what's hard to avoid recognizing is that Prince George has poisoned itself systematically and within the rule book since its beginnings. It makes no difference whether it's the sensorium being abased—ears, eyes, nose, respiratory, or the political system. And so we're clear that this is something more than a malcontent's rant, let's go back to the headwaters, to the deep background of human settlement, to test it out.

The development of Western cities since the time of the Greeks has evolved around the concept of a central marketplace, or Agora, that focuses both commercial and civic activities and then surrounds them with the human necessities of housing,

The Grand Trunk Pacific found a way to purchase the land, moving the defenceless Carrier band 15 kilometres upstream on the Fraser to Shelley Creek. In April 1913, it gazetted its plan for the new city of Prince George. That touched off another land-buying frenzy, and this one had choice downtown lots selling at $10,000 apiece—a price that wouldn't be seen again for nearly 60 years. A building boom ensued, and for the next few years development was swift and confident. At the end of the Great War, the population of Prince George was close to 5,000.

The railroad planners' street layout was elegant and logical. On the north side, edging the Nechako River, were the industrial zones for saw and planer mills. Separating these from the business section of town were the rail yards. The residential areas began south and west of downtown, with three crescents curving around the schools and radiating outward from there. An elevated plateau to the southeast of downtown, separating it from the Fraser River, was named the Millar Addition, but it wasn't so much an addition to the city as a named response to the topography. The northwest edge of the plateau is separated from the downtown by a clay hill named after Lord Connaught, one of Canada's less memorable governor generals. The hill was the site of the city's original water tower, but by my time was mainly a refuge for crows, hobos, and teenage drinkers until it was turned into a civic park in the late 1950s. A few of the crows left for greener pastures, but not much else changed.

---

education, and recreation in a relatively efficient balance. But the recent evolution of contemporary technological systems is leading us toward a commercial monoculture—the city as merchandise, social life as a retail mall that gives up to scrutiny only its superficial proprietors and profit pathways. I'm talking about Athens in the 3rd-century B.C., or medieval Italy's Sienna, cities that understood that commerce was necessary but that it was one element in a larger community and world. The past 40 years in Prince George has been one long regression in the complexity of its community and its various environments.

The original layout of Prince George followed the classical rule book, right down to the part about bringing the traffic into, or at least near, the central commercial core. Urban planners have believed that this is a precondition to successful modern economic activity even though it isn't always pleasant for those subjected to the heavy traffic that comes with it. They're probably right.

But in practice, modern urban planning has developed a number of sub-rosa pro-

The Grand Trunk Pacific's layout had limitations. The main one was that it could house only about 7,000 people without bursting its seams. Not a problem, for a few decades. By the early 1920s, the building boom had become the victim of a lumber industry bust, and the city's population was hovering around 3,000. It fell further during the 1930s, and didn't begin to recover until the Second World War began. After Pearl Harbor, Prince George was designated as the second line of defence against a Japanese invasion and a sizable army base was built out on the ancient river flats west of the city. For obvious reasons, and not just because the construction of Mosquito bombers required strong, light spruce, the area's forests again became attractive. The population began to surge anew.

After the war, growth continued, but it was 1952 before the city began to burst the original street plan. With the Kenny Dam in place, the city's river flats were safer for industrial development, and the PGE (Pacific Great Eastern) gave the region commercial access to the south and the port at Vancouver. From the gravel wastes that replaced the backwaters and sloughs came industrial yards that gradually filled with local manufacturing and fabricating, or later, when those businesses were bought out and closed, with warehouses and equipment depots. Other filled-in waterways became new roadbeds, commercial developments, and housing. The swamp just south of downtown below Connaught Hill and slightly east of the neighbourhood where I grew up was filled in and turned into the city's recreational facilities,

---

tocols that get in the way of good intentions. One of them is that planning is inevitably about supporting the political and commercial *Zeitgeist*, not about social evolution or quality of life. Planners got their start as a genteel but completely pseudo-scientific instrument for separating the wealthy classes from the noise, crime, and mechanical intrusions of 19th-century industrial life. It is genteel because it has done the job more gently than, say, steel fences and club-wielding police would have.

But along with power and authority inevitably comes obsessive behaviour. After the Second World War, planning began to pursue two impulses more obsessively than was healthy. It also went a little crazy with the authority it was accorded. One of the obsessions of planning has been with the radical separation of basic human activities—a pursuit our larger cities are only now rethinking even though Jane Jacobs has been debunking the destructiveness of radical separation since the late 1950s. The other obsession of planning has been with serving automobile transportation— nearly always to the exclusion of common sense and human well-being. One's primary

which in those early days meant a few scrubby baseball diamonds that could double as sites for outdoor skating rinks in winter.

Some of the development did improve the quality of life. At the end of the 1940s, the Junior Chamber of Commerce, with my father as president, decided that Prince George needed a community meeting and showplace. They purchased one of the several huge equipment hangars declared surplus and abandoned by the army after the war. By hook and by crook they dragged the building downtown and set it atop a patch of filled-in swamp across from the old wooden hockey arena. Once set, they laid a hardwood floor, built a foyer, and named the structure The Civic Centre. It served for everything from teen dances to weddings to magic shows and indoor sports events for the next 30 years.

Today, the elegance and simplicity of the Grand Trunk's city design is hard to detect. Some of the early buildings fell victim to natural and man-made misadventures, while road widenings, redevelopment, and the inherent temporariness of softwood structures took care of much of the rest. Sometimes, these forces came together. When a new civic arena was built against Connaught Hill next to City Hall after a heavy snowfall brought down the old wood-frame one, it required, in somebody's mind, a new traffic layout, and so the ball diamonds that had been nestled beneath the hill were moved out of town. The land lay derelict for more than a decade, and was used for a new public library, a swimming pool, some pointlessly complicated

---

human right, in the eyes of post-war urban planners, has been to get to whatever commercial destination one chooses without undue obstruction or delay.

In large metropolitan centres, this obsessive compulsion has carried a certain dark logic—it prevents suburban dwellers from having to spend all their non-work waking hours sitting in traffic tie-ups. But in smaller cities and towns, that logical basis is absent, and in its place has come an asinine mimicry of large-scale urban systems. The consequences are costly, inefficient, and frankly antisocial.

In Prince George, the most destructive phase of urban planning began in the early 1960s, with the building of two modestly scaled shopping malls. More or less simultaneously, and probably under pressure from the mall developers, traffic patterns were rerouted throughout the city—to get people to and from the malls more easily. A few years later, the brain-trust at City Hall commissioned a University of British Columbia planning professor and then Vancouver city alderman of South Asian descent named Setty Pendakur to devise a downtown traffic plan that would attract retail commerce back

new roadways, and dozens of franchise retail outlets. That was the way things were: commercial life always took precedence over civic life. Never mind that the new ball diamonds were too far for most kids to walk to, and that their displacement atomized the cultural habits of the city. Progress and money were talking, and those were the only voices that got a hearing in Prince George.

I'd planned to take Max into town, as far as it was going to be possible, along the routes that were used in the old days. That way, we'd get a view of the two pulp mills on the north side of the river, and we'd enter town across the 1914 railroad bridge that was an adventure all on its own. The bridge had been built with a lift section for riverboats—gone before I was born—with two automobile lanes cantilevered precariously onto each side of the track later on. The auto lanes were narrow and slippery in winter, and it seemed that every two or three years a car or truck would plunge through the railing into the river, generally with fatal consequences. It was hard to find anyone who could traverse that bridge without recalling some near-lethal crossing they or someone they knew had made. After a schoolmate of mine lost his life in one of the accidents, I never crossed the bridge without a mortal twinge that reminded me life was crueler than advertised.

---

to the beginning-to-fade downtown. Pendakur, cheered on by downtown businessmen already panic-stricken by the drain-off of activity to the two malls, devised a plan grounded in two goofy principles. First, his plan set up the downtown to compete with the malls on the malls' terms: commercial-only uses, easy auto access, and convenient parking. A series of one-way thoroughfares was set up in the core even though most of the streets so designated were wide enough to handle six lanes of traffic.

That wasn't Pendakur's worst blunder. To give the downtown that shopping mall "feel," the plan changed the two primary retail streets, George Street and Third Avenue, from four-lane thoroughfares with parallel parking to two-lane semi-malls with angle parking. Each intersection was larded with concrete curbing, and tacky-looking canopies were set above the sidewalks to increase the mall atmosphere—and obscure the building facades, some of which were still the original (and now decaying) clapboard. Together, the measures had roughly the effect a beaver dam has on a creek. The traffic or water slows, debris accumulates, flora and fauna sicken and die, and the creek

The stink from the pulp mills that assails us long before we can see the city is a pungent, sulphuric aroma just short of acridity. You taste it in your food after an hour or two beneath its blanket. Worse, it stays on your palate for days after the wind has returned the cloud, always temporarily, back up the river.

Max wrinkles his nose. "Is that stink here all the time?"

"Depends on which way the wind is blowing," I tell him. "You'll get used to it."

Max doesn't like what's in his nostrils, but he has trouble connecting it with the unremarkable buildings across the river and the fluffy white plumes billowing from their modest smokestacks. When we crest the hill and begin the descent into town, I point out the source of the stink, and make a fatuous mental note to take him out to see where the effluent out-pipes enter the Fraser.

"Are we going to have to stay around long if this gunk is in the air?" he asks.

I don't bother to answer. He's been educated to a kind of environmentalism that's quite different from my Protestant sense of good and evil causalities. To him, what matters is the affront to his person. What matters to me is fairness.

Halfway down the hill I recognize that we can't use the old bridge to get into town. The new route takes us past the provincial jail, under expansion for what seems like the two-hundredth time, and into town on a new bridge that couldn't offer anyone adventure if they greased

---

slowly strangles and begins to stink. The beavers like it fine until they've chewed down the surrounding trees, but then they leave.

Soon after Pendakur's traffic scheme was in place, many of the smaller buildings in the downtown area began to fall—some to accommodate several idiotically large parking garages but in most cases merely to create ground-level parking for the businesses that remained. So much parking was created that by the mid-1970s a visitor was able to ask me, in perfect innocence, if Prince George had recently experienced an earthquake. In the next decade, downtown Prince George began to die. Its demise was helped along by the construction of the Pine Centre, one of those large, enclosed malls so generic in its architecture and range of franchise outlets that it could be situated anywhere in North America. Welcome to the future, Prince George, British Columbia.

Mr. Pendakur was a nice enough man. But it's likely he didn't spend more than a few summer days in Prince George before he retreated to his university campus office on Vancouver's Point Grey to apply his theoretically sound and conventional principles.

it with olive oil and anchovies. I'd planned, once we crossed the Fraser, to turn south and drive in along Patricia Boulevard, a pretty street that overlooks the eastern edge of the downtown. We can't do that, either, damn it. The City has sealed off Patricia Boulevard with the bridge approaches, and we can't get there without having to drive nearly an extra kilometre into town. I can't show Max the way things were because I have to live with the way things are.

4

So I don't subject Max to downtown Prince George. It's too damned depressing for a kid. We skirt it, driving south along Queensway and up onto the plateau, then turn west onto Patricia Boulevard past the Catholic church and into the Millar Addition. Another turn, this one south again onto Hemlock Street, and a half block along, I pull over across the street from the house where I spent the first 18 years of my life.

The white clapboard siding my father was once proud of is now buried beneath a coat of crumbling stucco, and there is an unedged

---

He evidently knew little about the principles of creek hydrology and was almost certainly poorly informed about snow removal or the effect heavy equipment has on curved concrete curbing. For what his traffic-management scheme did to the downtown, the people of Prince George should have hung him in effigy if not in person.

One of the reasons that didn't happen was that within a few years most of the politicians who'd hired him to save the downtown were gone: retired, dead, moved on. So were many of the downtown businessmen, their stores replaced by a decaying potpourri of pawnshops, dollar stores, downscale hotels, amusement parlours, and cafés that change ownership faster and more absolutely than the seasons. A provincial government office complex, built in the 1980s, didn't help. It merely gave the city's growing EI- and welfare-collecting subcommunities a slightly warmer and more centralized place to waste their days. A new Court House built in the 1990s has done little more than add a few people trying to avoid criminal sentences, along with their lawyers.

Now, like every other city in trouble, Prince George is talking about building a casino.

gravel driveway in the front yard that spills stones onto his once-immaculate lawn. The vegetable garden, my mother's pride and joy, is grassed over, and the crabapple trees my father planted, enormous now but largely barren, badly need pruning. The elm tree I can remember him planting next to the garage has grown so large it needs a chainsaw taken to it if it isn't soon to devour the building it dwarfs.

"Not a very big house," Max says. "The whole family lived in that little place?"

"It seemed big enough when I was your age," I answer. "People lived differently then."

I'm grateful that he doesn't ask what the differences were because I'd have a hard time coming up with an answer. I restart the car and swing it left around the last two corners—one street east and one back up in the alphabet, Hemlock to Gorse.

It is just after 6:00 p.m. when we pull up in front of a hot-pink Dodge pickup truck and park beneath the conical elm trees of Gorse Street. The house we'll be staying in belongs to Barry and Joy McKinnon. It is among the oldest homes in the city, but Max isn't very impressed by its antiquity. That's because "old" in Prince George is relative. The house was built in 1915, one of three houses constructed next to one another using essentially the same floor plan. Most of the other houses nearby, like my parents' house less than a block away, were built right after the war in the 1940s and 1950s, as were the majority in this part of town.

Since the mid-1970s, I've been able to stay with Barry and Joy when I'm in Prince George. We're friends, but that isn't the whole reason I stay with them. The house I grew up in, 1432 Hemlock, is less than a block away from 1420 Gorse, and I played in Barry's house many times while I was a child. In the 1940s it belonged to John Steward, the city manager, and through the 1950s and 1960s to the Toronto-Dominion bank manager, Steve Cavaghan and his wife Dot. Their son, Eric, a year younger than I was, was one of my playmates until I beaned him with a baseball throwing high-skies in their side yard.

The Millar Addition has aged more gracefully than most of Prince George, even though it's the first and worst affected when the wind carries the pulp-mill sulphides into town. Barry and Joy's house, not large by today's suburban standards, has the graciousness of a much larger home. Its two storeys are rare for the area, and extensive renovations have protected the exterior from the elements—the original clapboard siding lies beneath vinyl—and the windows, most of them, are new. Unusual for the north, Barry and Joy's interior renovations have retained the flavour if not the exact floor plan of the original.

Nearly all their changes are improvements over the original. The ratty greenhouse the Stewards built at the rear of the house is now a spacious deck with an outdoor Jacuzzi and dozens of impossibly lush potted petunias, while the vegetable garden that once filled most of the open backyard is now mostly grassed over and is protected by a solid wood fence 2.5 metres high. These fences are popular in Prince George today, along with locked doors and security systems. When I was young, none of those things were necessary, and the big fences were impractical. Back then, nearly everyone had large vegetable gardens to mark boundaries. That was enough: unless you were dead drunk, you didn't take people's property, and you didn't steal their food.

Barry and Joy are in the backyard when we arrive, sitting around an open firepit, biting, as the local jargon has it, the heads off a few weasels. They have a son, Jesse, who's a year older than Max, and he's lounging in the Jacuzzi. Judging from the glower on his face as I introduce Max to him, he's already got a serious case of adolescent hormones. Barry hands me a beer without asking if I want one, and we go back to the firepit and leave the two boys alone to construct whatever relationship they're going to have. Barry has lit a fire even though it's summer and the day has been sunny and warm. He knows, with the shadows lengthening, that the air will cool off in a hurry. And anyway, campfires are part of living here, even when you're within walking distance of downtown Prince George.

I plop down in a lawn chair, twist the top off the beer—it's a Kokanee in a glass bottle—and ask Barry what he knows about the clearcutting around the Bowron River.

"Oh, I know about that, yeah," he says. "I've been in there, actually. Collecting firewood. Last fall, I think. It's a real mess."

"I can imagine."

"We can take a run out there if you're interested. Take my truck and overnight at one of the forestry camps. You should know about it." Max has wandered back by this time and has draped himself in my lap. "Want to see the biggest clearcut in the world?" Barry asks him, half ironically.

Max shrugs. "That'd be cool," he answers. "I guess."

_____

As this summer evening unfolds, we find ourselves toasting hot dogs over the open fire, and at various points neighbours and friends join us. John Harris, like Barry an English instructor at the college, drops by on his way out of town for a few days; Bill Bailey and his wife, Carol, appear and stay for the evening; and Noel, an elementary school teacher who lives across the street, comes over to sit for a while, along with several people I've never seen before. I've met Noel on previous visits, Harris I hope to see later in the week, but I've known Bill all my life. We were in first grade together, and were close until adolescence tricked me into thinking his slow sweetness was merely slowness. Years later, I woke up and recognized the will and intelligence behind that deceptive exterior. Bill forgave me for my arrogance by pretending he hadn't noticed it.

Here, as the light fades, I settle into the unhurried music of Bill and Barry's conversation, and begin to feel the sense of comfort I've never experienced anywhere else. The light, rich and slightly smoky from the fire, feels right as it plays its departure through the tops of the elms and birches, and so does the crisp night air that creeps in. Even the one or two behemoth-size mosquitoes cruising us for their evening meal feel right. I'm home.

We're drinking a lot of beer, and Barry voices the local cosmic worry—whether we ought to drink off all the homemade stuff he and Noel made or make a run to the beer store before it closes. I recognize this as Barry's subtle way of cutting himself out of the drinking circle while wondering aloud if we're not about to fly out of control, and whether we should, maybe, pack it in and get some sleep. For a guy who talks as if he lives inside a giant brewery and is proud of it, he's a surprisingly moderate drinker.

I have a photo of Barry someone gave me years ago that I haul out whenever I need to remind myself of who he is and—not incidentally

—why I don't live in Prince George. There are about 10 people in the photo, taken at some party that probably started like this one with a summer afternoon beer around the firepit and got out of hand before sundown. I'm able to deduce this last detail because the photo was shot in daylight, which in this latitude means any time before 10 p.m. during most of the early summer. It's an important detail because it keeps the photo from showing that the people in the photo resemble small rodents transfixed by the headlights of a car or truck just before it runs them over.

What strikes me about the photo is that, of the people in it, Barry alone seems to see that there might be something bearing down on them. Judging from his expression—somewhere between disgust, fear, and resignation—it's a semi-trailer truck filled with freshly cut logs. The photo reminds me of why I like Barry so much, and that, if I'd stayed in Prince George, there would have been two people in that photo looking as trapped as he does.

It's that combination of disgust, fear, and resignation that allows him to live relatively comfortably in Prince George—as comfortably as he would have as, say, a court poet in Vienna at the end of the last century. This is not to suggest that he's a naturally comfortable man. He isn't. But his poetry illuminates his discomforts so eloquently it resembles a nightingale trilling in an English country estate—or a formal garden in the courts of Vienna. By his own description, Barry is a whiner, not a fighter. His whining is so well mixed with irony and self-deprecating laughter that it's been hard to tell when he's serious. I've concluded, over the years, that he isn't. Not all the time, anyway.

But it occurs to me here, watching him, how little any of us really know about our friends. Because we're decently fed, clothed, and sheltered, have jobs to go to and families to come home to, and can manage to keep our personal woes hidden, we assume that the people around us are basically happy and fulfilled, and that we need not worry about them.

Once in a very rare while, this turns out to be true. But much more often, something happens that reveals that our happy, fulfilled friends are drowning in private miseries too deep and opaque for anyone to fathom. Then it comes to us, maybe, that we're all being bamboozled, that our common sense has been buried beneath an onslaught of commodities and distractions, and that our attempts to wade through them have made us insensible to the human condition and to one another. At that moment—this is one of them for me— we can see, if we want to, that the vast consumer mall in which we're all condemned to live out our over-provisioned lives hasn't obliter- ated or even much alleviated the misery of human life. It has merely rendered it temporarily invisible to us—and thus virtually impossi- ble to respond to in wilful and effective ways.

But on this lovely evening, as my attentions shift from Max with his eyes nearly glazed over with boredom, to Bill's explanation of how fragile the local economy has grown, to Barry's troubled, intelligent distractedness, I get something more than that. Here, the miseries of the human condition have crept close to the edge of *not* being private. The complaints I'm hearing—concerning a city no one can figure out how to care about, and not just about personal or occupational courtesies not properly paid, or how deep the water has gotten—are also about that clearcut I've yet to see, 60 kilometres to the southeast.

5

While Max and I wander around town over the next two days, I ask anyone willing to talk what they can tell me about "the clearcut on the Bowron." Most are dimly aware that there's a big one somewhere near town, but don't see it as outrageous or remarkable. One or two haven't heard about it, and when I offer details, they respond pre- dictably: too bad, but what can anyone do?

A small minority are passionate. One old acquaintance insists that the clearcut is "500 square miles," another believes it is larger still, maybe "5,000 square miles or kilometres." "The bastards are scared to tell us how large it really is," he insists. Both have heard about being able to see it from outer space, and hence, I suspect, their inflated estimates of its size. The others willing to hazard a guess—not many —think it is about 50 square miles, or 50 square kilometres. Everyone, at one point or another, offers the familiar clichés about the price of progress. Very few think they're paying too much.

On our third morning in town, I leave Max with Barry and Jesse, and drive down to the *Prince George Citizen* offices to talk to Ken Bernsohn, who wrote a book about logging in the early 1980s while he was a freelancer for the logger's trade magazines and was then hired by the paper to offer an expert view of the local forestry scene. Bernsohn's book, *Cutting Up the North*, managed to be critical of some elements of the forest industry without getting anybody steamed up —no mean feat. I'd talked to Bernsohn briefly a few years before, but at the time, I'd just picked up a copy of *Cutting Up the North* and didn't have anything more than general questions to ask. I'd gotten the impression from both the conversation and (later on) the book that, while he didn't much like the way the big corporations operated in the north, he very much liked and admired the people who actually did the physical work in the industry—from the fallers all the way to the local owners and managers. Now, I want to see whether the clearcut on the Bowron has changed his mind.

Bad luck. Bernsohn isn't in town—on holiday somewhere south, which in Prince George as often means Thailand as Vancouver. But Bev Christensen, who's an old hand at the paper and has known me since I was an 11-year-old *Citizen* paper boy with an attitude problem, spots me at the counter and waves me over. Bev and I have always liked one another, but our conversations, in the 30-something years since I gave up delivering the paper she writes for, somehow haven't evolved past basic adult–child awkwardness. She seems to think of me as an adolescent who's unaccountably developed a brain, and I can't help thinking of her as, well, an adult with a brain.

That I am, on this visit, a columnist for a major newspaper— and therefore a sort-of celebrity to some of the local media—simply makes this more silly and awkward. Every few sentences Bev stops mid-phrase, sighs, and shakes her head as if talking to me is amusing but somehow pointless. This has the predictable effect. I feel as if I ought to be throwing snowballs at her, or whatever the situational equivalent is.

I recall Barry mentioning that Bev has been working on a book about an Alcan proposal to raise the Kenny Dam again, use the stored water to generate hydroelectric power and sell it to the government. When I ask her about it, the bemusement vanishes. When I want to know what's wrong with raising the level of the dam again, I get a dismissive scowl.

"Well," she says in a consciously laconic sort of way that suggests I must be impossibly dumb for not already knowing what she's about to tell me, "you know they'll have to fill the dam, and that'll squeeze the water flow in the Nechako down to a trickle, and, of course, once they've got it filled they'll discover that they have to divert the flow permanently so they can generate the electricity. They say not, but I don't see any reason to believe it. Plus I'm told the diversion will raise the water temperatures in the Nechako enough that you can kiss the remaining salmon goodbye when they try to spawn."

The snarky adolescent she imagines I'm hiding surfaces for this one. "All 15 or 20 of them?"

"Don't be snide," she snaps. "There's still fish in that system."

Maybe. But I have a hard time believing it coming from Bev, just as I generally do. I understand, in a theoretical sense, that the salmon runs on the Fraser *weren't* ended by all the dynamiting the railways did in the Fraser Canyon back in the early part of the century. But after innumerable visits to Hell's Gate, the site of the worst damage, a part of me simply can't believe there can be many fish left. That I've never actually seen a live salmon anywhere in the Fraser or Nechako rivers, least of all in the famous fish ladders at Hell's Gate, may be anecdotal evidence, and no doubt I visited Hell's Gate at the wrong time of year. But I still find the idea of substantial salmon populations in the Upper Fraser and Nechako watersheds tough to swallow.

Half-heartedly, I try to explain this to Bev, but it just confirms to her that I'm still a crazy adolescent, big-city newspaper column or not. She clams up about Alcan *and* about the salmon. Is she worried I might scoop her book?

"Listen," she says. "If you really want to find out what happened down on the Bowron, you should probably go up to the Forest Service offices and get the story from the horse's, er, mouth."

"Good idea," I answer. "You don't happen to know who's in charge here these days, do you?"

"Northwood Pulp and Paper is in charge, and that means Noranda," she says, with that "you're impossibly dumb" look again. "You already know that. As far as the Forest Service goes, it seems like the government sends in a new bunch every year or so now to rejig their operations. I'm sure the current head will have his name on his office door. Tell them who you work for and you'll probably get to watch them pee their pants on the spot."

I'd like to go directly to the Forest Service offices. But Barry has arranged a lunch at Harvey Chometsky's new cappuccino bar and art gallery, Other Art, and I'm about to be introduced to the newest incarnation of Harvey. In his last one, he'd been sinking into semi-oblivion as a hard-drinking young poet, the home-base identity he'd used for years to make his forays into the world beyond Prince George. A year or two before that, he'd worked as a typesetter and editor for a small press in Vancouver, and he'd seemed pretty happy. When he vanished and showed up again in Prince George, he told me he'd loathed Vancouver's soggy climate. Barry says it was because he hated the writing community; it let him know it had seen other northern Rimbauds come and go long before he arrived. Since I was one of the northern Rimbauds who preceded Harvey, I worry some about his spiritual progress, and occasionally about his physical survival—particularly since he turned 30. When you're 21, pretending that you're what Rimbaud would have been if he'd grown up with a chainsaw under his bed is just fine. If you're still at it when you're 35, it might be less a matter of misunderstood genius than arrested adolescence.

Harvey's credentials as a northerner are better than mine. I was always a downtown Prince George city-slicker, but he's from a little place called Penny, one of the railway whistle stops southeast of the McGregor River system along the Fraser, about 80 kilometres from town. It's rough country out there, part blackfly bog, part postcard-beautiful cedar-hemlock forest, with pockets of very good farmland along the river's narrow flood plain. When I travelled through the area in the early 1960s with the Forest Service, it was a mix of heaven and hell, with blackfly riots in summer, and three-metre snowbanks in winter. The extremes account, I suspect, for Harvey's taste for them.

Max and Jesse are in the den when I return, locked in on late-morning game shows on the big 27-inch television, and they barely glance up. I can hear Barry in the backyard chopping wood.

"Hey, kiddo," I yell from the doorway. "Want to go downtown for some lunch?"

Without muting the volume he waves the remote as a greeting. "Where to?" he hollers over the TV din.

"At Harvey Chometsky's place. Downtown. It's a cappuccino bar."

He puts the television on mute and cuts to the chase. "What kind of food do they serve?"

I can't answer that one, so I finger a time-out and wander out to the back deck to ask Barry.

"Oh, hell," he says, slamming his double-headed axe into the block. "I don't know. Coffee. And poofter food, I guess."

"Anything a kid will eat? Max wants the menu before he'll come with us for lunch."

Barry laughs. "The food's all vegetarian," he answers, using the same intonation on "vegetarian" as he would on "puke." "If Harvey's got anything there at all. Listen, Joy left some stuff in the fridge for the kids. And I can nuke up some chicken noodle soup for them if they want."

Max has followed me outside and is taking this in. "Is the food really crappy there?" he asks Barry.

"It's okay." Barry shrugs and mentions a few inedibles he thinks might be on the menu. He's making the fridge food sound more attractive, even to me, which could mean he's trying to warn me, in his genteel fashion, not to eat anything when we get there. More likely he wants to talk over something and doesn't want the kids around to hear it.

Max and Jesse take a pass on lunch at Other Art, Max because of the food, Jesse because he's already deep enough into puberty that being seen in public with either of his parents is only a little less uncool than crapping in his pants. I decide that leaving Max to his own devices—even if the main device is a television set—isn't such a bad idea. After three weeks together we need a break. And I'll find out what's bothering Barry, if anything.

Other Art is close enough for us to walk, but we defer to local custom and take Barry's truck. He's sold the blue Ford 150 he's been driving since the early 1980s, and the hot-pink Dodge I parked in front of when I arrived turns out to be his.

"Where'd you get this beast?" I ask as we climb in.

"My father found it for me when he heard my Ford was dying. I think he got it off an auto-body repair guy who'd fallen into a vat of LSD or something."

"Interesting colour."

"I like it," Barry says, without irony. "It runs good, it's a pickup, and it kind of lets everybody know I'm one of those pansy profs from the college. It's smaller than the Ford, too," he adds. "The gas consumption on that sucker was killing me." He guns the motor. "If I'd done this in the Ford," he says, "we'd have had to stop at a gas station before we could drive to Harvey's."

Other Art is located on the north end of George Street, once one of the two most active streets downtown, but now dammed up by angle parking and largely derelict. It's close enough to City Hall that Harvey could break the window in the mayor's office if he threw a rock from the roof of his building. As we angle-park in front, get out, and tramp up the steep stairs to the second floor, I remind myself not to mention this to him.

The café is laid out pretty much as you'd expect for a recently opened coffee house on a short budget: scrappy tables and chairs, counters and display cabinets that don't quite fit, along with a sense that at any moment the waitresses may trip and launch a latte over everyone. But at least there's someone in the place beside us to spill coffee over. Eight or ten people, half of them young tree-planters, are spread around the room sipping coffee and either reading or talking quietly. I can't see Harvey anywhere, so Barry and I settle at a window table with a view of the roof of Barry's pink pickup truck and the Keg & Cleaver franchise across the street.

Harvey's taste in painting runs more to Salvador Dali than to Tom Thomson or Emily Carr, and he seems to like his Dali with infusions of LSD Punk. A half-dozen large unframed canvases line the side walls, featuring abstract, bright, semi-figurative anti-landscapes. If Barry and I were being cynical, we'd be making jokes about how the painters had managed to get so many different colours on the end of a chainsaw.

"You know, this really isn't half bad," I say to Barry, trying to see beyond the paintings to the purely mercantile side of the place. "Harv could make a decent living running this if he'd toss all the punk-rock stuff back into the alley and make some sensible arrangement with the local crafts people and artists."

"Fat chance," Barry answers gloomily. "Besides. Harvey doesn't see this as a living. He doesn't just want to run a coffee house, he wants to start a franchise with it, so he can hire managers to do the work and make him a millionaire."

"He wants to get rich selling gourmet coffee and funny art in Prince George?"

"Wait'll you talk to him. He's wall-to-wall business slogans. When he isn't counting his imaginary capital as it accumulates. He figures he should be a millionaire in about six months, if everyone would just co-operate."

"I can't see many of the people I know around here paying money for this sort of stuff," I say, gesturing at the artwork on the walls. "It looks like he's just trying to piss people off."

"I know. I've tried to tell him to get it on with a few of the landscape painters who hang out at the Art Gallery, and so has Harris. Harv just tells us we don't know what we're talking about. Which is true enough. But neither does he."

Harvey hasn't showed up at work yet, even though Barry phoned him at home to say we were coming in for lunch. "He's playing at being fashionably late," Barry complains. "Does he owe you money or something?"

While I'm trying to remember if he does (the answer is yes, but not much), Harvey appears from the back of the building, lugubriously tying an apron around his waist. He's gained weight since I last saw him, and his wide grin makes him look like he's got a couple of donuts stuck in each cheek. But he hasn't gone completely straight. He's sporting a messy Fu-Manchu and his hair is still long enough that he's got it tied into a ponytail.

"Gentlemen, gentlemen," he says as he approaches our table, rubbing his hands together like some caricature of a German shopkeeper from a 1930s movie. "And how are we this fine day?"

"We're fine, Harv," Barry grumbles half under his breath. "Cut the glad-handing bullshit."

It takes a while, but Harvey does squeeze off the hype pipe long enough to explain his new persona. The short version makes reasonable sense: he got tired of being broke all the time, and with his girlfriend, Lila, who has both the experience to start a business and the capital, he dreamed up a combination cappuccino bar, art gallery, and crafts gift shop.

Other Art has the right basics for success if you squint enough to blur the loose ends. Harvey *does* want to feature local painters, and the gift shop will be strictly local craftspeople, including his new T-shirt sideline. There's no real flaw in the business plan until you get to the part where Harvey takes over the Chamber of Commerce and turns it into a more socially caring instrument of public will.

Nothing in any of this, so far, is out of character for Harvey. He's always thought big, even when he was printing up his own poetry chapbooks and expecting the cultural capitals of the world to crumble into submissive awe in the face of his insights. And since I don't think Harvey's *really* going to change, this new persona seems, on the whole, a positive thing—at least it'll prevent him from ending his days collecting beer bottles along the side of the highway.

Collecting beer bottles along the highway just happens to be the fate Barry has had nightmares about for years, except that in Barry's nightmare it isn't Harvey pulling the little red Radio Flyer wagon along the highway, it's Barry himself. One possible reason for his irritability with Harvey might be that he suspects Harvey is planning an entrepreneurial takeover on the nightmare, so that when it becomes reality, there will be Harvey holding the franchise rights on beer-bottle collecting, offering Barry a particularly bug-infested stretch of the road for a too-large portion of the take.

This beer-bottle-collecting nightmare isn't as silly as it sounds. It's a direct product of Barry's ongoing real-world nightmare. About 10 years ago, the college he's taught at since the early 1970s began "downsizing" its liberal arts programs in order to emphasize a series of half-baked job-creation schemes aimed at turning Prince George into an industrial hub of the north. The college entrepreneurs didn't seem to realize that every other community college in North America operating under the influence of the local Chamber of Commerce has tried to do the same thing, or that the current model everyone imitates—Silicon Valley—isn't exactly a shining example of government–industry cooperation.

None of the college's other job-creation schemes—a chopstick factory, a gigantic slaughterhouse and meat-packing facility capable of supplying all of B.C. and Alberta, the proposal to hyper-develop architectural and management software that was already obsolete or public domain—came to anything, except to make the lives of everyone teaching liberal arts totally miserable. The cutbacks were permanent, and they reduced Barry to teaching remedial English and study skills instead of the literature and creative writing courses he's eminently qualified to teach. Worse, the college administrators have been terrorizing him more or less continuously, calling on him to justify every element of his occupational existence whenever he tries to redesign a student course or (to hear Barry tell it) asks for a paperclip. Several times, they've attempted to eliminate his job altogether.

"It's enough to make me want to join the Commies," Barry says ruefully. "But of course those humourless bastards would just give me more of the same, so what's the point?"

It doesn't matter to Barry that what's happened to him is happening to liberal arts teachers and their programs everywhere. "I'm trained to teach people the pursuit of beauty and truth," he says, "and they've got me teaching morons how to write timber estimates when there isn't any timber left to estimate, or how to produce personal resumés that hide what assholes they really are."

But while Barry takes every one of these humiliations personally, another part of him has learned to see the comedy in them, and he's become a genius at making jokes at his own expense. This, I suspect, is what keeps him from slipping into a serious depression over what they've done to him. The trouble is that his jokes are so good they make him more visible and more vulnerable to the humourless college administrators trying to exterminate him.

I admire Barry more than it's polite to let on. It requires real courage to keep a sense of humour in a town like Prince George—assuming that you're not drunk, stoned, or brain-damaged by some leaking industrial solvent. But in our here-and-now, it's what is making Barry such a rotten audience for Harvey's bushy-tailed business optimism.

After almost an hour of non-stop sloganeering, Harvey announces that, well, he'd like to stay and chat, but he has several business meetings to attend. "But listen," he says, as if to reassure us that he enjoys our company even though we aren't part of the real world, "if you're going to drive out to the clearcuts, I might want to come with you. A guy can't be all business. I need a break once in a while."

I see Barry's face start to crack up at this zinger, and recognize what's going through his head because it's going through mine: we've been here less than an hour and we need a break from Harvey ourselves.

As we watch him bustle off, Barry offers to drive me to the Forest Service offices. I take him up on it because I don't have a clue where the offices are now. The main office I worked out of 30 years ago was in the basement of the provincial government building on 3rd Avenue, but that was taken over by the expanding criminal courts in the mid-1970s and is now used for storing criminal records. The equipment depot of my day has been the city's art galley for years.

Anyway, Barry and I need to talk. All we've done since leaving the house is crack jokes about Harvey. And I'd noticed, while Harvey was giving his motivational-speaker impression and Barry was tuning out, that Barry looked as haggard as Harvey did manic. More haggard and stressed-out than he usually does, I mean.

But as we're winding our way west across the city, Barry spends the time assuring me that even though Harvey irritates the hell out of him, he hopes that Other Art succeeds. "Hell," he adds, "we need people on the other side. And Harvey's always been a good friend. Maybe they'll put him on the college board of governors and he can save my job."

6

The Prince George offices of the B.C. Forest Service aren't what I'm expecting. The modest two-storey building set back from the street behind a scratchy lawn is no surprise, and assuming that the equipment warehouses for the firefighting, cruising, and Silviculture operations are behind them somewhere, the scale is about right.

It's the decor. The building has been "done"—sided in unplaned cedar and stained a greyish-black. Forest Service colours are forest green and white. When you ran across a green truck in the bush, you knew who was around. For the same reasons, Forest Service buildings—depots and ranger stations alike—were painted white with dark green trim.

The B.C. Forest Service—Prince George District, at least—has been subjected to the Disney makeover that's splattered across the rest of civilization. This building's trim colour is a garish shade somewhere between mauve and hot pink, and there's a lot of it. Even sillier, the entrance has been tarted up with faux log pillars the same colour. The effect is so jarring I have to touch the pillars to ensure they're not fibreglass.

Barry sees this and grins. "What?"

I gesture at the building. "What's wrong with Forest Service green?"

"Charcoal is the right colour," he says. "All the Forest Service does around here now is burn slash after the companies have finished clearcutting. And rubber-stamp their applications to cut more."

"Then, what's the hot pink about?"

Barry jerks his thumb over his shoulder in the direction of his truck. "What's wrong with a little pink paint here and there?"

"You work at the college," I say. "That's how everyone expects you to paint your truck. But when the Forest Service starts running around in pink, doesn't it make you wonder?"

"Wonder what?"

"I dunno," I admit. "Maybe I'm getting old."

Getting old or not, it's clear that I've been away a long time. The Forest Service of the 1990s is a leaner and meaner—read "much smaller"—operation than when I was there. The number of live bodies driving their green trucks out to the bush every day has shrunk because the job of estimating timber volumes was privatized, and Silviculture has no doubt been reduced to a few overworked inspectors trying to make sure the tree-planters are really sticking seedlings in the ground like they've been contracted to do.

Since seeing that first clearcut on the Yellowhead Highway I've realized that I know as little about today's forestry methods as I do about the state of the forests. I haven't been in the bush locally for almost a quarter century, except for day trips to fish for trout or to collect fiddleheads along the roadsides in spring. Spending a couple of years in these forests robbed me of any desire to be anywhere wild if I can't have a hot shower at the end of the day.

On the drive up, when I asked Barry how they fight forest fires these days, he said he didn't know, but then chuckled and said he suspects they're farming it out to the U.S. Air Force. I looked puzzled, and he laughed.

"Wait'll you see how they handled fire control in the Bowron," he says. "You'd swear to God they spend more time dropping napalm on the hilltops than fire retardant."

"Slash-burning?"

At the bottom of the barrel, half-hidden in the muck like one of those 550-kilogram sturgeon that once inhabited the Fraser River, is this monster: the most important public agency in British Columbia has made no comprehensive record of its activities.

Not surprised, somehow, that there is no written history of the B.C. Forest Service? If you're not, take it as a demonstration of how profoundly cynicism has addled your common sense. That successive governments of British Columbia and their officials have—deliberately or with a gun stuck in their ear—chosen to make no summary of the specific acts and events that have brought the province's forests to the state they are in *should* be shocking to everyone, including those who want to continue the cutting. And it isn't just the government that doesn't want a history. No one from the corporate sector has been interested in compiling the narrative either, and British Columbia's universities, two of which have departments dedicated to training professionals to oversee the forest industry, have likewise looked away.

There *are* historical documents for anyone wanting to track what has been done.

"Supposedly. But about half the fires burn out of control because they don't have the budget to hire enough people to keep the fires where they want them."

Once we're inside the building the Disney entrance gives way to a government office out of the 1960s or 1970s. A map of the Prince George Forest District has been mounted on the wall just inside the door, and across from the entrance and its small, chairless waiting area stands an imposing wooden counter that looks as if it came from the old downtown offices. A portrait of Queen Elizabeth II on the wall reminds whoever finds themselves at the counter that B.C.'s forests belong to the Crown—and a few others with money, expensive clothes, and a taste for coronets.

Barry and I line up behind several others waiting at the counter, and I eavesdrop on what a middle-aged man in overalls is asking for —permission to cut some trees on a private woodlot. The clerk, a sour-faced woman in her thirties, is making it clear that if the public is being served here, it's with officious reluctance. Every third word coming from her mouth is "No." *No, the Crown doesn't permit that. No, we don't give out that sort of information to the public. No, I can't advise you what you should do.*

The man soon backs away from the counter, defeated and grumbling, and I see that my chances of getting anything about the clearcuts on the Bowron from this woman are slim-to-none if I request the information as a private citizen. Barry must be thinking the same

---

The Sloan Royal Commissions on Forestry in 1946, 1956, and 1966 contain valuable data and analysis, but each one treated B.C.'s forests as an inexhaustible resource and mostly projected the practices and trends of the immediate past into the future. It wasn't until the 1976 Royal Commission headed by Peter Pearse that there was any inkling that the forests aren't infinite or that forestry practices need to be examined more closely to ensure that the industry isn't merely clearing the province of trees so British Columbia can be turned into a string of water reservoirs for thirsty California.

Pearse's report, commissioned during Dave Barrett's accidentally elected social democratic government of 1972–1975 had some of its recommendations implemented before the commission reported out, but was treated with a combination of hostility and indifference by the succeeding right-of-centre regime. The result was that the 10-year increment of inquiries into the state of the forest industry set by Sloan in 1946 was ended. Hear no evil, see no evil.

The motives for the ongoing silence about British Columbia's forests are simple

thing, because he leans over and whispers in my ear, "Flash her your press card. These suckers aren't about to admit what year it is unless you scare it out of them."

I tell him that I left my press card stuck in my snap-brim reporter's hat back in Toronto.

"I'm not really worried about credentials. If someone demands to see them, I'll tell them to phone the *Globe*. I don't have a clue what my editors would say if they do phone, but it doesn't matter because they'll never get through the automated switchboard. *I* never have."

While Barry and I talk, the surly clerk has been browbeating a pale young woman who is there to obtain maps. She isn't quite sure of the area she needs them to cover, or the scale. Everyone in the lineup knows she doesn't have a hope. Eventually she figures it out, too, and with a sigh, gives up. I step up to the counter, nod to the Queen, and then try to penetrate the algae fog in the clerk's watery-green eyes.

"Yes?" comes her interrogative, dripping the insolence of a tyrant on a winning streak. It isn't a question so much as a statement of her lack of interest.

I give her my name first, careful not to mumble. Then, with more force, I tell her whom I represent, and the city I'm from. The first word that stirs the algae behind her eyes is "Toronto." While it swirls around those three syllables, I tell her what I want. There's a momentary pause, during which Barry later claims he could smell circuits

---

and very similar to one another. From the bite of the first European axe into the first trees, the treatment of B.C.'s forests can be accurately summarized with two words, each of which has an exclamation point tacked permanently onto it: *Whoopee!* and *Whoops!*

The B.C. Forest Service, established by the first *Forests Act* in 1912, has operated pretty cheerfully on that sort of basis. It has participated uncritically in the changing *Zeitgeist* of the forest industry, whatever it happens to be. From its beginnings, the Forest Service has given enthusiastic aid to anyone able to afford the price of a device for cutting down trees, whether it was pioneers clearing the land to make a little bit of Europe in the wilderness; locally based loggers—gyppos or magnates—out to make a fortune and move on; or today's post-national corporations out to spread fiscal joy to their offshore shareholders.

In the Forest Service's defence, I probably ought to point out that not being able to see beyond the obvious trends and tropes of the present hasn't exactly been a capital crime in the 20th century. It is also true that around the time things really

PARADISE, 1990 / 43

fusing inside her brain as her fear of whatever authority she imagines
I represent launches her back in the general direction of the human
species. "Just a moment, sir," she squeaks. "I'll get someone who can
handle your request."

The next few minutes would be hilarious if they weren't so depressingly predictable: clerks scurrying this way, officials scurrying that. It
makes me feel like I represent the Gestapo, not the *Globe and Mail*.
Even Barry confirms my Gestapo identity, unconsciously taking a
step away from me, distancing himself from what I've become to the
clerk.

A sudden decorum settles in—if not a logic and proportion—and
I'm ushered into a spacious office where I'm attended to by three senior officials of the local Forest Service. We sit down and exchange
pleasantries while they offer me tea poured into porcelain teacups
from an ornate silver tea service. One of the men introduces himself as
the "regional manager," a term I find puzzling enough that it atomizes
his name and those of his assistants. They look like foresters and senior rangers, these men, not corporate managers. All three are about
my age, all slim, physically fit and informally dressed—as befits men
who've worked their way up from the bush through the Forest Service
hierarchy. But who—or what—turned them into managers?

Over the next half hour I listen politely as they tell me a longer
and more convoluted version of the following story. I'll summarize it
as accurately as I can, and in the plain English in which I heard it:

---

got going, at the end of the 1930s, the Chief Forester of the era, Ernest C. Manning,
warned of the long-term results of overcutting without reforestation. So did his suc-
cessor, C. D. Orchard. Both warnings were ignored.

On the positive side, B.C.'s governments have had, from the beginning, some
conscience about—and considerable success in—preventing the wholesale alienation of public forests in British Columbia. But until the mid-1950s, the Forest Service
took no interest in what happened to the publicly owned forestlands once the private
sector's loggers had removed the trees. Since then, constantly shifting and mostly
fanciful theories of how reforestation should be conducted have had little to do with
anything that could be substantiated by hard science. Nearly all of them have a great
deal to do with self-congratulatory optimisms about trees being big vegetables and
forestlands being vast, untended farms.

Unfortunately, along with the awakened interest in replanting the forests has come
a parallel buckling of will in the face of industry pressures—mostly from the large

Everything started with over-mature spruce forests in the Upper Bowron River valley, a forest just at the beginning of a renewal cycle that in nature is generated by uncontrolled forest fires, wind, insects, and disease. The trigger in the Bowron appears to have been a series of windstorms starting in 1974 that levelled small patches of trees across the valley. Now, as everyone knows, blow-down in a mature forest tends to snowball, bringing down more and more timber, partly because the roots of the trees adjoining blow-down are loosened by the uprooted trees, and partly because the felled trees create unnatural openings in the forest canopy for further wind damage. So, the Forest Service decided to permit limited salvage logging of the blow-down to prevent further damage by shaping the forest.

Unfortunately, the patches of blow-down were ideal conditions for insects to breed, and the Forest Service personnel and the working loggers soon noticed, once they were in the area, that spruce beetles were moving in and that they were moving much more swiftly than the Forest Service or its salvage loggers are able to. By 1980, there was a spruce beetle infestation of unprecedented seriousness in the Bowron, one that had to be acted on swiftly if huge volumes of timber were not to be simply wasted. The decision was made to salvage-log the whole area.

Between 1980 and 1987 the companies harvested 53,000 hectares of timber, most of it spruce and balsam fir, with a little

---

multinationals who began to take over ownership of the industry from the locals after 1965—to increase the permitted volume of the harvest. Reforestation has become, in reality, one of the incentives to increase the annual cut, even though it amounts to counting the number of egg-laying hens the day after they've been hatched as chicks. The Forest Service has become, if anything, an ever-more-pliant servant to the industry over the past 30 years. Meanwhile, ownership of the industry has grown more or less completely remote from the communities living near the trees being harvested—those same communities that will have to face the music once the trees, and possibly the forestry corporations and its pliant Forest Service, are gone.

Let's be blunt about this. While the Forest Service has presided over the consuming of B.C.'s forests, it has been as silent as the forests themselves concerning the wisdom and sustainability of the harvesting methods. B.C., perhaps particularly in the northern areas, where the government and the mainstream media don't pay close attention, is losing its tree cover, and its communities have utterly lost control over the

Douglas fir mixed in. They took out about 15 million square metres of lumber—enough to build 250,000 homes—with an economic value of more than $800 million. The government received about $27 million in stumpage fees. Since then, the Forest Service and the companies have been busy reforesting. By 1992 almost all of the logged areas will have been replanted.

This explanation is presented to me in such a genuine "what else could we have done?" tone that the only way I can question either the narrative or the facts contained in the narrative is to call into question the honesty and professional integrity of the men who are sipping tea with me. Even if I had a coherent alternative view—which I don't— or sufficient cynicism about corporate-controlled government agencies—which I do—simple courtesy would stop me. This may be an official story they're giving me, but it's also *their* story. They aren't lying to me. From their perspective, they aren't even stretching the facts.

I *like* these men. They remind me of the guys I worked with when I was 20. They're older now, and they're more world-weary and smarter. But the same earnestness and sense of mission makes them identifiably Forest Service. They're decent people, in other words, who've been caught up in a situation so completely that they don't see its indecency.

I need more facts about the Bowron, along with some official documents and names that will establish the facts. "Do you have a

---

disposal of benefits from cutting these trees. Parallel to this, technology advances, along with artificially cheap energy and transport, have permitted the corporations to make radical reductions to the number of jobs, which are what sustain the smaller towns and cities. The only component that has been thriving since the mid-1970s is the forestry corporation shareholders and their profits.

Is so extreme a characterization of the state of forestry in northern B.C. fair? Maybe not, because there are always exceptions—companies that log in sensitive ways or go out of their way to create jobs. But if you're standing at the intersection of Victoria Street and Third Avenue in what was once downtown Prince George, it's a characterization that will feel pretty accurate.

Beyond all this, the forests of the Canadian north are a story everyone needs to hear. But the trees themselves don't talk, and until very recently, no one thought to speak

summary of this that you can give me?" I ask dimly, not quite sure what that would entail.

"No," one of them answers, as if he's never thought it necessary until now. "But we'll put one together for you as soon as possible."

"Is there a map of the areas affected?"

"Give us 10 minutes," another says, and leaves the room, presumably to instruct a draftsman to produce a map.

It is while we wait for this map to appear, making idle chit-chat, that one of them remarks that the clearcut is the largest contiguous clearcut in the world, so damn large you can see it from outer space. His pride grates, and my pose of journalistic objectivity falls apart. But at first I ignore the remarks, partly because I'm distracted by a large framed photograph on the far wall showing a long line of log-filled trucks proceeding in a zigzag convoy across a treeless snow-covered valley. I count 22 trucks before my hosts realize what I'm staring at.

"That photo was taken in the Bowron at the height of the logging," one of them says with the same pride in his voice I'd heard from his colleague when he told me the clearcut could be seen from outer space. "Twenty-four trucks in that convoy. That was a common sight out there for a couple of winters. You did hear that it's possible to see the clearcut from outer space, didn't you? It was quite a show."

I can't stop myself. "I heard what you said," I answer. "But I'd feel better if I thought people could see the clearcut from Prince George.

---

on their behalf. I'm not sure, to this day, that those currently taking up their cause ought to be trusted. I include myself here, whenever I step away from my always-shaky neutrality to try. Canada's forests are not, to begin with, a single coherent, connected forest, but rather a patchwork of often profoundly different biotic entities defined by their altitude, latitude, hydrology, topography, and how much topsoil the glaciers left in their wake as they acceded and receded.

The forests of northern British Columbia are among the least glamorous on the continent. The dominant species grow slowly, they're neither noble nor grand, and they aren't characteristically covered in the kinds of picturesque mosses and lichens that attract nature photographers or professional ecologists. That's why, I believe, this clearcut in excess of 50,000 hectares has gone undetected and undiscussed in most of the places where it should have set alarm bells clanging.

The chosen methods of harvesting the forests of northern British Columbia for human use, and the scale of the harvest, on the other hand, are progressive and

People around here don't seem able to get their heads around it. I wonder what they'd think if they could?"

The chill is instant. "I'm sure," the regional manager says, "that you're aware there were no other choices open if the spruce beetle infestation wasn't to get completely out of control. It was cut it or lose it."

"Don't you lose it anyway if you cut it?"

A chasm opens between us: these men believe that a forest is a resource only if it is cut and used. Somewhere along the line, I've come to believe that it is a resource only if it is left alone. The Forest Service officials haven't missed the difference, and are now on red alert —literally. Isn't the *Globe and Mail* a business-oriented newspaper? Why did they send this tree-hugging crypto-commie to bother them? I'm wondering the same thing, actually. Two of my instincts are warring—the one that tells me to distrust anything a government official tells me, and the one that tells me these men are too honest to make their living by telling themselves and others things they know are lies.

What began as a handshake meeting becomes dissembling: they're covering their professional asses with half-facts and larded estimates of the number of jobs created during the cutting, and I'm backtracking so that I can regain their co-operation to give me a shot at whatever additional information they have available.

We're saved from ourselves when a skinny technician with a scraggly beard—he looks enough like one of the cruisers I worked with in

---

uniform even if they aren't coherent or logically consistent. Once you peel back the professional and government rationalizations and push away the slimy "positive spin" the industry puts on its doings, the harvesting of trees has been, then and today, determined by two things and only two things: the technology available for harvesting trees, and the size and greed of those employing the machines. This was true with horse loggers using hand winches and saws at the turn of the century, and it is true of today's post-national corporations using tree-snipping mega-machines.

So long as the harvesting technologies didn't require massive capital outlays— until roughly the 1960s in North Central British Columbia—the forests had a certain degree of protection. But when the major forestry corporations moved in, building pulp mills that demanded unprecedented volumes of wood fibre, the volume and scale of logging increased to accommodate them, and the Forest Service meekly altered its methods to suit, well, the suitors. Small wonder it hasn't been interested in recording its history.

1963 that I catch myself wondering if he's that man's son—brings in a rolled map and spreads it across his chest. It offers the only thing all four of us are likely to agree on at this point: the physical dimensions of the clearcut. We leave the office and the silver tea service and reconvene in the outer office where a drafting table provides a surface large enough to lay out the map. The clearcut is a jagged green star on the bottom right corner of a map of the eastern half of the Prince George Forest District.

"That's 53,000 hectares?" I ask. "What is that—53 square kilometres?"

"It's 53,000 hectares," the regional manager confirms, carefully.

"It looks bigger than 53 square kilometres," I remark, shrugging.

"It's a large area," he answers. "But the beetle infestation was a severe one. The worst anyone has ever seen in this area."

7

The history of forestry in British Columbia runs through the middle of a universe of ideological chaos, honest misconception, and self-serving bullshit. So even if the details can't be added up to anyone's satisfaction, let's try to piece together what we know of the story, beginning with its depressingly consistent plot. As a preamble, I'll offer a one-sentence summary of the Forest Service's philosophical history. It goes something like this:

> The purpose of the Forest Service is to serve the needs of the forest industry, and to support its aspirations, whatever they are at any given time and location.

No difficulty swallowing that bloodless bit of management Newspeak? Not so fast. Behind it are a number of rhetorical questions that will get everyone fist fighting, because in the real world, there are different answers to them: Who else might the Forest Service serve? Can a Forest Service simply conserve forests? If local communities don't get any of the profits from harvesting the resources around them, should they allow them to be harvested at all?

But what if we look at this in a slightly old-fashioned way and suppose that the forests of British Columbia are a resource that belongs to what used to be called "the commonwealth," which is a theoretical state of physical and spiritual being aspired to by all serious democracies. It means we want to share what is essential to life on a fair, if not necessarily equitable, basis.

Let's also assume that there is no longer any such thing as a truly rhetorical question, and rejig our inquiries to ask, in the circumstance of British Columbia facing the possible North Africanization of its forests, how we define *wealth*, and *commonality*? Is wealth strictly a matter of monetary profits legally derived and distributed? Or is it also reflected in the quality of life—human and/or natural—within the commonwealth. How literally, in the Global Village and within a globalized economy, can we define the term *commonwealth*?

It isn't necessary to brandish the spectre of threatened owls and rare rodents to raise quality-of-life issues in forestry. This is a matter of the air people breathe, the water they drink, even the stability of the ground they build and live on. And at a very slight remove are questions about the general well-being of things: derelict cityscapes, decimated forests, polluted waterways, stinky, toxin-infused air. If the wealth from these forests is paying for limousines in Hong Kong or cocaine in New York City but not providing enough jobs or profits to maintain the city of Prince George, then is that wealth offering accurate and adequate service to the commonwealth or even to the forest industry?

So let me put the only positive spin on this I can. Since there is no agreed-to, acknowledged-in-public history to the B.C. Forest Service, then my version is as valid as any. I'm not being flippant. I spent a couple of years working for the B.C. Forest Service, and what I saw happening then is the only sure place I have from which to begin. I will start by admitting what I did in and to the forests, and I will testify to what I saw other men do. Some of what I did and saw I'm now ashamed of, but there are other things in my reckoning that fill me with pride, and with longing for things and people I didn't appreciate nearly enough while I was among them.

––––––––––––

When I started to work for the Service in September 1963, the logging method used in northern B.C. was to mark out small plots of seed trees, mow down all the others, and bring in big Caterpillars the summer after logging to bare the ground so that spruce and pine, which can only reseed in bare ground, would be able to regenerate. There were flaws in this system, some of which were visible to me at the time. The obvious ones were that regeneration, if it occurred at all, would take a very long time and be erratic. The seed plots were small and few, and rarely placed in any relation to the topology that would protect the trees from being blown down in the first windstorm—and when the trees were protected, the plots weren't well situated to facilitate the spreading of seed. Loggers complained, often with justification, that most of the seed plots blew down in a couple of years. There were other complaints—somewhat more fanciful— that the opened-up ground, along with the huge mounds of debris that resulted, were fire hazards, and even prone to spontaneous combustion. A more complicated argument was that scarification, as the earth-baring procedure was called, did nothing to release seeds from the spruce and pine cones. That, the argument went, could only be done by fire.

But in my day there was a powerful prejudice in the Forest Service against deliberately starting forest fires. Since the other role of the Forest Service was to coordinate the fighting of forest fires, the prejudice wasn't easy to get around. It was rooted in common sense: only an idiot deliberately starts a fire in the bush, and idiots aren't very talented at controlling fires once they've started.

Nearly all the loggers' criticisms of the plot-regeneration system of the early 1960s were accurate, except maybe the one about forest debris constituting a fire hazard due to spontaneous combustion. That could result only from the logging and scarification crews throwing empty whisky and beer bottles around, a situation that occurred, well, no more than 10 to 20 percent of the time.

The only way to prevent forestry debris from acting as kindling for lightning strikes or careless campers is to incinerate it so there's no volatile carbon there to burn. Ironically, the theory behind the current method of treating clearcut forests prior to manual replanting is to mimic nature, and to a degree it does. Spruce, pine, and fir cones release seed best when subjected to fire, which likewise serves to clear forest floor debris and release mineral nutrients into the soil. Fire also, obviously, kills insects and eradicates diseases. In pre-European British Columbia, lightning-generated forest fires regularly cleared vast tracts of land for regeneration. It was an integral part of the natural cycle.

Because of this, forestry theorists can truthfully argue that subjecting tracts of land that have been completely cleared of trees to "controlled burns" reproduces part of the natural cycle: 1) it frees some seed from cones if it doesn't burn them to ashes, which it generally does because they're no longer high in the trees but lying on the ground with the other logging debris; 2) it releases whatever chemical nutrients remain in the wood after logging; and 3) it bares the soil for replanting. But it certainly isn't mimicking the action of periodic forest fires in a productive sense, because the key ingredient—carbon —isn't there after a forest has been logged. Forest fires leave vast quantities of carbon littering the ground to feed the regenerating seedlings. Burning off a logged forest transforms most of the carbon that's left to ash, and most of that is washed into the creeks and rivers before the new growth can use it.

I could dress this discussion up in much more grandiosely scientific language, but that would hide the depressing truth that the "science" behind reforestation in the north is either skimpy and fanciful, or non-existent. The regeneration schemes of the past 50 years could have been worked out over a coffee table by an average sampling of loggers and Forest Service assistant rangers in a single morning. That's probably how they *were* worked out: a bunch of guys sat around and projected a scheme that served their short-term interests and employed the technology and manpower readily available at the time. When technologies changed, or external events exposed how self-serving the scheme had been, another session became necessary. This approach is no doubt a big help for the coffee industry, but hasn't been much help to British Columbia's forests. And it ain't science.

I didn't think about macroeconomics or ecology as much when I was 19 as I do today. But I understood the concept of public service fairly accurately, and I believed that the Forest Service was supposed to belong to the public. I wasn't the only one who thought about the Forest Service this way, either. It was, remember, the early 1960s, and the cynicism about government we now take for granted didn't exist. The Forest Service was full of young men like me, often reasonably bright, but usually without any burning ambition to collar the hard-assed world we'd grown up in: idealists without a clue or a cause. We were just kids who didn't want to go where we could feel the world tugging us to go.

We thought the Forest Service was there to serve the forests and, maybe, the people who lived in and around those forests. Consciously or not, the Forest Service of the period fostered that attitude. The wages were low, and you didn't get a job without passing an entrance exam that was a lot harder than the one that gets people into Rotary or the Club of Rome. I couldn't have imagined joining the armed forces, but since I wanted to be part of something larger than the financial ambitions of my family, the Forest Service seemed like a haven. I would go and work for the forests. Was that all an illusion?

8

The idea of the Forest Service, with its built-in notions of public service and nurturing forests, captured my imagination well before I joined. Once in, the pleasure of being in the bush was greater than I imagined. I also found the technical elements of the work—map-making, timber volume estimation, elementary surveying—pretty stimulating. The pay was lousy, but the mix of hard work, science, adventure, and the mild degree of regimentation that crew work made necessary was exactly what the doctor ordered.

Beyond this, there was an unexpected bonus. Joining got my ass out of town, and once I got used to the isolation of the bush, I recognized that I was escaping from my destiny without having to run away from it. It was only a tem-
porary escape, sure, but no one was going to pick on me for taking it. If they did, I had a ready answer: I was working hard in the toughest country in the north—literally no one I knew had ever been as deep into the bush as we were working. At worst, my quorum of imaginary critics would decide that the Forest Service

would either toughen me up or scare me back into town where I belonged. They could think whatever they damned well liked so long as they got off my case.

Working in the bush didn't scare me back to town. It didn't scare me at all, at least until I began to understand a few things about it. It did toughen me up, between my ears and otherwise. On an average day I walked between five and ten miles through heavy bush, and that improved my balance and lower body strength—always the weakest parts of my constitution.

I got stronger in less tangible ways, too. Concentration is a mandatory skill if you have to compass a straight line across topologies that modulate crazily, undermining definition with their combination of complexity and monotony. I learned to see what I saw, and I learned to remember it absolutely and in detail for a few seconds. Then I learned to capture the next set of details without forgetting the others: remembering where you've come from is almost as important as knowing where you're going.

Beyond that, the Forest Service imposed a curriculum for my intellectual and spiritual education, and it has stuck with me. It showed me, first, how stimulating it could be to live among things on the terms they set out. Such lessons were as rare at the beginning of our era of short-term commercial attentions as they are today, and I sucked them up even though I sensed they'd disable me for most of the occupations the rest of my life was conspiring to cram me into. In the bush, you see, physical details are an end in themselves. The texture and firmness of the bark on a fallen tree obstructing your path tells you whether it is safe to cross or walk along. The depth of moss in the undergrowth tells you the depth and age of the forest itself, and the species of trees around you betray elevation, topology, and nearness of the groundwater. The marks on their trunks and branches—or on the moss or snow—tell explicit stories about game populations and their proximities.

Such details weren't of idle interest. They defined how you moved, where you moved, and sometimes, why and when. Second by second, hour by hour, day by day, these details were at you and on you in the bush. Their immediacy bred mental habits, habits of the kind that don't lend themselves to staring into the far distances, either at the scenery or upon visions of private fiscal splendour. The habits I developed there have prevented me, more or less permanently, from projecting my theories and will before seeing what I'm up against. Before I joined the Forest Service I'd felt hopelessly abstracted and incompetent. When I finished high school I wanted to do something decent with my life, but all I'd been able to come up with was to fight in a war—the Spanish Civil War—that had been over for 25 years. Now, miraculously, there were things I could do that made sense: I could pay attention.

So, forestry, in the eccentric way I came to understand it, was about being "out there" instead of "in here." I'd been given a way to pay attention to the specific claims of precisely those things in life that *weren't* me and didn't offer entrances for the addled expectations of a society that already seemed as stupid to me as it was aggressive and myopically self-involved. The bush served up a hundred tactical tricks I still remember and use, and it created a permanent appetite in me for practical reality and its scenery-free exhilarations.

But saying so makes working in the bush seem more romantic than it was. For nearly everyone else who worked there, it was simply gritty and dangerous. A lot of loggers got killed, and the work sure as hell didn't lead anywhere near the Contemplative Life. If you were

logging, it was about 2.5-centimetre-thick steel choker-cables flashing
through the air at throat level; a just-fallen 25-metre spruce rumbling
down a blind slope too fast to elude; or a log slipping across a sawmill
carriage to trap and crush an arm or leg.

But I was in the Forest Service, a cruiser, where you were as far
away from the gears of the industry as you were from the moon, and so
the bush meant the unexpected discovery of a pristine meadow at the
depth of a tract of timber replete with a 1,500-pound lily-munching
bull moose, or a cache of perfectly dry moss and lichens for a campfire
four metres into the branches of a spruce tree, accessible because the
snowpack was nearly three metres deep. It meant making precise maps
with both sophisticated and pioneer instruments in conditions as
extreme as those anywhere on the planet. I snowshoed, I fought forest
fires, I boated on lakes no one had previously laid eyes on, I braved
infestations of blackflies and mosquitoes so thick they would crowd
between my eyeglasses and my eyes if I ran out of repellent. I learned
to run precise compass lines across topologies that defied perspective,
and I trailed racketing yellow Caterpillar tractors through wastelands
of shattered trees and glacial rocks as they scraped the ground clear
for reseeding. I suppose there were a few too many flights in helicopters with half-drunk pilots, and landings that ran too close to unstable
fires or bottomless swamps, and I was shot at more than once by
hunters too drunk to aim straight. But those were minor hazards
compared with what the loggers faced.

I was happy moment by moment, because each moment brought
something new and usually unforeseen, and I never once thought I'd
experienced it all. The bush, I'd later realize, was like the future—one
surprise after another, the unexpected heaped atop the unforeseen,
one amazement following the next—a tsunami, a flood, a roiling cascade of particularity. Yet the first practical lesson the bush gave me
was also its primary one: when I let my attentions wander, I was
likely, both literally and figuratively, to step into a quagmire without
a bottom—or I'd miss a wonder that would never repeat itself.

The Forest Service also gave me back, briefly and for the last time
in my life, something similar to the orderly universe of my childhood.
The difference was that the rule book of the woods was practical and
the rules testable. The bush and its specificities were cruel to braggarts

and posers. They turned myth and magic inside out. Maybe that's why the first cruiser I worked for, the man who taught me most of what I learned about being in the bush, was named Thor.

No one ever asked Thor where he hailed from because it was evident from his name and accent that he was Scandinavian. There were rumours that he'd been a professional forester in Norway or Sweden, and his encyclopedic knowledge of the bush seemed to confirm a kind of training not possible for mere mortals like us. His English was fluent when he had something to say, which wasn't often. He had no small talk, and I never heard him allow an argument on his crew. He spoke, you listened, and then everyone shut up and got down to it. I didn't think he was a god or a genius, but I did recognize, and very quickly, that he was a walking sanctuary from bullshit.

Thor's gift was for simplification. He was deliberately *non-cognizant* of anything but the bush and the specific job at hand. He quickly set about simplifying me, starting my first day on the job. He showed me what to wear in the bush for different kinds of weather, no options, and was equally clear about what I shouldn't under any circumstance put next to my skin—denim and polyester. One wanted what could help cool or heat the body: in winter, nylon that was watertight, and beneath that, wool that can shed moisture but retain heat; in summer, only the lightest cotton would do under bug- and water-shedding oilskins or nylon.

Thor simplified the way I walked, the way I looked at roads, at trees, at topology and landforms. He taught me never to take a step in the bush without thinking about where I'd been and where I was headed; he taught me how to fall into and across and over things with hurtful spines and jutting knots and butt-ends without injuring myself. He taught me when I could walk along a rotting log and when it was too dangerous; how and where to cross a stream; and where and how to land a boat without a dock or even a perceptible shoreline. I did everything he told me to—it was perhaps the only time in my life I've been completely cooperative—and he was never wrong.

At the time his lessons appeared to be purely practical. They were much more. Without trying to, he taught me stillness, and along with it, the true purpose of, and occasion for, eye contact. When a sleeping moose suddenly awakens and stands up 3 metres away from you, how still you can remain can save your life. Stillness and eye contact were the only effective devices you had when you needed to confront—or disappear from—encounters with the bears common in the bush. When you were lucky enough to meet a wolf or coyote —much rarer events than encounters with bears or moose—eye contact and stillness were the language you shared with them, and your sole means of prolonging the event. Thirty years later I can recall the quiet of the bush, the silence of my body, the tranquil, egoless attention in the animals' eyes.

Thor was not a hunter. The only animal I saw him kill besides trout was a grouse, which he decapitated with his boy's axe from a distance of 10 metres one morning while we were compassing lines. No one else on the crew knew the grouse was there until it was dead. Thor plucked the bird on the spot and cooked it over a small campfire for lunch. As he chewed on a drumstick, he allowed that he'd killed it only because it was time to eat and the grouse was "as dumb," he put it, "as a barnyard chicken." That was his version of being loquacious.

Other than that, I never saw him tempted, even though we had dozens of opportunities with moose, deer, bears, and wolves. The only other weapon he owned was a sawed-off single-shot .22 rifle, which he carried during hunting season to alert the brush-shooting hunters, who were forever firing—accidentally—at Forest Service crews. After a month on his crew I was carrying one, too. I fired mine as rarely as he did his, and never in the direction of an animal unless it was wearing a hunting vest.

What animated Thor was being in the bush. To him it was alive in ways I and the other green kids he trained to be woodsmen never quite were. His imagination was kindled by the way the slope of a heavily wooded hillside could trick the eye into following it; or how a barely perceptible rise in terrain changes balsam fir into spruce, or spruce into lodgepole pine. He was fascinated by the way water is never still in a forest, but moving down, always down, and away. He had two bases for judging other human beings: what they knew about how to behave in the bush, and how they handled the inevitable discovery that he had all the relevant knowledge. No one passed his tests, but I noticed that he responded to my failures without rancour or any visibly elevated sense of his own superiority. He went on delivering his lessons about the bush to whoever he worked with, whether or not his students were willing to learn.

Thor even simplified food. In his mind, there was just one acceptable meal. It consisted of a plate-filling sirloin steak, fried with onions, with a can of peas dumped over it. Everything else a man might eat was ketchup, including the occasional feasts of trout he showed us how to catch on his multiple-hook lines, or the eggs he sometimes planted atop his breakfast steak instead of peas. Even the grouse we ate for lunch was silliness to him. And never mind that his diet wouldn't take most people past the age of 30 without bypass surgery. It provided the calories and the protein we needed to keep up with him.

I worked with Thor for most of a year, but we didn't become friends. As far as I could see he had no friends in the Service. To him I was just a kid on his crew, a greenhorn. I was one of the teachable ones, but when he'd moulded me into a capable woodsman, he treated me no differently. I didn't take it personally because I saw no reason for a teacher to be interested in a student.

Thor's lessons could be as harsh as the bush itself. Once, when I'd grown overly confident about my woodsman's skills, he took away my axe and compass and invited me to pursue a theoretical shortcut across a wooded hillside I'd been nagging him to follow for several days. I blundered off cross-country and was lost in 10 minutes. When he rescued me three hours later from the wooded basin in which I'd trapped myself, I was blubbering in terror. The basin, he showed me on the map when we returned to camp, was barely a half-mile across.

This lesson was meant to teach me not to believe in what my senses were telling me about the bush—and not to take shortcuts. The first place a man becomes lost, he said, is inside his own body and brain. A man becomes a woodsman only when he believes what the instruments—his compass, the clues the forest gives up—tell him; a woodsman does not believe in anything outside particularities. He might have added, but didn't, that a woodsman doesn't believe in either the Forest Service or his own testicles. It was advice straight out of a Joseph Conrad novel, and it still seems like the best anyone ever offered me.

I heard, years after I left the Service, that it ended badly for Thor. Even while I was there he'd been under pressure to write the Assistant Ranger exams and move on and up. Thor liked cruising, and maybe he disliked change. Cruisers, he often told us, had the best jobs in the Service, and I think he was right. We were first into the wilderness, and our work involved by far the greatest degree of separation from the office and from the noisy harshness of logging.

By one account, Thor got into serious trouble when he refused to go along with deliberately underestimating the timber in the Finlay River valley, and when he continued to decline the Assistant Ranger exams for several more years, he was fired. That makes sense to me. The Forest Service, under orders from the government, was discovering that the virgin timber that covered most of the lands to be submerged by the filling of the Peace River Dam was not, despite appearances and some preliminary cruising, big or good enough to log. If the stands of huge timber there were mere half-grown scrub it would allow the dam builders to avoid a two-year delay in filling the dam, and a probable invasion by hysterical ecologists. Presto! Shrinking trees.

But by another account, a supervisor found an icebox filled with Forest Service–issue T-bone steaks in the back of Thor's pickup and canned him for theft, and to set an example. That explanation seems equally plausible. He'd sent me home more than once with a half-dozen sirloins when we finished a cruise earlier than expected. He didn't like the Forest Service administration, and he wasn't above petty theft. When I was transferred out of his crew to one being sent up to cruise the Finlay River in helicopters, he made it clear I shouldn't go, hinting darkly about "Forest Service collusion," and warning me not to get involved in its "Buddy System." He didn't tell me what the Buddy System was, and I was too naive to ask. It sounded paranoid and nutty, and I wanted to ride around in helicopters. What 19-year-old wouldn't?

It was the 1960s, governments were still trusted by most people, and the multinationals were just beginning to creep north. I'd seen plenty of co-operation between Forest Service crews and loggers, and it seemed fine to me. Mill owners didn't see anything wrong with dropping into a Forest Service camp for a morning cup of coffee before work started, and I'd seen a few bottles of rye change hands, too. I didn't see anything harmful going on, nor did I see any undue attempt to influence us beyond getting us to see that we were all in the same boat, and that the boat seemed to be going in the right direction when the loggers got enough trees to cut. That was the way things were. We were working men, and so were the loggers. That the loggers' work was harder and more dangerous than ours gave them a certain kind of authority. I left Thor's crew and went north with the choppers.

I didn't stay long, but not because it wasn't fun. There was something else. Around the time I left Thor's crew, I had my first serious girlfriend trouble, and nothing Thor had taught me helped me with that. After the summer ended the girlfriend left town to go to university in Vancouver, and after a couple of months in the helicopters I quit the Service to follow her.

I'd waited too long, and she dumped me a few days after I arrived. I stuck around for several months working as a truck driver, hoping she'd change her mind, but she didn't. One soggy winter morning I woke up and recognized how much I disliked Vancouver. I didn't miss Prince George, but I did miss the bush.

I retreated north and reapplied to the Forest Service. There was a job for me, but it was on a Silviculture crew. That meant I'd have to work much closer to the industry and to the business of cutting down trees. The loggers called us "markers," meaning that we went into cruised timber sales with backpack spray guns of bright blue paint to mark which trees the loggers could take, and those that would be left as seed plots for the wind and the other post-logging hazards to bring down.

Silviculture was okay, but it didn't thrill me the way cruising did. I wanted to go back to cruising even if it meant taking a pay cut. But when I applied, there was a problem. I'd begun to rise in the estimation of my supervisors, and they made it clear that my next step was forward, to become an assistant ranger, not sideways to cruising. After a summer smoke-jumping and a winter among the markers I quit the Service again, this time for good.

In a way, I quit because of Thor. Until I met him, I'd let my family,

the town, and simple circumstances push me along, ducking opportunities and responsibilities alike. But now it seemed possible that I
might be competent at something of my own devising, and that my
competence might just be as strange and consuming as Thor's passion
for the bush. What seemed to my supervisors a step forward was for
me a step backward toward the past. I didn't want to succeed—not
their way, at least.

9

And so it's a sunny August morning in 1990. Barry and I are on the
street in front of his house, packing camping gear into his pink truck
and trying to decide if we can squeeze four of us—Barry, me, and
the two boys—into its lumpy front seat. The alternative is to take the
Mazda into the clearcut, something I'd like to avoid. Actually, we're
not so much trying to make the decision as we are dodging the torrent
of mostly contradictory advice Joy is giving us.

"You can't all fit in that truck seat," she's saying. "You'll end up
trying to choke one another to death before the day's finished. Jesus
Christ, Barry, put Jesse and Max in the back if you're going to go in
one vehicle. Open up the tailgate or something."

"Oh sure," Barry says. "So they can fall out and be run over by a
logging truck."

I see Max sidling toward me at the remark, even though he caught
Jesse's "my parents are at it again" shrug.

"Don't you be getting any ideas," Joy says, shaking her finger at
me. "You can't take that silly car of yours on those roads, Fawcett.
You'll run it into one of those truck-eaters out there and that'll be the
end of it."

Max takes another step closer. "Truck-eaters? What are those?"

"Relatives of the Sasquatch," I tell him. "Joy's exaggerating a little
bit."

"Well, you sure as hell can't go out there without maps," Joy rattles on. "Don't you have one of those forestry maps that tell you where the camps are? Where are you going to camp tonight, anyway?"

"He's got maps," Barry replies irritably. "And so do I. We'll stop at one of the forestry camps out there. Don't worry about us. We'll be fine, for Christ's sake. Fawcett's still a card-carrying woodchuck."

My woodsman's licence has long since expired inside my head, which is where it counts, but I do have a map of the Bowron. It's the one that the Forest Service managers sent one of their draftsmen off to make for me before they realized I wasn't there to slap them on the back and say what fine guys they were. Since they could hardly deny me the map once offered, I have a perfectly serviceable map with an outline of the clearcut and notations of every forestry road and campsite in the area.

While Barry and Joy haggle over whether we ought to take the Coleman stove or cook everything over a campfire, Harvey pulls up in his near-new leased van and announces that he's coming with us.

That solves a raft of logistical problems. Max is tired of my company, Jesse would rather be dragged behind us on a chain than be forced to ride with his father, and I share Joy's concerns about whether my car will survive the forestry roads. Jesse cheerfully agrees to ride with Harvey, and Max, who finds Barry's gloomy sense of humour more entertaining than Jesse's hormones, wants to ride in the pink pickup. I'll be swingman.

Harvey's in a cheerful mood, but he's also impatient to get on with it. Even here, he's a busy guy. Okay by me, because it stops Barry and me—and Joy—from dithering. We end up tossing a bunch of food into the coolers, taking everything rather than trying to select. We pack the Coleman in along with the coolers, sleeping bags, some tarps, and a selection of axes, saws, and fishing tackle, lift Jesse's trail bike over the tailgate—and we're ready to roll.

———————

It's as hard to gain perspective on the clearcut from the inside as it was listening to Barry or the Forest Service managers talk about it. The roads leading in pass through other clearcuts, some of them 10 or 15 years old and starting to fill in, others as freshly desolate as I'm expecting the big one to be. We're not even certain when we're inside it, until, near the heart of the Bowron River valley, the vistas open out.

When they do, I'm not sure how we got there. There are denuded hillsides in every direction, kilometre after kilometre of them, to the horizon and, likely, beyond. Only near the peaks of the hills, and in the small and intermittent greenbelt strips along the river itself, can adult trees be seen. Near the crowns of most of the hills within sight there are rims of dead and whitened trees. They were the ones, Barry tells me, he'd been talking about in the Forest Service offices, killed by under-supervised slash fires that swept out of control. It's the bizarre set to the surreal, and the visual music isn't pretty.

"It goes on and on," Barry says when we stop the vehicles at the top of a rise that allows us to see in all directions. "Into the next valley to the south and beyond even that. I've never been able to find the end of it."

Harvey clambers up onto a stump by the side of the road and removes his yellow and white baseball cap. "Man, this is something," he says, mopping his brow. "Those fuckers really lost their minds out here."

I assume that Harvey is joking about this, but he's serious. His theory about the clearcut—one that I'll hear more than once in the next while—is that it was the product of what he calls an "industrial riot" during which everyone in the local forest industry went temporarily crazy. Once the logging companies got their equipment into the valley and began cutting down trees without any limits on what and how they cut, Harvey argues, they slipped into a state of "productive" insanity, and with the big multinationals behind them, successfully pressured the government and the Forest Service into letting them keep cutting. The rationalization: no end to spruce budworms and the damage they might do.

It sounds loony at first, but as Harvey elaborates it makes a strange sort of sense. The impetus for cutting was, at first, morally attractive —salvaging trees that were doomed to be killed by insects anyway. Tack on the idea of the clearcut as a hoof-and-mouth style quarantine zone in which the infectious species is made of wood instead of sporting hooves, and you can see how enlarging the cutting zone to stop the infestation must have looked and felt like forest philanthropy to those doing the cutting.

But as we gaze out across the Bowron River valley, which was the recipient of all this economic philanthropy, it's hard to ascribe generous motives. It is numbing to look at, this landscape without distinguishing features—there are no ruins, no gaping wounds, nothing to focus on except here and there the uniform pattern created by planted

seedlings: a block of spruce here, and block of lodgepole pine there.

Later in the day we'll find a few things—higher in the hills there are huge stacks of abandoned logs that someone decided it was "uneconomical" to haul out; logging trails that run right down into the waters of the Bowron River, once a notable salmon-spawning stream; mountains of half-burned slash pushed into the draws. But for now it is a gigantic nothing that almost defies description, a hell of choking weeds and underbrush, some of it a washed-out green, but more of it, even in August, burned brown by the summer sun with panoramas intercut by a grey-brown network of forestry haul-roads and log landings. The river, once we get down to it, is unexpectedly clear, despite the banks fouled with logging debris. Near one bridge there are several car bodies rusting in the water, but you find that in any river in the north. From the look of them, the cars were dumped before the logging began. When I examine the river more closely, though, I see sludge caking the bottom, something that wasn't there 25 years ago.

In the next five or six hours we go high and low, back and forth, trying to get a unified sense of what we're seeing. The boys lose interest, and Barry grows increasingly silent and gloomy as the day wears on, while Harvey talks more loudly, though less about what he's seeing and more about himself. I try to see the clearcut through my own eyes, but after a few hours I give up and take out the two cameras I've brought. They're identical MX-bodied Pentax semiautomatics, one equipped with a good 200-millimetre lens, the other with a 1–4 standard 50-millimetre. Framing what I'm seeing with the cameras might help me to understand what I'm looking at.

The cameras help, but only because they reveal how impossible it is to capture any sort of coherence or perspective. It is like trying to photograph zero: nothing distinguishing itself from zilch. After a while, I have trouble focusing the cameras. Am I trying to see the foreground or the background? It really doesn't matter—nothing stands out, and nothing provides background.

While I was in the Forest Service, I learned that the key to moving within the bush was to foreshorten one's visual field. It was an aesthetic principle as well as a navigation tactic: the closer you were, the easier it was to read the relevant terrain. And sure enough, when I push back the underbrush here, I find spruce and pine seedlings suffocating beneath the mass. I also discover that even at the higher elevation, most of the gravel a few centimetres beneath the topsoil is smooth and rounded, evidence of an ancient lake or glacial torrent. But then, abruptly, the gravel base sharpens, calling up some unwitnessed ancient cataclysm of falling rocks shattering against one another.

There are no animals to be seen or heard, and no evidence of them otherwise—no droppings or scat, no nibbled foliage. There are no birds, and even for the time of year, few insects. A solitary bumblebee dashing here and there in the fireweed can be heard 30 metres away—until drowned out by the tire grind of a tree-planter's pickup truck crossing the valley 8 kilometres away.

The boys respond as, well, *boys*. Jesse wants to get the motorcycle out of the truck and drive the silence away. Max, more cerebral, grows quiet, establishing eye contact with me every 20 or 30 seconds as if to ask: *Is this real?* We tune into one another, and that soon takes the form of a rock-throwing contest. We establish our targets with the simplest head movements, nods, and shrugs. None of the others can see what we're aiming at. Stumps, mostly.

As the day wears on, my sense of outrage, strong in the first hours, begins to slip. There is so much of this, it is so total, that something akin to boredom overtakes me. I want to leave, to get, if not out, then at least to the edges of this, where the real world—or the world I'm comfortable in with its familiar systems of sound and colour—will engage my defeated senses. I can't see enough to give the clearcut the definition and substance necessary to hold it in memory.

Even Harvey, with his optimisms about all the profits the clearcut meant for the loggers, winds down, lapsing into silences broken only by such mutterings as "Oh, fuck" and "Holy Jesus." Finally Barry, after poring across his map, announces that he's had enough. "Let's drive out to Narrow Lake," he says. "There's a camp Bill and I stayed at a couple of years ago that wasn't bad."

For as long as I can remember, the Forest Service has been building and maintaining wilderness camps like the one at Narrow Lake. These days the camps are among the few remaining indications that the Forest Service remembers it has a responsibility to provide services to the public and not merely to the logging companies. The campsites aren't the usual public relations gesture of contemporary governments. They're more a "we use them you use them" production. Most were placed along the edges of logging operations, initially as work camps for cruisers, or more recently, tree-planters. They're to be found near waterways, on lakes or creeks all across the north, and the facilities are minimal but usually intelligently built and placed. There's customarily no fee for their use, and the only rules are that you're supposed to respect what's left of the environment, and not spread your garbage around. These rules are taken seriously by a few people, but most ignore them.

Barry has used the camps from time to time over the years, for fun or for firewood-gathering expeditions, and he's a conscientious camper. Right after we set up camp, he and Jesse wander off with some green garbage bags to clean up the site. Max and I join them, and within 20 minutes, we've filled three of the bags with debris: empty cans, most of them shot full of holes, shards of broken beer bottles, bits of plastic and cardboard, a couple of dozen metres of shredded monofilament fishing line.

"Hunters," Barry mutters as he jerks a twist-tie tight around the neck of a bag and tosses it behind Harvey's van. "They're such fucking animals. The fishermen are better campers," he adds. "But only a little . . ."

"That's because the fishermen usually aren't as drunk as the hunters," Harvey chirps, picking up the garbage bag and placing it behind Barry's truck. He hasn't participated in the campsite cleanup. I can't tell whether that's be-cause he thinks it's pointless, or because he's worried we might deprive someone of an entre-preneurial opportunity. "It's a little hard picking up your garbage when you've got a rifle in one hand and a 26-er of Canadian Club in the other," he adds.

"Don't get me wrong, Faw-cett," Barry says. "There are lots of good people in the north. But you know how it goes. More people means more assholes."

Harvey flinches at that. The one predictable thing about the Chamber of Commerce mentality—anywhere—is its belief that more people is the cure for every problem. "Why don't we see if we can catch a few trout for dinner," he says amiably.

Barry's gloom steamrollers that. "Nah," he says, using his foot to nudge the garbage bags to a neutral position between the two vehi-cles. "These lakes are fished out. You'd need a boat to get far enough out to have a shot at what's left. Besides, we don't have any worms. I'm going to pull that trail bike out so Jesse can mess around."

That's enough to kill Harvey's enthusiasm. He strolls to the back doors of the van, opens them, and begins to rummage around. "You and Max go ahead," he says to me. "If you really think it's worth it."

I help Barry lift the motorcycle out of the back of the truck while the two boys watch, but once the heavy work is done, Jesse takes over. He straps on his helmet, cranks the bike twice to start it, and is gone in an ear-splitting cloud of blue exhaust and road dust.

"How long are you going to be gone?" Barry shouts after him.

I yank the spinning rods we've brought from Barry's truck, then park my butt on the tailgate while I show Max how to tie the spinner and weight so the lure will travel far enough across the water to reach the fish. I've probably got it wrong, but we can adjust it at the lake with the selection of weights I shove into my pockets.

I've fished before, but it's never been a passion. The serious fishermen I know practise it as a kind of Zen—it's the casting that counts, or the choice of spinner, bait, or fly. Others, more cerebrally, enjoy the process of outsmarting the fish, something that's always struck me as a minor sort of accomplishment, similar to feeling superior when you see a goldfish bumping against the glass sides of an aquarium.

I happen to like the taste of lake trout, but I've inherited my father's impatience with exacting tasks that don't have an immediate payoff. When I was a kid, he and his business friends occasionally paid big dollars to fly in to remote lakes—lure-hits-the-water-fish-hit-the-lure kind of lakes—but I rarely saw him fish when the fish weren't plentiful. I resemble him enough that I understand people who toss sticks of dynamite into lakes. I wouldn't do it myself, but I know why they do it.

The bushes come almost to the shores of Narrow Lake, thick alder and willow tangles fronting wind-tilted balsams and spruce, so Max and I navigate our way 50 metres along them to a sandbar that projects out into the lake. As soon as we're outside the radius of Barry's cleanup, we find more garbage—more shot-up cans, shards of brown beer-bottle glass, huge wads of toilet paper, and disposable diapers. There is enough fishing line festooning the bushes to make Max ask if it is some sort of decoration instead of what it is—too many fishermen or a few very, very bad ones.

The two of us cast off the shore for 20 minutes, until Max decides he's got the hang of it and I'm convinced we're not going to catch any fish without dynamite. At least half of our time is spent extracting our lures from the trees behind us, which are too close and dense. When we quit, we're both satisfied: me because I've taught my son the rudiments of a minor woodsman's skill, Max because we did the deed, didn't kill anything, and he won't have to eat fish. Just in case we did catch something, he spent the last 10 minutes yakking about how much he's looking forward to roasting the hot dogs we've brought over the campfire.

Barry doesn't seem disappointed when we return empty-handed. It suits his mood. "You know," he says, as if it's his fault, "you never catch anything any more. Everything is fucked."

Now that he's clear of the cut zone, Harvey's optimism returns. "It's probably the lure," he says. "Or, wrong time of day. There's lots of fish out there. We just don't have the right equipment to catch them."

"Cut the Chamber of Commerce crap, Harv," Barry interrupts. "There's just no fish left, and you know it." Then he changes his mind. "Well, Bill told me there were fish in Slender Lake, but we'd never get these rinky-dink trucks in there. I wish I had a four-by-four. But shit, those cost too much to run, so what's the use?"

He's nosediving again, and I distract him by asking where Jesse is, even though I can hear the trailbike off in the distance. That back-fires because we hear the bike suddenly racket up, then go silent.

"Oh Christ," Barry moans. "He's cracked it up. I'd better go get him."

"Hold on a sec," Harvey says. "He may just have stopped to look at something."

We wait for three or four minutes. The silence is pleasant, but it isn't the silence of the clearcut an hour ago. A breeze is rattling the stiff aspen leaves, flies and bumblebees are busy all around us, and off in the distance, there are ravens shouting at one another over some opportunity they're about to exploit. Behind that, there's a growing rumble as a vehicle approaches along the edge of the lake from the north. Through the interval, Barry stares in the direction Jesse's gone, his jaw getting more rigid as the seconds pass. Then, just as he's about to press the button on a full-panic rescue mission, we hear the bike crank up again.

Barry turns to Max. "You want to take a run on that sucker when Jesse gets back?"

Max glances at me and, when I shrug, makes his own decision. "Nah, I don't think so. I'll just hang out with you guys. Maybe after a few hot dogs."

10

The year I joined the Forest Service, someone gave me a translation of Albert Camus' *The Myth of Sisyphus and Other Essays*. I carried the book everywhere I went for the next two years, reading and then rereading each essay, sometimes by a gloomy campfire in the rain,

sometimes sitting in brilliant sunlight by conifer-darkened streams, sometimes by flashlight in a canvas tent during a snowstorm. The essay that most caught my imagination was one titled "Summer in Algiers." From the first sentence it was gourmet mind food, life-affirming, infused with the beauty and permanence of the North African landscapes Camus cherished, yet appreciative of the headlong obliviousness with which his native city's inhabitants lived their lives.

I remember sitting atop one of the clay banks high above the Nechako River just north of the city, reading the essay for the umpteenth time and thinking about what it was telling me about my own world. It must have been late summer, one of my weekends in town, and the leaves on the cottonwood trees below me on the river flats were betraying the first faint hints of yellow and gold. The warm breeze was sawdust sweet and clear of forest fire or burner smoke. I was looking south, across the city's spreading grid of streets to the Fraser River beyond, with its mix of blue Nechako and muddy brown Fraser water. Above that were the vistas of forests and rivers and lakes and mountains without end.

Camus, writing the essay in exile during the darkest days of the Second World War, seemed to be saying that sensory gratification and the pursuit of the moment were just as important as history and permanence. Without the former, the essay hinted, the latter would wither. And without the latter, the enterprises of the present were doomed to be inarticulate and sterile.

Where I was sitting, little more than 20 years later, I could detect nothing that felt permanent. Prince George was as headlong and ephemeral as Camus' Algiers, but history seemed as remote and abstract as the nearest star. Mine was a city that drew energy only from the future, even though there were inflated claims everywhere that the city was on the leading edge of a continuum that had taken millenniums to build to its current velocity and technical force. For all that, Camus' description of Algiers seemed a more accurate depiction of Prince George than the Chamber of Commerce slogans about putting your head down, working your butt off, and letting the unstoppable forces of progress perform their magic. Yet it was sheer—if not quite pure—capitalism Camus was describing. And the way he figured it, that energetic magic could combine with the instinctive human ardour for democracy and beauty, and the resulting fission would allow citizens to take their pleasures, gather their fortunes, and build a great city. Simple.

If Canada's northwest didn't have quite the grandeur or scale of North Africa or its depth of history, its untouched forests and rivers were more beautiful and vital, and they held the infinity of resources necessary to make a city powerful and its people, eventually, wise and generous. I was as convinced of this future as was the Chamber of Commerce.

But instead of being filled with lust for wealth, I formed the ambition to write, someday, an essay about Prince George that was as marvellous and deep as "Summer in Algiers." And I wondered, as the creamy clouds scudded across the enchanted afternoon skies, if I would have to, like Camus, write my essay from exile in a world darkened by destruction and misery that would seem as infinite as the resources did here.

A few days after Max and I return from camping in the clearcut, after visiting dozens of places around town I hope might stir his imagination but don't, I remember the valley of the Salmon River. A few kilometres north of town on the Fraser, it is the site of many memories from those sweet days when everything seemed not only possible, but effortlessly likely. By coincidence, my older son, Jesse, then just turned 20, has flown in to attend an anniversary celebration for his maternal grandparents, who still live in the city. His presence offers me the opportunity to take both my sons for a swim in my old haunt, and incautious as always, I seize it. Maybe the beauty of the place will make them understand, in some small way, my attachment to Prince George.

In the early 1960s, the valley of the Salmon River had been a wilderness of lofty cottonwood trees, and abundant wildlife, of which my friends and I were not the least. By mid-July the flood waters dropped, and for a few weeks, grew crystalline and warm, transforming the river into a succession of gentle swimming lagoons and riffles mild enough that we could raft from swimming hole to swimming hole on air mattresses before the Salmon poured its sparkling waters into the muddy Fraser.

To get there in 1990, my sons and I cross the Nechako River on the old bridge, climb the hills out of the city, and pass through the ragged upland suburbs in silence. This will be one place, I feel certain, where I won't have to propagandize. Its beauty will seduce them by itself. And as we begin the gradual descent through gently sloping farmland into the valley, I'm flooded with intensely particular tableaus from those now-distant days along the river: Butch Neilsen's grin of pleasure as he pauses before diving into a sparkling pool; Don White's look of anticipation as he nudges his 1953 Chevy through the branches at one of the semi-secret parking spots; Lorraine Spiekermann's expression of terror as her husband Claus pulls her from inside a log-jam by her hair after she lost her balance and slipped into its roiling, lethal midst.

Like everything in the north, the Salmon River wasn't ever wholly safe. There were near-drownings, more than a few drunken arguments and fist fights, and, I suppose, one or two accidental pregnancies. Our encounters with the river, and with one another along its banks, left us slightly older and perhaps wiser, but no less enamoured of being alive. It was our place, and we left no garbage, smashed no beer bottles against the river's banks and boulders. We would, after all, be coming back the next week—or the next year.

At first glimpse in 1990, little seems to have changed along the Salmon. I pull the car off the highway and park in the same glade where my friends and I parked our cars 25 years ago. Then, abruptly and horribly, I see that it *has* changed.

The first hint is the deeply grooved four-by-four track snaking among the cottonwoods beyond the old parking spot. As I lock the car, I notice several plastic six-pack collars littering the gravel underfoot. I lean down, frowning, and pick one up. As I walk from the parking spot to the swimming lagoon some 100 metres away, I pick up 32 more. I don't pick up the Styrofoam cups, the empty pop and beer cans and bottles, or the jagged shards of broken glass that are everywhere. I leave the mounds of stinking disposable diapers where they've been dropped, and I ignore the cardboard, the plastic grocery bags, the car mufflers, and the other rusted auto parts that've been dumped.

The deserted gravel beach next to the swimming lagoon looks like a cross between a landfill and a war games site. Then there's the river itself. From a distance, the water appears to be clear and clean, but when we near the bank and look down, we can see shards of brown beer-bottle glass jutting through a layer of iridescent slime that coats the bottom. Neither Jesse nor Max will want to swim here. And neither do I.

Because I read somewhere that six-pack collars are lethal to birds, I pick up and remove as many as I can find. I have 61 of them before I give up. My sons pick up a few, too, but they quit sooner than I do, recognizing the hopelessness of the project. As I'm stuffing the collars into the trunk of my car, it comes to me that this might be the truest product of the unleashed capitalism everyone is talking about. Whatever happened to the enchantment and to the sense of democracy that makes what is public both the property and the responsibility of everyone?

As we drive back to Prince George in silence, I begin to think in a new and very personal way about what becomes of creatures that foul their own nests. From a lifetime of evidence it's easy to deduce that such creatures have had some essential part of their survival instinct disabled. They have become, in that sense, mere beasts, driven insane by contingencies of the moment. Or is it more complicated? Are they responding to stimuli so toxic and overpowering that they have been transformed into social psychopaths, storm troopers of a new Apocalypse, in which the fires will be fuelled by their own careless-ness and inattention to detail? Is this the way things really are?

Maybe. But the explanation is too abstract, like Camus' history. More accurate to see the desecration of the Salmon River as a violation of natural and human sense. It is inexplicable and without excuse, and I am ashamed of it. But it is also, that way, my own.

As we near town, Jesse asks me how I could ever have cared about such a horrible place. Without answering his ques-tion, I try, once more, to recall what it was I cherished here: sunlight across the clear water, the brief, intense heat of the northern summer, the vitality in the faces of my friends, all of it intensified by what Camus asks me to value. But other memories now move against those ideal-izations: I recall that the hulks of abandoned cars even then had begun to litter the valley floor, and I remember the beer bottles we *didn't* bother to pick up. I recall watching, somewhere, a compan-ion smashing an empty against a rock. And I recall, with a shock of recognition, that the log-jams we'd played amidst weren't natural phenomena but debris from upriver logging.

My memories have lost their power to enchant me. So I don't offer Jesse and Max any lame excuses about how the Salmon River was beautiful, once upon a time, before it was sullied by evil, stupid peo-ple. I don't blame its condition on today's vandals, or yesterday's. It is part of a culture that was there in my days, and well before my days.

Prince George is to blame for passively following the continuum that began, as much as anywhere, on the forested slopes of North Africa several thousand years before Camus penned his essay about sunlight and sand and human pleasure. From one rarely articulated point of view, the story at the root of all human development has been the story of the eradication of the world's trees. *The Epic of Gilgamesh*, the first story anyone ever considered important enough to write down, is also history's first logging tale. Across the now-treeless wilderness where Gilgamesh and Enkidu took axes to fell those giant cedars and kill the monster Humbaba, Iranians and Iraqis have recently spewed a decade of artillery and poison gas shells at one another, and American smart bombs that don't seem smart enough to tell the difference between weapons facilities and people's homes have been and gone and been again. Some history. Some continuum.

In the 35 years since I left Prince George, the forest primeval has come to a woeful end. The monster that Gilgamesh and Enkidu battled and defeated all those centuries ago had its final apotheosis in a valley southeast of town, and it turned out to be a bunch of scruffy, allegedly diseased spruce and pine trees the logging companies flattened in just a few years. After visiting the clearcut it is easy to see that progress and history have limits, and many people now believe that both have ended. We're going nowhere nowadays, even though the Chamber of Commerce doesn't recognize it yet. Maybe, given what progress brought to Prince George, we ought to feel relieved. Maybe its end will force people's gaze from the bloody, treeless horizons, force them to look at where we are, what we've done, and what we've got left.

But for the rest of my life, and probably for the rest of my sons' lives, we're going to have to live with this truth: we're the barbarians responsible for creating places like Salmon River and the clearcut in the Bowron River valley. Every one of us.

ALEXANDER MACKENZIE'S SUPERMARKET, 1993

11

A young man in a red shirt patched with scraps of gingham leaps from a scarred 8-metre birchbark canoe into the shallows of a chilly mountain lake and lifts the boat's prow slightly to guide it onto the gravelly shore. Above him, a pair of North American robins crouch against the branches of a flimsy alder. As another eight men clamber from the boat, the female robin abandons the nest and its three pale-blue eggs, while her mate dives at the men's heads, hoping to divert them from the nesting tree. But the men aren't interested in robin's eggs. They busy themselves with unloading the canoe. That accomplished, they shoulder it, then carry it across a bridge of land to a nearly identical lake. After a cursory examination of the canoe's hull, they nose it carefully back into the water and, without stopping to take in the scenery, return along the path for their baggage.

They are mostly half-blood voyageurs, these men, and except for one, all are as colourfully clothed as the red-breasted robin buzzing them. They dress themselves in bright colours for the Indian tribes they encounter, to signal that they're neither game animals nor members of hostile tribes. They're traders, no more a threat than a used-car salesman is today. Or rather, they're the same kind of threat—aggressive, loudly dressed men with things to sell or trade for more than they're worth. Their leader is a 29-year-old Scot named Alexander Mackenzie. He is dressed more drably than the others, possibly to distinguish him as the man in charge.

Here they are crossing the Arctic Divide, the point of land beyond which the streams and rivers of this part of North America cease to flow north toward the Arctic Ocean and begin to run south and west into the Fraser River watershed and, eventually, the Pacific Ocean. It is June 12, 1793.

Beyond Mackenzie's laconic recording of the passage in his journal, history has little to reveal about what they do here, and nothing at all about what they are thinking. Thus, I can't tell you what sorts of things the men say to one another while they carry their canoe and its baggage across the Divide, and I have no clue about their private thoughts. These aren't men who record private thoughts—not even Mackenzie. They don't dally with or indulge their emotions, and they aren't given to ceremonies. They happen to be in one hell of a hurry, because they need to get to the Pacific Ocean and return to where they started from before the snow flies. So far, they don't really even know where the Pacific is, despite vaguely understanding that it is somewhere to the west. They are probably hoping they've seen the last of the mountains. They haven't.

It is possible that none of them recognizes what they're passing across here, at least not at first. Their Great Geographical Point of Passage takes place on a modest gravel bar between two cold lakes. It is dotted with scrub alder, Russian willow, and alpine spruce, and there is an Indian trail to ease their way, but there's no brass plaque to mark the spot as the Arctic Divide, no tourist kiosk with a representative to officiate over the comings and goings, no fast-food outlet. The only marker is a wooden post festooned with items for swap. Mackenzie takes the time to remove several fish hooks, a net, and a beaver trap from it, replaces them with some of the trade goods he carries—a knife, some awls, and one or two colourful beads. If he lived today, deep in his mercantile soul, a cash register would be going *cha-chinggg*, but since the invention of cash registers is in the distant future, Mackenzie hears nothing but the racketing of the robins. Maybe. These robins are at the northerly extreme of their range, and are, I confess, my authorial intrusion, not figures of recorded history.

At the south end of the second lake—now named Portage Lake —any doubts Mackenzie may have about what they're crossing will be dispelled when he sees that the short creek that drains the lake flows south instead of north. This will provoke at least a smile or two among the travellers. In theory, their labours will now be easier, paddling with the current and not against it as they have had to do since leaving northern Alberta a little more than a month before.

The smiles will soon be disappear. After Portage Lake drains into Pacific Lake, also small and cold, the waterway drops down to become the James Creek/Herrick Creek/McGregor River tributary of the Fraser River. When Mackenzie and his crew pass through it they will be the first Europeans introduced to plan-versus-reality, northern B.C.–style. The tributary is one of the wildest waterways in North America. Mackenzie, in his understated way, notes that the Indians call it, simply, "The Bad River." For Mackenzie and crew that will turn out to mean that the river is well past anyone's definition of commercially navigable. They do more wading in icy water and cursing than navigating—or thinking about how rich their venture will make them.

How can I substantiate the badness of the Bad River? Try this: These strong, able men cross nearly 2,000 kilometres of wilderness in 91 days during the spring and summer of 1793. It takes them four miserable, danger-filled days to get through the 18 to 25 kilometres of James Creek alone. The reason one must estimate the distance of the Bad River this loosely is that the stream bed changes so completely from one year to the next that one year the passage might be 18 kilometres and five years later 25 kilometres. In it they wreck their canoe, and lose most of their rifle ball along with a worrisome portion of their other supplies. Only some dumb luck saves them from drowning, when their canoe strikes a midstream snag broadside instead of coming up beneath the hull to shatter its keel. The experience is so distressing that the famously tough Mackenzie, when they reach the wider and calmer Fraser, falls into a depression deep enough that he fails to record the hard-to-miss junction of the muddy Fraser with its largest tributary, the then-blue-watered Nechako. He also misses the site of what will one day be Prince George—and the Carrier Indian village that was or wasn't there, depending on which side of today's land claim dispute you support.

Two hundred years later, plus a week or so, I find myself travelling to the Arctic Divide for a re-enactment of a historic ceremony Mackenzie himself almost certainly didn't perform. This being the late 20th century, the impulses behind the re-enactment of historical events have more to do with the tourist industry than with respect for the past. Even though this event turns out to be purer than most, and is almost completely free of commerce or tourists, its relationship to historical verity is marginal. That I'm part of it is on the hilarious side of the margin.

Whatever else my presence here signifies, I am proof of how much easier life has become over the intervening centuries. Unlike Mackenzie, for instance, I didn't have to start my day at 3 a.m.—daybreak at this latitude and season—and I haven't paddled here in a canoe. I'm travelling from the south, in the cramped but relatively comfortable jump seat of a Cessna 185 float plane. Behind me in the plane is a group of similarly minor dignitaries flying up to meet three canoes full of students from Lakehead University in Thunder Bay, Ontario, who are celebrating the bicentennial of Alexander Mackenzie's overland voyages across North America to the Pacific Ocean by re-enacting them with as much authenticity as 20th-century safety regulations allow.

Not counting the two flights (Toronto to Vancouver, Vancouver to Prince George, six hours of boredom at 39,000 feet plus one slight earache), my re-enactment has involved nothing more strenuous than a 30-minute flight out of Prince George, during which all I'm required to do is sit on my fanny and gaze at the scenery. By contrast, the 20 or so outdoor recreation students from Lakehead University are into their third summer of retracing Mackenzie's paddle strokes. In this last leg of their voyage, they left the town of Peace River in Alberta on May 16 and are planning to arrive on the Pacific Coast at Bella Coola on July 22 after following Mackenzie's overland trail out of the Fraser system, up the Blackwater River south of Prince George, and thence over the Coast Range of the Rocky Mountains. Between now and late July they've got to cross the roughest country in their voyage, and get through a half-dozen more ceremonies like ours, including the invented-for-the-occasion Rivers Festival in Prince George at the end of the week. Although they don't yet know it, they're also facing a series of unpleasant confrontations with the Carrier and Chilcotin Indian bands south of Prince George that will ultimately prevent them from following Mackenzie's exact route through the mountains. But for now, all of those are unseen blips on a distant horizon.

It has been two years since I visited Prince George. My last trip was a 1991 quickie to launch the gardening book I'd written, a book that had been very much influenced by my growing up in northern British Columbia. The publisher named the book *The Compact Garden*, but if I'd had my way I'd have called it *The Contingent Garden*. It offered a gardening method that employs whatever assets one has without exploiting them, and suggests that gardeners ought to concentrate on pleasing themselves when and where that's possible— gardening aesthetics be damned and no whining about how many options the neighbour's garden cuts off. That's what you learn early on if you want to have a successful garden in northern B.C. The season is a short, miraculously bright respite from the gloomy cold, I counseled, so pay close attention to the specifics, and make the most of the assets you're given. The backbone of the book had been applying the unique common sense that gardening requires in the north to the more crowded if warmer southerly climates I'd gardened in since, but not until the book was in the stores did someone point out to me that I'd spent most of my life loudly recommending that people practise pretty much the opposite: restraint, careful consideration, not being ruled by the concerns of the moment. I'd had no answer except to mumble lamely that gardening—and northern B.C.—operated by a different rule book.

I wasn't *quite* invited to the Alexander Mackenzie festivities just because I wrote a book that recommends northern-style smash-and-grab opportunism in the garden patch. In the mid-1980s, I wrote another book that began with a fanciful journal I claimed, tongue-in-cheek, had been penned by Alexander Mackenzie himself. From there the book went on to dramatize and then loudly condemn northern B.C.'s almost wholly mercantile history, and to paint a doomsday portrait of its future. This second book, or maybe the fact that several professors at the College of New Caledonia have been teaching it to their English students, is what got me invited to speak

to the dignitaries and local citizens attending the Mackenzie bicentennial. Though I'm pretty sure that the people paying for the festival
haven't a clue what I really think about Alexander Mackenzie and his
enterprise, I'm glad of the opportunity their invitation presents. For
one, it will be my first real shot at lecturing some politicians about
their crappy behaviour while they're in power.

Intoxicating as that feels, the invitation isn't the only enticement.
For one, it's midsummer, my favourite time of year while I lived here,
because the sun rises at 3:00 in the morning and sets at 11:00 p.m. For
another, my private life has changed dramatically since 1990, and I
need the reality check Prince George has always provided. Two years
before, I left Vancouver after two decades and moved to Toronto.
Later in this same summer I'm planning to remarry.

Leaving Vancouver was disorienting, but once out I began to see
just how little of that city I'd been comfortable with, and how many
things about it I'd come to loathe—its soggy weather, the hornet's
nest of self-aggrandizing ethnic and preferential enclaves that transformed it from a city of 700,000 in the 1960s to a series of self-
involved banana republics of 20,000 to 100,000 people crowding
contentiously against one another. By moving to eastern Canada
I'd put myself farther from Prince George than I'd ever been, but the
more extreme climate of Ontario quickly felt comfortable, and within
a year I was more at home in downtown Toronto than I'd ever been
in Vancouver.

I liked Toronto because it is, as Prince George had been in a different way during the 1950s and 1960s, filled with immigrants who
aren't being made to feel like outsiders. The sense of community in
the heavily Italian downtown neighbourhood I moved into had an
inclusiveness and a generosity that felt familiar. It wasn't quite home,
but it reminded me that I had once *had* a home, and that I'd been
missing some of its human amenities for a long time.

Moving to Toronto hadn't been all welcome and good times. Soon
after I arrived, the *Globe and Mail* fired me as a columnist. They'd
done it, I decided, because I'd been having too much fun at the
expense of some of their advertising and ideological faves. But once I
cooled down I recognized that it probably had more to do with their
deciding I could hardly carry on the role of their West Coast House

Communist when I was living a kilometre from the paper's Toronto editorial offices and showing up at the same cocktail parties as their editorial board. *C'est la vie.*

Leaving Vancouver also meant leaving my son Max for long periods while he was at a vulnerable age. I was compensating by spending hours on the phone with him talking about hockey and baseball, and flying him out to Toronto for every conceivable occasion. But moving was an admission that the struggle I'd waged to remain a primary influence in his day-to-day life was over, and that I'd lost. Once again, *c'est la vie*, but this time, not so easy to live with.

———————

The man responsible for getting me to Prince George was Kent Sedgwick, the local head of the Alexander Mackenzie Trail Association and one of the chief organizers of the Prince George Rivers Festival. A soft-spoken, heavy-set man, Kent has been in Prince George since 1970, first as a geography instructor at the college, and after 1983 as a member of the city's planning department. I met him at one of Barry McKinnon's backyard campfire drink-downs several years before, and we'd chatted briefly about the frustrations of doing planning in a city so chronically ruled by short-sighted concerns. Or maybe I'd nattered at him about those things, and he'd listened politely as long as he could stand it, and then quietly defended his chosen home. I recall that he countered my high-handed dismissals of this and that by stressing the need for moderation and patience. There was a good side to Prince George I wasn't seeing, he insisted.

He'd made these arguments in defence of his adopted home so calmly that I thought he was just another of those guys who've reached that life condition that occurs within some civic bureaucracies where, because they think the Mayor is peering over their shoulder, they never really say what's on their minds, even to themselves. If not that, then maybe he was crazy the way people around here get. Or, brain-dead.

If this was Kent's story, I'd have no way to blame him. He's had the thankless job of trying to patch the mess of Prince George's early big-city wannabe civic projects with the subsequent onslaught of private developments that mostly look like they came out of an architecture kit of the "worst and don'ts" of the past 40 years. He's also had to work in the deregulation frenzy that has existed everywhere since the late 1970s. Around here the frenzy has bordered on civil anarchy—or at least developer insurrections that parallel the cutting of the Bowron in their extremity. Enough to make a good man crazy *and* brain-dead, in other words.

The second time we meet, Kent turns out to be both sane and thoroughly—"exceptionally" is a better descriptor—functional. He'd merely learned camouflage and the virtues of a thick skin, which were all I'd seen on our first meeting. Here, I'm discovering there's more to him, and more to the way he sees his adopted home. And, of course, because he makes plans for a living, he has one for me. There's the lecture on Saturday, and the next day a barbecue where I'm supposed to be one of the minor dignitaries. But the itinerary item he's included that has interested me most from the moment he approached me is the first one: flying up to meet the Alexander Mackenzie brigade as they cross the Arctic Divide.

Predictably, one of Kent's virtues is forbearance. With me, it's getting a workout, because I'm not handling being a minor celebrity in my hometown very graciously. From the moment Barry picked me up at the airport I've been yapping and pontificating at everyone who comes near. Partly, this is my way of working out what I'll say on Saturday when I give my lecture, trying different routines on different people. But that's no real excuse, because I'm mostly jabbering, and not listening to what's coming back at me. All the way out to Tabor Lake and the seaplane base we're flying out of, I've ragged on poor Kent like a nine-year-old, complaining that they've changed the roads since the 1960s, closed the Federal Experimental Farm, torn down this and that—as if Kent himself were responsible. Only when I catch him rolling his eyes at one of my zingers do I begin to realize how over-the-top silly I must appear.

"Well, you know," he keeps repeating in his low-key, reasonable way, "that it looks a little different from my perspective. You win a few, you lose a few, and you keep trying to make life better. That's what this is *really* about."

Eventually we get to Tabor Lake. Tabor is the lake closest to town, and many of the leading families in the city once had cabins along its western side. In those days, its shoreline was also dotted with a series of church picnic sites, one of which has been recycled as today's float-plane base.

Aside from proximity to town, the reason for Tabor's popularity was that it is shallow, and therefore warm enough to swim in for two months each summer. But like nearly all the warm lakes, it is—or was—infested with leeches. As Kent's car bumps along the road to the lake, I have a recollection of my mother trying, in her exasperated way, to teach me how to swim. I was just beginning to co-operate when one of my older sisters came out of the water with the tail of a fat black leech glistening in one of her nostrils. I lost interest in learning to swim, and it was years before I'd put my face in water that wasn't enclosed in concrete or porcelain. Hard to concentrate on the Australian crawl when you're constantly checking your nose to make sure something gross isn't swimming up it.

Leeches are not Tabor's worst problem in 1993. Off the edge of the seaplane dock, and as far as the eye can see, the water is so choked with lake weed it would be virtually impossible to draw a canoe paddle through it.

Kent sees me staring. "It's been that way for a few years now," he says mildly.

"Eurasian milfoil?"

"It's actually Canadian pond weed," he answers. "Phosphate run-off from the Grove Fire in 1961 caused it, along with the fire retardant they dropped. They've been looking for ways to clean it up, but so far nothing has been acceptable."

"The whole lake is like this?"

"Pretty well," he admits. "There's a few clear patches where the water is deep enough. I understand they're going to start experimenting with a mechanical harvester soon."

"Any fish left?" I ask. It's a dumb question, but I ask it anyway because Kent will give me a straight answer. I know others who would try to tell me the Russians dropped the weed into the lake just to screw with the local fishermen. Or, now that Communism has been defeated I suppose they'll have shifted the blame to lesbians or environmentalists. Chances are I'll hear space aliens get the blame if I ask around enough.

Kent laughs. "Generally speaking, game fish don't thrive in this much weed," he says. "And when the big fish go, so do the minnows. Sooner or later. But you know that, of course. The funny thing is, someone caught a ling cod in here several years ago."

I'm beginning to appreciate this man's unperturbable balance, even while he's forcing it on me. Still, I'm not about to ask him for the sunny side of pulp mills. I'm way too likely to get it.

On the flight up to the Divide something happens that reminds me once more of how utterly dependent on contingency life here remains. Just as we begin to move over the McGregor Mountain Range, the Cessna's motor conks out, and I'm staring at something I've *never, ever* wanted to see mid-flight: a motionless propeller. As the nose dips, the pilot reaches down and claws at a lever near his feet and I catch a flicker of fear in his eyes. Then the motor catches, the propeller becomes a suddenly pleasing blur, and the plane levels off. The pilot laughs, loud enough that we all hear the merriment over the din, and he yells something about switching tanks: happens all the time, ha ha. The way he peers out over the nose of the plane and busies himself with the instruments makes it clear that he's given us the only explanation we're going to get. He's screwed up, but hey, it didn't kill us. Never mind that if that fuel-starved engine had quit while we were taking off or just before landing, we'd all be dead, or swimming in water cold enough to make us dead very quickly. Ha, ha.

Whether it's harmless pilot error or the near-death encounter I suspect, one small good comes of it. It reminds me that I'm mortal, and that puts a clamp on my bullshit hose: I stop thinking of all the things I want to say and start to pay attention to what's going on around me.

Our route has taken us north across the Fraser and up the snaking McGregor River. Below us lies a remarkable aerial panorama of James and Herrick creeks. As rugged and chaotic as I'd imagined, the view is a jumble of white water, rock, mud, and uprooted trees where riverbed shifts of 200 to 400 metres are common. Off in the distance, a small forest fire is burning its way up the side of a mountain, even though we're not yet into fire season. I have an instinct about how Mackenzie must have seen this, as a half-created jumble where the basic elements of creation—water, stone, wind, even fire—hadn't quite stabilized.

It's no wonder going through James Creek threw the man into depression. When his passage to the Pacific, instead of becoming easier, warmer, and more hospitable, proved so much more difficult, it must have dawned on him that the Great Overland Trade Route he was searching for was taking him straight through a part of the world so undesirable and difficult that God hadn't bothered to finish it. For Mackenzie, this place was more than the divide between one river system and another. It was the divide between dream and nightmare, where he learned that the unfinished geography of North Central British Columbia was going to prevent him from becoming a rich man.

I wonder if the kids from Lakehead University we're going up to ceremony with have any sense of what they're about to enter. That they're a week behind Mackenzie's pace during a year in which high water has been early and moderate suggests they aren't fools. Then I remember that nobody can adequately prepare for what they find in this part of the world.

12

The pilot bounces the Cessna onto the glassy surface of Portage Lake, and taxis it up to an open area on shore where we can see someone in a mackinaw waving us in. The plane bumps the gravel shore, our greeter pulls a rope from around a pontoon and secures the plane to a beach snag. The air is much chillier than at Tabor Lake, particularly when the fast-moving scuds overhead momentarily obscure the sun —a mackinaw isn't a bad choice. The lake water below the pontoons is faintly amber from the conifers that run down to the shoreline, and it is difficult to see anything below a depth of a metre unless it moves. When the water settles, it is like a mirror, mottling darker as the clouds move by.

It is beautiful here, in the spare way extreme landscapes sometimes are. I stop for a moment to take a deep breath of it into my lungs before following Kent and the others across the Divide. As I do, a chilly puff of breeze shills the lake surface, clearing the air of the last traces of aircraft exhaust and permitting the faintly acrid scent of black water to reach my nostrils.

I've been to this place innumerable times before, but always in imagination. While I was young I daydreamed about it, having been told by an elementary school teacher that it was an important historical spot. I pictured it with a stone cairn like the one across from the railway station in town, but with the sides of the continent sloped away in a Scuffy-the-Tugboat cartoon topology, northward to the Eskimos and southward to the United States.

Later, when I was in the Forest Service, the Arctic Divide again preoccupied me, but somehow I kept missing opportunities to get here. I suppose I finally made it, in a different way, when I wrote the book that begins with Mackenzie's voyage, but by then I'd left the city and no longer really expected to get this far into the wilderness again. So, it's more than exciting to confirm that history has a material existence. Instinctively I grind my heels, trying to make a mark that will somehow set me for eternity the way the muddy footprints of dinosaurs fossilized and became stone eons before we came along.

Kent's hand is on my shoulder. "Let's go meet the others," he says, apologetic that he's had to interrupt a private moment, but properly insistent on his agenda. Remembering Mackenzie's 817-pace estimate of the Divide's width, I count out my steps as I walk along behind Kent. When we reach the crest of a small rise and I see that two centuries have diminished the passage from Arctic to Pacific, I give up the count before I reach 300.

Three big re-enactment canoes, 25 footers like Mackenzie's but skinned in fibreglass and Kevlar instead of birchbark and pine pitch, have been beached for a couple of hours at Arctic Lake. The students, about half of whom are women, are finishing lunch, fiddling with equipment, or talking to the dozen or so people already there to witness the ceremony. A few are milling around a helicopter that arrived just before we did, helping to unload a fourth, slightly smaller canoe the helicopter carried in from Prince George. It's there, Kent explains to me, so experienced canoeists from Prince George can guide the kids safely through James Creek into the Fraser.

"Very smart," I say, conscious of sounding wiser than I feel. "That stretch of water between here and the Fraser is a killer."

"You're the one to say," Kent says. "You wrote the book about it."

His expression doesn't tell me one way or another if he's giving my chain a gentle yank. I guess I'm supposed to know that, but I don't. And I don't get to ponder, because he introduces me to the leader of the Prince George contingent of canoeists who'll be providing the experience for the Lakehead students. This man's name is Lyle Dickieson, and Kent seems to think we ought to be acquainted, or at least have lots to talk about.

Dickieson and I have never laid eyes on one another, and it's a meeting between different species, not just different men. Conversation is a struggle even though there's a world of things I ought to be asking him about. Our respective centres of gravity—physical and otherwise—are so different that the usual points of contact evaporate.

Lyle Dickieson is a man of medium height, with curly, sandy-red hair and square, powerfully muscled shoulders. He'd be ordinary-looking if he didn't give you the feeling that more of him was in contact with the ground than most men could muster if they plastered themselves against it face down. There's something about Dickieson that is so solid he makes me wonder if he hasn't been chiselled out of rock. Yet he doesn't crush my hand when he shakes it, and I don't float into the air in his presence from the sheer contrast. He merely radiates a kind of focus and competence that makes what normally passes for self-confidence seem cheap trickery. He's an adult, in other words, in a world that has more or less exterminated adults in favour of clamouring victims, wounded children, arrested adolescents, self-aggrandizing entrepreneurs, nincompoop neurotics, bullshit artists, incompetents, and people like me.

Dickieson reminds me that there *is* a difference between competence and confidence, and that I used to be clearer about it than I am now. If he was Superman, he'd wear the same ordinary work shirt he's wearing here, and he'd make no big deal of his job. I catch myself wishing I did know him, and, more urgently, that I could think of something to say that won't be so stupid it'll expose me as the city-slick wuss his mere presence has made of me.

Do I tell him I've owned a 16-foot Peterborough cedarstrip since I was 16 years old, or that I once ran it through the Isle Pierre rapids sideways because my partner and I were eating lunch and didn't recognize where we were until it was too late? Not relevant. Neither is the story about my cedarstrip rotting away on its rack beside my house in Vancouver until my ex-wife gave it away. No, this man can probably do the Ft. St. James–to–Prince George trip with one hand tied behind his back. He's probably got a canoe like my Peterborough folded up in his wallet.

Guys like Dickieson used to be fairly common in northern B.C. They were a community resource, self-contained men so absorbed by the physical demands of living that they never dithered over whether what they were doing had value. I don't mean to suggest that they were abundant, just that there were enough of them around to allow others to feel secure about how the world was being handled—or to provide models for handling it oneself.

I don't know a thing about Dickieson's personal life except that there's something about him that says, *Don't ask*. His experience and abilities evidently haven't made him rich or famous, just more substantial than other people. After a few minutes of observing him I recognize that I'm not the only one he doesn't have much to say to, and that I'm not the only one who's in awe of him. He's already developed a group of admirers amongst the Lakehead canoeists. They're crowding around him respectfully, asking him questions about what lies ahead in James Creek, or simply staring. His answers are rarely longer than a few carefully considered words.

When the leader of the Mackenzie re-enactment, a professor of outdoor recreation at Lakehead named Jim Smithers, wanders over to speak to Dickieson, he's similarly deferential. Smithers is a man in his sixties, immensely fit in a craggy, gaunt sort of way that makes him seem larger than he is. I can see he's a professor before he speaks, and when he does, his diction tells me that his sense of self is pretty cerebral, despite what he's been doing these past few summers. His body language says he's disappointed by the sparse crowd, but not quite insulted. Except with Dickieson, it translates as a slightly irritable

curtness. Hard to blame Smithers for feeling a letdown. He's probably been up since four this morning preparing for the ceremony.

I had expected that Smithers would play the role of Mackenzie, but he doesn't. Not his style, apparently. When he does speak, he's laconic and directorial, and his voice has a diffident edge, as if he'd prefer to get back out on the  water but knows he has to put up with this particular bit of nonsense as he has with hundreds of others like it.

As I watch, I begin to warm to him. He doesn't have the presence Dickieson has, but I can see from the way the kids from the brigade respond to his direction that they like and respect him. To have gotten as far as he has with a project this logistically complex and physically demanding has to have required an iron will and immense organizational skills—not so different from the qualities Mackenzie himself had 200 years ago. That Smithers doesn't have Mackenzie's public relations touch and isn't much of a showman has probably cost his project some publicity along the way, but may have helped to retain its integrity.

By putting them through the hardships of this re-enactment, Smithers has likely made interesting human beings out of these students. They aren't merely fit-looking and tanned the uneven way you become when you're living outdoors and can't avoid the sun. There's a calm economy to the way they go about their business, and they seem to fit comfortably into their skins. They've become strong and toughened, if not tough, and that kind of strength might stay with them. Who's to say they won't simply turn out to be the playground supervisors, nature trail interpreters, and park wardens they set out to become. But if they want more out of life, Smithers has helped them develop admirable qualities that won't easily dissipate into slinging bullshit around the barbecue when they reach middle age.

After some minor dithering but very little grumbling or bickering, the canoes are relaunched onto Arctic Lake so that the expedition can be *officially* landed at the site. History only counts, I guess, if it is photographed and videotaped. I lean over to ask Kent which station is filming the arrival, and he explains that the cameraman isn't from a television station. He's a private citizen helping the expedition by making a video diary of this part of their voyage.

"Isn't the *Citizen* or the television and radio stations covering this?"

Kent grimaces. "I'm here," he says. "I've been doing radio spots about the brigade every so often for CBC."

"That's it?"

"'Fraid so," he answers. "The local media say they don't have the budget to do coverage." He seems regretful that others don't know what's taking place here, but there's no bitterness in his voice.

"Ain't corporate profits a wonderful thing?" I mutter half audibly. Kent doesn't quite catch the remark, or pretends he doesn't.

The official re-enactment begins, and the first canoe crunches onto the gravel of the Arctic Divide. The young man playing the role of Alexander Mackenzie manages to step out onto the shore without falling in the water, but there is no cosmological thunderclap or public applause. But it's okay, and it satisfies the cameraman and the videographer, and is, I guess, a thrill for the history buffs.

The stilted choreography makes me wonder how this *really* went down 200 years ago. It's unlikely, for instance, that Mackenzie would have been first out of the canoe. The lightest and most agile of his men would have been first to alight—and first to get an arrow through the throat from hostile Indians, or, if you're more interested in slapstick than interracial history, the first to lose his balance and fall into the water. Alternately, if Mackenzie had been a modern-style egomaniac and control freak, he'd have been at the stern, steering the canoe like a macho character from a James Dickey novel. But as the leader of a venture that required he do more thinking and writing than the others, it's most likely he'd have been mid-canoe, protected there from accident, deliberate harm, and most of the hard work.

As I ponder these sorts of considerations, the first two speeches of the ceremony are delivered without my hearing a single platitude. Then it is time for the obligatory First Nations Interface, and a perfectly authentic hereditary chief of the Sekanni band from McLeod's Lake steps forward to greet the faux Mackenzie.

It occurs to me that this is actually something of a faux moment all round. If this were 1793, Mackenzie and his men would be *leaving* Sekanni territory, and the chief would be waving goodbye to them (and trying to bargain for one more iron implement), not offering fatuous media-friendly ceremonial greetings. On the south side of the Divide, the waterways are salmon streams, and thus would belong to the Carriers, who guarded their territory against the gentle but culturally threadbare Sekannis by killing them on sight.

When Simon Fraser happened by Stuart Lake a few years after Mackenzie's run, the Carriers he encountered were naive enough to believe that the pale-skins and the tobacco smoke constantly issuing from the mouths and noses of the Euros meant they were dead men, and the Carriers treated them, like all visitors from the spirit world, with cordial circumspection. But this late in the non-smoking 20th century the Carriers are neither credulous nor very polite, and they're not about to show up here to shake hands with ceremonial white men wanting to legitimize their version of history. Among other things, the Carriers are involved in a more than half-serious bid to gain property rights to most of downtown Prince George, and they've got negotiatory dibs on pretty well every other worthwhile asset in North Central British Columbia.

As one of their chiefs will say a few days from now, when they refuse the expedition permission to follow Mackenzie's route up the Blackwater River, "All [Mackenzie's party] brought was influenza, smallpox, and alcoholism." In fact, Mackenzie's party was remarkably free of diseases and booze, but later visitations from white people in boats with axes and trinkets to sell weren't so clean. The Carrier village at the mouth of the Blackwater River, for instance, where Mackenzie left the Fraser and headed overland after a friendly enough welcome by the inhabitants, was later wiped out by smallpox and other diseases brought by Euros. And during the 1950s, the site was made useless

even for archaeological reclamation when it was used as a log mar-
shalling area and river-drop by a logging company. So if the Carriers
are testy about seemingly innocuous ceremonial incursions into their
space, they have reasons.

The Sekanni chief is introduced as Harry Chingee. He's like nearly
all the Sekannis I've met over the years: gentle, sweet-tempered, and
unhurried. He's been obsequiously cheerful and polite during the
run-up to the official ceremony now taking place, but he has also
looked slightly uncomfortable, as if he's realized that this ceremony
isn't going to be his people's game any more than the last 200 years
have been. He says the right things in his short speech, but you can
tell he's struggling against the impulse to tell us all to clean up our
mess and go back where we came from. Being Sekanni, he'd let us
make the decision about whether he means the mess here at the Arctic
Divide or the general mess of the past two centuries.

Since I'm one of the Euros, I can't quite agree to us all being kicked
out. We've got no place to go. But I'm with him about the mess in the
here and now. As I gaze around the Divide, there's abundant evidence
that white guys, and I mean upper-case, careless jackass White Guys,
have *been* here, hacking down trees for their fishing camps, getting
drunk, shooting up the place, and leaving behind large volumes
of garbage. The ground we're standing on is literally crusted with
rusting food cans and broken glass, and so are the shallows of both
lakes. Then, as I tune out the speeches and the blah, blah of tourism
industry platitudes, I spot something at least as interesting as the
arrival of these costumed university students. It is a nestling starling,
and it is dead.

Starlings are even less native to northern B.C. than white Euros.
They are on this continent because in the 1880s, a misguided amateur
naturalist by the name of Eugene Schieffelin decided to release, into
the wilderness of New York City's Central Park, breeding pairs of
every bird mentioned in the works of William Shakespeare. The gentle nightingales and skylarks disappeared within weeks, slaughtered
by the weasels, rats, or muggers. But in the summer of 1890, Schieffelin came back and released a flock of 60 starlings. The birds thrived,
and soon began to breed. And then they began to spread. By 1910
they had reached Massachusetts, and by 1920 they were in Toronto.

The starlings arrived in Vancouver shortly after I did in 1963. With the soft living conditions of the West Coast—the mild climate, verdant agricultural fields running the length of the Fraser Valley, and incontinent grain terminals dotting the shores of Burrard Inlet, there were hundreds of thousands of them nesting under the city's bridges within a decade.

Despite their iridescent black plumage and their skills at mimicking the songs of other bird species, starlings haven't won any popularity contests in North America, and they're not likely to in the future. As well as the agricultural damage they inflict on berry and fruit crops, and with the guano they splatter below their mass nesting sites, they're natteringly loud and belligerent. Robins virtually disappeared from Greater Vancouver for 20 years after the starlings arrived, and even when the robins reappeared—after population-restraining measures had been quietly taken against the starlings when their local population reached 4 million—one still couldn't trust that the lovely trilling at dawn and dusk wasn't some mimicking starling.

So let me say that I feel a sort of low-grade resentment toward starlings, even this poor dead nestling, that must be similar to what Harry Chingee is justified in feeling toward us.

While I'm pondering this, the moment of history ends, and it's just 40 or 50 mortal men and women milling around a chilly point of land high in the mountains trying to figure out what to do with their bodies and their too-active minds. I catch Dickieson's eye, and he grins ever-so-slightly at me. Then, not to waste the connection, he asks if I'd mind giving him a hand carrying the Prince George canoe across the Divide.

I respond accurately for the first time since I arrived in Prince George: I say, "Sure. Glad to."

I don't whine about my bad back—the reason I gave up river canoeing 15 years ago—or think about whether it is an honour to be asked. I see that there is work to be done, that Dickieson is asking nearby bodies to help, and I'm the nearest body. This is good luck all round, but nothing to be high-fiving myself over, and it ain't exactly an exoneration of the "Planet of the European Guys" we're here to celebrate. Dickieson nods to several others close enough to have heard our exchange, and together we get on with it. By the time we get the canoe up onto our shoulders there are eight of us, and the job is easy. But it's still a thrill, and I let that carry me across the Arctic Divide.

13

By 8:30 the next morning I'm behind the wheel of a rented Ford Taurus on Highway 16, headed toward the clearcut on the Bowron to see what the changes are, if any. This time, I'm on my own: no Max, no Barry or Harvey, and no Kent Sedgwick. Kent seemed slightly relieved when I told him I'd be busy with my own things for a day or two, Max is starting high school in Vancouver, Harvey is busy, busy, and Barry has been so listless since he picked me up at the airport that he hasn't been out of the house except to go up to the college.

The only thing I've brought from the last trip are my cameras and my Buck knife. I've borrowed a boy's axe from Barry, and I've got one of his sleeping bags in the trunk even though I'm planning to be back by the end of the afternoon. That last item is there because the Forest Service trained me to take precautions in the bush even if I'm only walking to the outhouse, and today I have good reasons to travel prepared. Where I'm going even the tree-planters have abandoned. If my rental car breaks down or I run into something, there won't be another human being within 30 kilometres.

In 1990, we entered the clearcut near its midpoint, from the northwest along the Willow River Forest Service access road, and retreated back to town along the same road. This time I'll enter from the top by the Forest Service access road into the Bowron River valley so I can drive the length of the clearcut's east side. Once I've done that, I'll exit around Narrow Lake—or south of there if I can get through —and drive southwest by whatever passable roads meet Highway 97 at the old mill site of Dunkley. That'll give me an idea of how heavy the cutting adjacent to the clearcut has been. One of the stories going around is that the Forest Service has deflated the true extent of the clearcut by reserving strips of trees around its edges and then continuing to allow the companies to mow down the timber on the other side.

At first I can see little change. But once I acclimatize, distinctions become apparent. Since it is June, the colours are different—the greens brighter, and reds and oranges absent. There are also fewer browns and greys; fewer dead trees and less exposed earth. The rows of pine and spruce seedlings, barely visible in the underbrush in 1990, are now poking green tops above the scrub. Barry had mentioned something about the Forest Service experimenting with selective herbicides to retard undergrowth, and sure enough, here and there I see patches that betray its use—the willows dead, no fireweed, and armies of evenly spaced, chest-high lodgepole pines on the march across the valley floor.

I'd also heard from someone—Kent, maybe—that one of the Indian bands had proposed grazing sheep in the clearcut as a way of reducing underbrush growth, but when I saw neither sheep nor Indians I wasn't surprised. It had sounded more a proof-of-righteousness scheme than anything practical—or rather, while herding sheep is eminently more practical in the long term than spraying herbicide over everything, having band members sit out in a clearcut during blackfly season watching sheep feed—and trying to keep the sheep from being driven insane by the flies—wasn't a job any self-respecting hunter-gatherer wanted, no matter how far along the eco-path he'd come. And in the end, never mind: trees grow. The ones here were doing better than I'd have predicted.

After an hour of driving from one half-recalled spot to the next trying to shoot duplicate photos so I can compare them with the ones I shot in 1990, I begin to see where these new details are leading. It doesn't warm my heart in the least. The little rows of trees are growing, yes, but they're more sparse at higher elevations, and, generally speaking, the higher I go, the more slowly the forests are returning—when they're returning at all. Through the camera's 200-millimetre telephoto lens the high elevations appear *more* bleak than in 1990. The fire-blackened snags have faded to a vapid shade of charcoal, and where the charcoal has washed out there's no distinguishable colour at all. I drive to a spot where the skid roads reach high enough that three years ago we'd been able to get Barry's truck up to the bottom edge of a stand that had supposedly been left to seed the slopes below, but which the Forest Service had burned during its cleanup. The road has since deteriorated, and I have to park the Taurus at a landing and climb the last several hundred metres on foot.

It's worth the effort. Compared to a clearcut, a burned-over forest is noisy and alive. As fire-killed trees dry and the wood hardens, the surfaces open to the elements and internal structures grow brittle. They creak and groan without a breeze, and with the merest puff, they crack, whistle, and shriek. Twenty years ago I stumbled across a road southeast of Tabor Lake that led me deep inside the huge Grove Fire that had fried nearly 20,000 hectares of prime timber in the summer of 1961. It was a still, early summer day more than a decade after the fire, and though some of the trees had fallen, enough were still standing to make an orchestra. The music they played kept me there for several hours, and when I left they'd half-convinced an atheist that trees have souls. So when a puff of wind brings the small hilltop burn on the Bowron to full voice, I'm only slightly less spooked than the first time. But I'm winded by the climb, and enough years have passed since then that I'm now more interested in the sources of the strange music than in ascribing spiritual qualities to it. I sit down astride a fallen snag and try to hear what the melody riding the breeze has to say.

There is nothing I haven't seen or heard before, but as I look around me I see the "nothing" is loaded with fresh life. Among the groaning snags, fireweed and a tangle of low scrub is coming along. From the dead trees themselves, tiny colonies of lichen and fungi have emerged. Many of the plant species presenting themselves to the sunlight here will be false starts, replaced by the time the trees are down by a community of more light-seeking and longer-lived species.

That's the way things normally go in a burn. But I can find no seedling trees up here, and the acoustic weight of the dead ones keeps me from looking very hard. Within 20 minutes, it gets too spooky, and I stumble back down to the car, get in, and slam the door against it.

I'm still under that influence as I angle carefully back down the skid road to where the regiments of little pines and spruce are poking their crowns above the underbrush. It is now, somehow, less easy to believe that the land is regenerating. I get back on the forestry road, drive down to the Bowron River, and pull off into a clearing not far from one of the bridges. I need to ask myself what I've *really* seen—I mean, without tangling what I'm trying to see with what I'd prefer to believe.

I can see no evidence, anywhere in the clearcut, that wildlife has returned. There's no bear scat, there are no moose droppings, no deer pellets, no grouse rousing themselves to flight. This despite adequate feed available for any of those species. On the other side of the scale, there *are* young trees growing, literally millions of them if not quite as many million as the Forest Service claims to have had planted. Their rate of growth is much better at the lower elevations, that's all. What I discovered up in that alpine burn is that the only trees coming back have been planted by human beings. On the Bowron, nature isn't taking care of itself, at least not yet, or not in a commerce-gratifying way. Whether human beings are taking adequate care as compensation is an ideological question, which is to say, people aren't going to ask it unless they're already convinced they have the answer. My instincts are to find the questions that will undermine those certainties people have, whichever side they're on. But right now, my mind is a blank, or at best, what it comes up with is pretty silly: Do I prefer the wildness of English gardens, or the order and artifice of the French style?

When it's clear I can't frame a question that isn't too abstract or silly for the stultifying physicality that surrounds me, I get out of the car, stretch my arms as wide as they'll go, and then crawl up onto the hood of the Taurus. I lean back against the windshield with my head pillowed by my rolled-up leather jacket, and let the emptiness and silence soak into my pores.

It isn't *quite* empty or silent. The leaves of the young poplar and willow scrub gabble in the breeze, the river rumbles faintly, and here and there flies and bumblebees drone. After a few minutes the black-flies discover me, but I've prepared myself. Before I ventured out of the car the first time, I slathered the exposed parts of my body with enough mosquito dope to make me smell as inviting as the abandoned logging equipment that's everywhere. Within minutes, I'm asleep.

I wake up two full hours later, refreshed and possessed by an instant and fervent wish to get the hell out. I roll off the car, crawl behind the wheel, and start the motor without a second of reflection. The impulse to flee surges in the direction of panic, and as is always the case when you panic in the bush, I'm soon in trouble. Instead of getting out quickly, I find myself at the south edge, trying to make my way west along roads that get seedier the more I persist. After three dead ends, I wise up and backtrack to the Narrow Lake road I'm familiar with.

The relief I feel outside the clearcut draws me to the same campground where Barry, Harv, the boys, and I stayed three years ago. The campground is empty, and I park and walk around for a few minutes trying to convince myself that I've had this diversion in mind all along, and that I'm actually following a plan. The changes here are predictable: the facilities have been improved in small ways—there are more picnic tables—and some 45-gallon oil barrels have been painted Forest Service green and chained to trees for garbage collection. But from the look of the barrels they've been used as much for target practice as for stowing refuse, and there's more garbage littering the south shore of Narrow Lake than I remember from the last trip. Progress . . .

Still not sure whether I feel comforted or defeated, I drive back to town along the Willow River forestry road, coming out by Buckhorn Lake to Highway 97 as we did in 1990. When a logging truck nearly runs me into the bush, I'm grateful for the noise, the dust, and even the danger. It tells me I'm in the same universe I started from this morning.

I'm back in Prince George by 2:30, and it hasn't changed either. I've created a small logistical problem for myself: Barry's at the college for a mandatory professional development seminar, Joy's at work,

and I don't have a key to the house. I drive past the college grounds, dismiss the idea of finding Barry as impractical or impolite, and decide to kill the time by having a gander at the Mr. PeeGee phone booth on Victoria Street. Barry has been making jokes about the thing for years, but he mentioned on the way in from the airport that it has now become a serious target for pranksters and yahoos, and from the proprietorial glee in his voice, a few of them are his ex-students.

The phone booth is Barry's symbol of the city's moral and commercial degeneration—a symbol that nevertheless has the power to make him laugh because it is such a ludicrously ironic interpretation of the original Mr. PeeGee. The spruce log original, which stood outside the tourist bureau office across from the railroad station until it rotted away and could no longer represent Prince George's pride in itself and western white spruce, was itself pretty ludicrous and ironic. Both are unintentionally accurate representations of the state of civic pride and the ability of the city's leaders to imagine their civic intentions: both are stick-men not designed for complex expression. The latter-day version is different in that it has been downscaled, infused with a lot of plastic, and is the property not of the city but of the telephone company.

On close inspection, this new Mr. PeeGee turns out to be a much tougher customer than its ancestor, which, I suppose, fits. There are small nicks and cracks in his fibreglass skin that show where vandals have tried to make their feelings known, and the weather has already dulled its sheen. But the fibreglass has been laid down so thickly and solidly that it could probably survive a nuclear blast. Several major dents along one edge indicate where someone has tested it with steel pipe or an aluminum baseball bat, but this Mr. PeeGee still looks ready to put a lot more kilometres on the odometer before he's done. That'll make him, as Barry would say, the most permanent thing the corporations have contributed to the north.

The telephone receiver dangles, but when I pick it up and tap the hook a couple of times there's a dial tone. On an impulse, I push a quarter into the slot and punch in a number that has been stuck in my skull for 30 years. There's a pause, and then *droonkk*, as Mr. PeeGee places my call.

14

The number I've tapped in belongs to Bill Morris, and Bill answers on the second ring. That's a surprise. I never reached him on the first try before today. Bill used to be a perpetual-motion machine, and even now that he's semi-retired, I can't imagine much has changed. You have to chase him down if you want to talk.

"Oh, Brian," he says, as if we last spoke a week ago. "I heard you were going to be in town. I was going to call. . . ."

He wasn't, but it's nothing to be insulted about. This is modesty, not indifference: Bill never presumes. But in his voice I hear that he's pleased I've called.

"I'm selling the house, you know," he says in a matter-of-fact way. "With the shopping centre expanding and my parents gone, it's time to move on."

"Move on?" I repeat his words, startled. "You're moving on? Where?"

It's a strange thought, Bill Morris "moving on." He's been the most stable presence I know of in this town, always there, same place, same appearance—not one to do anything hastily, ever. His father died in the late 1970s and his mother a few years later, so he's likely been mulling over selling the house for a decade.

He reassures me. "Oh, I'm not really going anywhere. But you know, I am spending more and more time in the Ukraine each year. It's easy to travel there now that the Soviets are gone, and I've discovered dozens of family members I didn't know about. Come over for coffee and I'll tell you all about it."

"Right now?"

"Sure," he says. "Why not?"

Why not? There are few people in Prince George more interesting to talk to than Bill Morris, and no one with a better grasp on who's who and what's what. With my own family long gone, there's almost no one to whom I owe more. That I haven't phoned him before now is shameful and predictable at the same time. He's always been so lax about debts that it's easy to forget they're there.

Bill is a slightly built man with a prominent Adam's apple. He's one of those people who has looked like his high school graduation photograph his entire adult life: moppy brown hair, black-rimmed Buddy Holly glasses, his head tilted slightly forward as if he were trying to make a personable impression on the photographer but not sure he can bring it off. He's changed as he's grown older, of course, but only in minor ways: salt and pepper invaded the moppy brown hair when he reached his fifties, the Buddy Holly glasses were exchanged for gold-rimmed aviators, and his Adam's apple grew. In the past few years his forward tilt has become a slight stoop, and he moves more deliberately now, as if he's walking on eggs. But for all that, the sense that he's trapped inside his high school annual remains, a kind of Dorian Gray without the burden of personal beauty but with the same reluctance to let time scoop him up and bear him away.

He was running Third Avenue Billiards when I first met him. It was 1959 or 1960, and I'd begun to stop by on my way home from school every week or two to see if there were any new Shell Scott or Carter Brown detective novels on the paperback rack there that served as the city's "bookstore." I was also trying to work up the courage to leaf through the current issue of *Sunbathing for Health*, which for some incomprehensibly fortunate reason he'd placed on the lower left side of the floor-to-ceiling magazine rack next to magazines I was allowed to be interested in, like *Field and Stream* and *Argosy*.

Bill was always there when I came in, always sitting on a stool behind the glass counter filled with Zippo lighters, tobacco pipes, and small knives, always busy with something below the counter. He seemed so distracted by whatever he was doing that at first I wondered why the storefront wasn't permanently full of kids stealing him blind.

He cleared up that mystery the moment I did lift an issue of *Sunbathing for Health* from the rack.

"You're Hartley Fawcett's youngest, aren't you?" he asked amiably.

"Yes," I answered, trying not to look completely guilty as I slipped the magazine back in place. "How'd you know?"

The rhetorical question got me Bill's deep *cluck-cluck* chuckle for an answer. I picked up *Argosy*, opened it, and pretended to be interested in the photos of hunters and dead deer.

"You like to read," he said after a moment. It wasn't a question, but at least it wasn't an accusation. "Have you ever read Raymond Chandler?"

That's how we started. Bill filled me in about Raymond Chandler and why he was different from the Shell Scott or Carter Brown novels I'd been reading. I listened because he didn't try to tell me Chandler was better. That was Bill's way—without aggression, but more important, without judgment. I liked that and I liked him, and talking about books soon became my reason for visiting.

As the long winters and short summers of high school succeeded one another, Bill and I kept talking. After Chandler he encouraged me to read other writers like Hemingway and Faulker, Norman Mailer, and James Jones. Nice writers to know about, but the better gift was Bill himself. He was a storyteller, skilled at weaving tales from what, up to that point, had seemed flimsy local materials. Unlike the philosophy lectures and parables I got from my father—always circling around how someone had succeeded or failed to be a good businessman—Bill's stories were filled with slapstick. They were funny, but I never got the impression that Bill told his stories because he believed people were stupid. I think he understood that slapstick is both natural to and maybe even inevitable for people who find themselves this far north of civilization.

Bill's eye for others carried a built-in generosity. The pratfalls people took in his stories weren't into walls made of rough brick, but over things that were more forgiving and, usually, a little silly—a drunk logger parking his pickup in the wrong driveway and then trying to crawl into bed with his neighbour's wife, or one of the town hookers, Skinny-legged Phyllis, spraining her ankle doing a one-and-a-half gainer down the front steps of a prominent citizen's house after a 2:00 a.m. trick, then howling loud enough to awaken the neighbourhood. The protagonists usually—not always—survived with minimal injuries and a less-than-complete loss of dignity. If they weren't heroes, they weren't victims, either. By Bill's telling, people sometimes learned a thing or two from their falls, and unless it made for an even better story, they didn't find their way back to their banana skin.

He was foisting on me a genial sort of disinformation about the world, sure, of a kind that I struggle with to this day. I think he was trying to convince me to think well of the world, even when I knew better. It was worth learning and so was the corollary: goodwill needs to be tempered with heavy doses of laughter.

I may have learned things about the world from Bill, but I rarely learned anything about *him*. The pokerface with which he masked his private life left those who knew him—along with the town's gossips—very little to work with. He was a magician at deflecting attention.

Some people I knew, for instance, believed that Bill was writing a novel while he was running the pool hall. It's true that for years he was constantly and furiously scribbling on the pads of yellow foolscap he kept below the counter. But if there was a novel being written, he never showed it to me. When I asked him about the rumour many years later, he said he'd been working on a real estate course by correspondence. There was something in the accompanying laugh that left me exactly where I'd been before I asked the question, and I came away even less sure he hadn't written something.

It doesn't really matter. If he wrote a novel, he never let it reach the light of day. But in a way obtuse enough that he'd enjoy it, he got more than one book written by making me understand that writing books was something people like us might actually do.

Bill was a confirmed bachelor—code for something adults of that era didn't talk about, probably because most of them weren't very clear what the "confirmed" part involved. In Bill's case, I'm pretty sure no decoding was needed, because he didn't have a private life rooted in secrets the way so many of his more conventional contemporaries did. I don't mean that he didn't have a *life*. He did. He had his parents, he had his extended family, and he had a more eclectic community of friends than anyone in town. *That* was his life. He took scrupulous care of his family responsibilities, he was a loyal friend, he was a competent citizen. But his private life remained private, and he intended it that way.

For what I knew with absolute certainty about Bill Morris, he could have been building nuclear weapons in his basement. I won't even try to guess how differently Bill's life would have been had he been born 35 years later, or had he grown up in Vancouver or Toronto or New York City—and neither should any wiseass self-involved city-slickers haul out the sociological artillery and pass summary judgment. There was, in those years and in those kinds of towns, a way of living in which family and friends were enough—a man or woman could lead an affective and more fulfilling life this way than through what today's culture has declared the single self-actualized way of conducting oneself. Not all priests are molesters, remember.

When it came to human relationships, if Bill indulged in any transgressions of convention, it was the slightly mischievous pleasure he took from bringing together disparate elements of his accumulated community. One summer when I was at loose ends, he invited me to dinner with the attractive but middle-aged wife of a wealthy local logger. She and Bill played bridge together, and she was, according to him, interested in the "Arts"—and very bored with her life as a small-town married chatelaine. My qualification was that I was young, arty, and very, very opinionated.

The three of us had dinner on several occasions. Each time, we talked until past midnight. I took everything in with the open spirit I'd learned from Bill, and nothing came of those dinners except that I went home about equally puzzled and entertained by the not-too-subtle erotic teasing I got from the woman. Bill's way, Bill's world. What I learned from that wasn't going to get me an invitation to tango at the Metropolitan Museum of Modern Art, but those evenings made my world slightly larger than it had been, and seemed to entertain Bill.

Bill was good with fun, but he was fabulous when there was trouble. When I was 19, at odds with my father, and physically helpless because I'd broken my foot in a motorcycle accident, he put me on a $20-a-week allowance. He was helping a friend, no questions asked. I didn't even ask for his help, and there was never any sense that this was a transaction or that I had an obligation to pay him back. It was the way things were.

I was on Bill's dole for eight or nine weeks, and each morning I hobbled downtown on crutches for an hour of conversation at the pool hall. I read books so we'd have something to talk about, and I even made notes about things that might interest him. When we were finished talking, I hobbled my way home, stimulated and guilt-free about mooching.

"Home," incidentally, was a two-room shack I'd been given free use of by the father of one of my friends, a man who didn't much like my father and so gave me the keys with an undisguised glee. Unlike Bill, who never visited, this man occasionally came over with a bag of groceries, all on the same no-questions-asked basis, although in his case I had to endure some bemused laughter and a lot more useless advice than I got from Bill.

Strange? Maybe. This was before the existence of the Safe World of today, strapped onto us with all its suspicions and prohibitions, the hazard-regulated world that is somehow filled with creeps hiding razor blades inside Halloween apples, and where no darkened alley is without its pervert, no school or church without its molester. In the now-gone world I grew up in, people helped you because they recognized that you needed help. In my case, they helped me because they understood that I was young and stupid, and they believed that I had the right to make a few unsupervised mistakes, and that I might learn from them.

I think Bill genuinely enjoyed my companionship. Maybe I allowed him to see what might be going on inside the heads of his two nephews—a few years younger than I was—to whom he was devoted. And maybe be believed that I offered a preview, however addled, of the future. Whatever he got from me, he let me know I didn't owe him more than an occasional conversation.

Many of the characteristics I was drawn to in Bill are the ones I've been drawn to amongst the friends I've made since who have conspicuously decided *not* to load their genetic imprint onto the planetary future. Among these friends, many of whom are gay, there is a deeper commitment to friendships and to other kinds of relationships in which one's private stake is disinterested and unselfish. Their "families" don't require protecting by genetic Darwinism and aggression, and they see that the future—the human side of it—is best guaranteed by nurturing tolerance and civility. So, they act pretty much as Bill Morris did around Prince George.

Bill is standing in front of the vast two-car garage he's recently had built to house his aging Thunderbird hardtop.

"You can park that thing inside if you like," he says as I pull up, pressing the remote attached to his key chain. It's more or less an order.

The double doors lift and I guide the Taurus inside, not wanting to insult him. I climb out and look around. The building is insulated and nearly tall enough to play basketball in. I holler greetings over the door noise. "Pretty grand," I say. "We didn't have doors like that in the bad old days."

Bill beams as we shake hands, and I follow him out and along the concrete sidewalk to the house, where I watch him select a key to open the door. I recall his odd habit of locking everything, but don't remark on it. He's done so for as long as I can remember, one of several fuddy-duddy behaviours that stop just short of being eccentric. It occurs to me that locking doors isn't as unusual here as it once was.

Garage aside, Bill has done almost nothing to the house he shared with his parents. I don't even think he's moved from his old bedroom upstairs to their larger one downstairs, and the house retains the faint scent of furnace oil I remember from earlier visits, even though he's replaced the oil-burning kitchen stove with a modern electric.

We sit down at the oilcloth-covered kitchen table, and Bill pours a mug of coffee for each of us from an enamelled metal percolator bubbling away on the stove. I top up the coffee with as much milk and sugar as the mug will take, but it still tastes like he made it the last time I visited, which has to be five or six years ago. He sits down across from me and pushes an ashtray my way.

"Go ahead and smoke," he says. "You knew I quit, didn't you?"

I nod.

"Eventually you will, too," he says. "Everyone has to sooner or later."

He's off to the next topic without waiting for my answer. He seems animated and relaxed, almost contradictorily so. It takes a while for him to ask his questions, but eventually it's my turn.

"Tell me," I say, "what you've been up to aside from visiting the Ukraine."

"Oh, nothing much," he says breezily. "A little this, a little that. A lot of bridge, some real estate, though I'm officially retired, now."

He asks me, for the thousandth time, if I've taken up bridge yet, and for the thousandth time I answer no, this time citing Stephen Vizinczey's homily about writers needing to conserve their small reserves of brain power, adding that learning to play bridge with any degree of competence would suck up far too much of mine. Bill listens carefully to this and nods agreement with my logic, even though he'll ask me the same question the next time I see him. Then I stop talking and listen while he offers up his report on the spiritual progress of his nephews, his sister Mary's health, and so on.

Finally warmed up, he asks if I recall a man very much like himself, one who has been a lifelong single, a small business owner and a small-scale pillar of the community—a good person, well connected with the Chamber of Commerce crowd.

I nod. I know the man well enough to exchange greetings if we meet on the street, but we've had little beyond that to say to one another over the years.

"You'll love this," he says. "Do you recall that briefcase he carried everywhere?"

I don't, and Bill taps his own briefcase, still on the table: a caramel, calf-leather box case, expensive, with a combination lock. "Like this one," he says. "Identical, really. Well, I had dinner at his house several months ago, and after dessert, he plunks the briefcase on the table between us like a second dessert, and says, 'Would you like to smoke?'

"'Of course,' I says, 'Indeed I would like to smoke, but you know I quit.' And he says, 'I mean, *smoke*, Bill,' and he pulls one of those clear supermarket produce bags out of the briefcase, and damned if it isn't jammed full with marijuana.

"Now," Bill continues, "I suppose I've tried that stuff once or twice with you-know-who."

I'm not sure who, but I'm not going stop the story to say so.

"And of course, as far as I'm concerned they're welcome to smoke sticks of dynamite so long as they don't hurt anyone else with it and they don't start a lot of stupid fist fights. God knows the beer parlours are more peaceful around here since marijuana started trickling into town from wherever it is they grow it."

"Alaska," I say half-seriously. "Doesn't everyone in the north smoke Alaska Thunderfuck?"

"I'm sure they do," Bill answers. "Anyway, I tell him, 'No thanks, but you go ahead.' So he does, and it's very odd, you know, because he doesn't change in the slightest even after he's smoked a full fat one, except that he's a little more, well, talkative.

"So it gets me thinking, you know, that maybe he's been doing this for a while, and I coax him into telling me the whole story. And naturally, since he's been smoking marijuana, he talks my hind leg off, practically.

"Well, it turns out"—Bill chuckles, *cluck-cluck-cluck*—"he's been smoking regularly since about 1970, and I mean daily. It's the funniest thing, really. Because about the time he says he started smoking, I'm sure, is roughly the same time a kind of mellowness came over him that I swear to God wasn't there before. I'd see him around town at various events, business meetings and what-have-you—for a few years he was the president of the Real Estate Board, you know—and now it turns out he'd been smoking marijuana the entire time."

"You're saying he was stoned the whole time?"

Another cascade of cluck-chuckles. "Yes. All the time. 'Buzzed' as he puts it. Isn't that a lovely story?"

It's not his best one, but it's good. I've suspected for a while that buzzed businessmen aren't unknown up here. Or rather, they're unknown, but not exactly a rarity.

"How's your health, anyway?" I ask when the chuckles die back.

Bill's eyes flicker evasively. "It's fine," he says. "Some small things. You know how it is when you're getting up there in years." He doesn't want to elaborate, so I let it go.

We chat for a few more minutes, finish our coffee. On my way out, I kid him about his Thunderbird having a nicer place to live than he has, and we're about done.

"I'll try to make it up to your little talk," Bill says doubtfully.

"Or maybe I'll drop around again before I leave," I reply. "How's that?"

Bill's smile lets me know he's not coming to my lecture and that my counter-lie evened things up just fine. I catch a glimpse of him in the rear-view mirror as I'm pulling away. When he thinks I'm no longer looking, he lets his posture sag. I suddenly see a little old man: comfortably at home, at rest atop the forest of eggs that has been his life.

15

The McKinnon house is empty when I get up the next morning, and it's after nine. Barry is off teaching, Joy at work, Jesse at school. I reheat a cup of lukewarm coffee in the microwave, top it with milk and sugar, and stroll outside to the deck to shake off the fog from Barry and Noel's homemade beer, which Barry and I sat up past midnight drinking. The sky above me is a deep blue, but the air remains cool even though the sun cleared the horizon almost six hours ago. The brilliance of the light feels sweet on my skin, and the five or six big pots of pink and red petunias Joy has positioned around the deck clearly agree: the blossoms are big and ectomorphic, soaking up the sun's 20-hour-a-day generosity.

I finish the coffee, shower, and dress, and without breakfast or a clear notion of where I'm going, walk downtown. I recognize that I'm planning breakfast at the new home of Other Art, which Harvey has moved from its second-floor digs on George Street to the back half of the building that once housed the long-gone-from-downtown General Motors dealership right across from City Hall. Now all Harvey has to do if he wants to break some bureaucratic windows is toss the rocks across a small park.

City Hall is open for business but it isn't serving breakfast unless you're a corporate developer. Other Art is empty and dark, even though there are breakfast items on the menu posted in the window. Disappointed, I amble on past both to the Simon Fraser Hotel for a breakfast in its Coffee Garden.

I'm not going there because they serve fabulous breakfasts, but because this seems like a good opportunity to check on a civic institution that has existed for almost 40 years. It's called the Coffee Klatch, and it arose from the peculiar dynamics of the area's economy in the late 1950s and early 1960s. What created it was the influx of consumer franchises and corporate buyout money, which began to produce businessmen with no business to take care of, along with still-working businessmen overconfident enough of their future to sit around talking politics and philosophy.

Nearly all of these men were then in their forties and early fifties, and mostly of like mind: right of centre politically, pro industrial development and pro population growth, particularly if the people making up the new citizens were of European descent, handy with chainsaws, and weren't interested in joining a trade union. The Coffee Klatchers weren't quite able to track the idea that the buy-ups and buyouts that had become an everyday occurrence weren't optional, and to the slicks coming in on the multinational wave, they must have seemed a little like plump white bunnies in a lettuce-filled cage.

In its early incarnation, the Klatch convened at a circular double booth under the front window of the old Silver Spike Café on Third Avenue, and it rarely drew more than 10 people. When the Spike closed in the mid-1960s, the Klatch moved to the then-new Simon

Fraser Hotel. The first two malls had been built and their franchises were beginning to pick off the old retailers along Third Avenue and George Street, while the multinationals were aggressively buying up the local sawmills. The Klatch grew. For a few years as many as 30 men showed up each morning to gab about the present and future, and for a while, it was around the Klatch tables that the important municipal decisions got hashed out. The Klatch regulars had acquired mugs with their names on them, and as the group grew, more mugs had stencilled names.

And then, gradually, the old gang got older, the ranks began to thin, and some of the mugs fell into disuse.

I'd grown to like many of the men—they were *all* men—who made up the core of the Klatch, guys like photographer Wally West, lovely old one-eyed Danny Palumbo, or Spike Enemark, Occasional Poet, perpetual losing political candidate for the Liberal Party and a sometimes-member of City Council. While I was on the outs with my father—which by my late teens I usually was—each of them had given me his share of entertaining if unhelpful advice. Other Klatchers I'd admired from a distance, particularly the retired lumbermen whose tough-shit attitudes were as close to deep thinking as Prince George could muster.

In session, the Klatch dispersed equal dollops of bigotry and common sense. But either way, their talk was pretty entertaining, particularly for its members. They might suggest that the poor ought to be lined up and shot, but they'd also come out in favour of easy access to abortion on the grounds that if people aren't going to love their kids enough to take care of them, they shouldn't be obliged to bring them into the world, or—as the pendulum swings back—be allowed to have kids in the first place.

I occasionally heard them talking this way, but I haven't made a practice of arguing with them. In fact, I haven't had a personal audience since the day in June 1961 when I presented a petition signed by 40 or 50 of my fellow grade 10 and 11 students designed to get a teacher by the name of Emile DeKonnick rehired as the high school's French instructor. DeKonnick had been a skilled language teacher and was well-liked by the few students who really wanted to learn French. But his only qualification for the job was that he spoke fluent French, and some bureaucrat just hired out of Vancouver by the School District decided that DeKonnick's qualifications weren't good enough for the children of Prince George. This was one of the ways progress operated in those days: all the good teachers I had in the high school were either underqualified or slightly cracked—just like the bad teachers. If a teacher was willing to come north, he or she must have come straight from the bottom of the qualified-teacher barrel or somehow wriggled in unqualified. Either way, all teachers were suspect to the new, progressive bureaucrats, old or young. But, the bureaucrats naturally picked on the wrong teachers.

I'd been dragooned into presenting the petition to the school board chairman because I'd bragged that the chairman, Harold Moffat, was a good friend of my father's. That had been a stupid move, because I didn't know if what I'd bragged about was true. My evidence was that my father bought tools from Moffat's Northern Hardware, and that I hadn't heard him call Moffat a sonofabitch or a "bird," which was his more polite term of derision. I was guessing that if my father respected Moffat, they must be on friendly terms.

Presenting the petition to Moffat turned out to be a little harder than I'd expected. My first attempt, at his office upstairs at the Northern Hardware, failed because Moffat wasn't there. I tried to pawn the petition off on his secretary, who listened to my spiel with a deepening scowl on her face and then kicked me out, advising me that I'd be wise not to bother Mr. Moffat with any schoolboy nonsense. Undeterred, I decided to present the petition the next morning—Saturday—at the Klatch.

Big mistake. In those days, Saturdays got peak attendance, and there were a dozen businessmen crowded in and around the big oval booth in the Silver Spike's front window. Moffat spotted me as I approached, and the glint in his eyes told me the secretary had warned him. With a suspicion that I was worse than doomed, I stood at the edge of the booth and harrumphed until I was officially noted.

"What do you want, sonny?" one of the Klatchers snapped.

I resisted an impulse to run, and straightened my posture, hoping that an erect spine would stiffen my resolve. "I'd like to present this petition on behalf of . . ."

Moffat turned a cold eye on me. "You're young Fawcett, aren't you?" he interrupted.

"Yes, sir."

"I see you're the same kind of smartass your father is."

This got peals of laughter from the assembled group, and so did my choking denial that my father was a smartass.

Bewildered, I tried to continue: "I'm representing . . ."

That was as far as I got.

"Son, I'm not interested in listening to you represent anything," Moffat said. "The school board has been elected to supervise the schools, and we're not about to be dictated to by smartassed kids who think they know better than their elders. Now get out of here."

I got so far out of there I've stayed clear for 32 years and a couple of weeks. But here I am again, a few metres west of the Klatch, disguised, I hope, by middle-age and a couple of decades of absence from town. Five of the dozen or so Klatchers relaxing around a 6-metre span of teak restaurant tables at the Simon Fraser Hotel Coffee Garden had been in the Silver Spike the day I tried to present my petition, including Harold Moffat himself. I sit down across the garden from them—at what ought to be a safe distance—to observe. They've aged, some of them alarmingly, but I don't need to read the names on their mugs to identify them. They're the same guys, still talking louder than they need to, still playing to the crowd even if, in the almost deserted Simon Fraser, the crowd is now mostly dead, deaf, or imaginary.

Maybe that's what gets me noticed, despite the safe distance at which I've parked myself. I hear a booming voice calling, "Fawcett! Hey! Over here, young fellow!"

It's Wally West, the photographer. He's sitting next to Teddy Moffat, Harold's son, the only Moffat I've ever been on a first-name basis with. Ted's a contemporary of my older brother Ron, so he's not much older than I am.

I get up from my table and walk over to the Klatchers. Several of them, I note, go into defensive postures at my approach, leaning back in their chairs or turning sideways. Harold is engrossed in conversation with Hilliard Clare, a long-time crony and business associate, and doesn't look up.

"Pull up a chair," Wally says.

As I sit down, Wally goes around the table with introductions. A few are necessary, most aren't. I've been on speaking terms with about half of these Klatchers at various times, and some, like Wally West and Hilliard Clare, I have an admiration for that's completely genuine. Ambrose Trick is there, Bill Morris's brother-in-law. He's been, along with Harold Moffat, the unofficial leader of the Klatch for years, an ex-lumberman who has stayed around town, like Bill has, out of a love of the north. I see Harold Moffat eyeing me with a curious half-smile on his face, along with an arched eyebrow I recognize, even after three decades. He merely grunts and waves when the introductions reach him, and goes on with his conversation.

The waitress comes over with a mug of coffee. The mug has the name "Bill" stencilled on its side. I ask whose mug I'm borrowing and someone tells me not to worry about it. "He hasn't needed it for quite a while," Hilliard Clare explains.

I chat up Wally about the photographic archive he's recently donated to the city. Wally seems less impressed with his own generosity than with the idea that he's gotten City Council to preserve his photographs without it costing him anything. The archive is both enormous and of high quality, but there's no use trying to convince Wally that from a local history perspective, he's given the city a gift that is literally priceless.

I don't mention that I know some of his photographs better than he could imagine. Years ago, I spent hours gazing at the landscape photographs on the walls of his shop while he and my father talked, which they did a lot while my father was still a travelling salesman. The photographs gave a steely-grey undertone to my understanding of history, which in those days—as today—was mostly made up of lumber boosterisms and other sorts of business bullshit. It occurs to me that Wally's photos are probably responsible for my childhood notion that colour was a fairly recent invention in the world, but I don't tell him that, either.

Despite his sometimes remarkable instincts as a landscape photographer, Wally was completely faithful to the local *Zeitgeist*. He photographed steel bridges and logging trucks and sawdust burners amongst the mountains and rivers without end—and so was unconsciously documenting the things that mattered to him along with the things that were beautiful. His portrait photography—the money-making part of his business—was more conventional, and his eye for people was pedestrian. His gift was for the things that stirred the passion of those in his generation who fell in love with this place: the wood and water and steel. The best of the archive shows how intense and specific that passion was.

To the other Klatchers, of course, Wally is a businessman among other businessmen, and his archive of photographs gives him no more status than Spike Enemark's poems gave him while he was alive. The Klatch could tolerate such strange sensitivities among its members, but it didn't and still doesn't celebrate them. Some people take photos, some people compose poems, some people have gimpy legs or uncertain tempers or drinking problems. Okay, so long as they're kept out of sight or rolled out to provide a laugh. The Klatch was about men in business and men making money. It still is.

The conversation with Wally soon lags—he's not much of a talker beyond pleasantries, so I shift chairs and take a few minutes with Danny Palumbo. That's enough. Spike Enemark, whom I'd have most wanted to see again, died in 1989. Talking to Danny reminds me that Spike was a man I liked most for something he *didn't* do to my father.

He was a large man, Spike, and it was well-known that he was physically tough and unafraid of a scrap. For reasons I didn't understand, he and my father disliked each other—or, at least, my father disliked Spike. One afternoon when I was about 14 years old, my father and I ran into Spike coming out of the menswear store he then operated with Danny Palumbo on Third Avenue. The two men exchanged pleasantries I could tell were insincere, and I saw my father's attention fix on Spike's tie. He rubbed his fingers together as if to make sure Spike noticed they were covered in machinery grease, and reached out to separate the tie from Spike's shirt front. Then he ran the tie, slowly, between his grease-blackened fingers before allowing it to drop back onto Spike's white shirt.

I saw Spike's eyes widen momentarily, and settle on me. Then he turned on his heels and walked back into the store as if my father's act of insolence didn't interest him in the slightest.

16

While my father was still a salesman, during the summer months I sometimes travelled with him. What I recall most clearly about our trips together wasn't the countryside or the companionship. It was the circular analogue clock on the passenger side of the dashboard of his 1947 Pontiac. I remember it because the clock was my steering wheel, and I steered the car so diligently that my father grew irritable when he realized that I imagined I was driving the car instead of him.

I also remember why he didn't order me to stop. He'd done so once on a family excursion, and my mother had answered with her stock "Leave the boy alone," adding that I did a better job of keeping my hands on the steering wheel than he did. This got cheers from my brother and sisters in the back seat, a scowling *harrumph* from my father—and a hands-off-the-boy policy that continued even when my mother wasn't there to enforce it.

When he replaced the Pontiac, the fun went out of our trips. I became a mere passenger, and after a while I found excuses not to go. I didn't make another road trip alone with him until he was 78 years old, when I spent two weeks helping him rediscover his childhood haunts in northern Alberta, including a bridge he'd helped to build in 1923. I came back with a photograph of him standing in front of his Cadillac, pissing on the now broken-down bridge. I've framed that photograph and hung it on my office wall. Whenever I need to remind myself of what men of his generation were about, there it is.

He and I stopped in Prince George on the first leg of that trip so he could survey some of the real estate he'd accumulated. We got into town late, and the only place with rates cheap enough to suit him was the Downtown Motel, a recycled Travelodge built in the late 1950s between the Simon Fraser Hotel and City Hall. It was also the last motel of the several Spike Enemark had owned and operated in the last years of his life.

Now, in the aftermath of meeting with the Klatch, I pass the Downtown Motel on my way back to Other Art, and it brings back the odd tension I felt on that previous visit between the two now-elderly men as my father and I checked in. It was after midnight, but my father tried to bargain down the price of the room.

"Jesus Christ, Hartley," Spike had said, only half joking. "What bloody good is it being an Okanagan millionaire if you're still haggling over the price of motel rooms with blind old men like me?"

That shut my father up. He agreed to Spike's more-than-reasonable price, which he let me pay, but he grumbled about it all the way up to the room. The next morning he insisted I drop the key into the office when we checked out. I stopped to talk with Spike for a few minutes, and when I got into the car my father was scowling.

"What did you have to talk about with that stupid old bird," he snapped.

It's 11 a.m. by the time I peer into the front door of Other Art once again, but there's still no sign of life. I stroll along George Street and up Third Avenue under Setty Pendakur's misbegotten and now scraggly mall canopy, past the vacant shops, the fly-by-nighters and 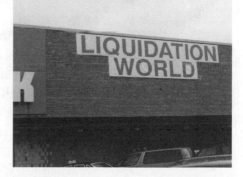 the junk shops, none of them selling anything people very much want. The exception is the block that houses the storefronts of Wally West's photography studio, Danny Palumbo and Spike Enemark's long-gone menswear store, and the Northern Hardware, which expanded into the building when Danny and Spike vacated. Beyond that block it's back to urban blight: a consistent downward spiral of retail decay so absolute that it is hard to see where it can end short of demolition. If the Northern Hardware ever goes belly-up, downtown Prince George will be ready for bulldozing.

Then there's the infinitely variable and unpredictable ways that human bodies spiral downward to oblivion. It's something best observed in places like Prince George, where people are born, grow up, and then stay around for the spiral.

Some bodies, like Bill Morris's, are fixed by the intensity of their youth, and never quite leave it behind, producing progressively ossified versions of the original. Others carry their baby fat into early adulthood, then lose it abruptly enough in their twenties that they become difficult to recognize. That's what I did, I'm told. Most people here pack on the pounds and lose whoever they were from the strain of hauling the pork from station to station. I've seen a few who put on muscle as if that were the physical manifestation of experience— people like Lyle Dickieson, I suspect—and become more solid and grounded than was imaginable when they were younger.

Then there's Judy Clark. Judy was a couple of years my senior the year she turned 18 and won the local beauty contest to become Queen Aurora number-whatever. That meant, among other things, that she was about as far above me socially as the aurora borealis. Back then she was a strawberry-blonde, with a willowy build and pert good looks. I thought she was unapproachably glamorous, but for all that, she never appeared to be too impressed with herself. She said hello if the occasion called for it, and was often friendly and courteous when she didn't need to be. I liked her, in other words. So did nearly everyone. Now, she's closing in on a half-century, having survived marriage and several kids. The strawberry-blonde hair is flecked with a little grey, but she's still attractive and personable in the same gamine sort of way.

That's what I see when I first glimpse her behind the reception counter at the *Citizen*, a post she's worked for the past few years with a kind of proprietorial confidence that makes you feel like she's there because *she* owns the paper and not the Southam newspaper chain. She recognizes me, sort of, and chats me up without asking why

I'm there. I can't tell whether she's been told I'm meeting with Paul Strickland, is covering up not being able to place me, or doesn't care who I am or why I'm there and is entertaining herself by playing Queen Aurora to the rabble. It doesn't matter either, because as we talk, I notice the lines in her face and the determined gravity of her demeanour. She's recognizably herself from 30 years ago: still slim, shapely, sure. But wait a minute—

Wasn't Judy Clark petite, willowy? Not this woman. Her hips are wider than I remember, and flatter. She's not big, and certainly not overweight. But she's voluptuous—not exactly the Venus of Willen-dorf, but closer to that than to Gidget. She's turned into a large, strong, well-constructed human female, and I suspect this is a fairly exact physical expression of a life filled by minor acts of will and not-enormous-but-frequently-overcome obstacles. How did that happen? Or better, why doesn't it happen to more people?

I'm saved from having to ponder that question by the appearance of Paul Strickland from behind one of the word-processing monitors deep inside the open-plan office. Paul is a very good small-town news-paper reporter, the kind Prince George has been short of in recent decades. He's soft-spoken, light-haired, fair complexioned, and plump —physically unremarkable to the point of deliberateness. His writ-ing style isn't remarkable either, but with the straitjacket style-sheets of today's corporate journalism, remarkability has become a burden most reporters can't afford. What is remarkable about Paul is that he reads widely—well outside the apparent necessities of his job—and is a scrupulous researcher. The takeover of small-town newspapers by the corporations, and the labour-relations hell that has resulted from their profit-driven downsizing, has turned most reporters into care-ful researchers. But his carefulness is more old-fashioned curiosity than ass-covering. He wants to know what's what, and why.

One of the ways Paul gets to know things is by wildly exaggerating a reporter's normal habits. He asks a single, simple question, normally an open-ended one like "What do you think about forestry"—or God—and then abandons you to the answer. It makes conversation painful, because he doesn't nudge you in one direction or another with the usual grunts or head shakes, or rattled chairs. He just stares at you, listening carefully and silently to your answers, moving only to write notes or adjust his tape recorder. As the interviewee, you're left to cope with utterly naked interrogatives, hanging on whichever of their hooks catch your mental flesh. If he ever gives up journalism, the police should hire him. He'd get more confessions than a priest or a fingernail popper.

Paul and I are nominally friends, but give-and-take conversation is out of the question. I suspect that he's simply lost the knack, or that his native reserve denies it to him. It's easy to calculate the effect he has on politicians or entrepreneurs with something to hide or efface with clichés and bullshit. In most of our past conversations, I've simply poured out literally everything that's in my head, along with whatever idiocies pop into it while he subjects me to his attentive neutrality.

Paul quickly suggests a cup of coffee and lunch outside the office. I say my goodbyes to Judy—a little too warmly apparently, because the slight arch of her eyebrows signals that she has no idea who I am, or worse, that she finds my appreciative gaze no more interesting than she did while we were in high school. Paul and I walk a half-block north along Dominion Street, passing under the street-straddling and perpetually empty parkade the city built on Second Avenue in the 1970s, and he enumerates our coffee-drinking options without tipping his hand about which he'd prefer. I stop in front of a scruffy-looking deli and gaze in through the mud-splattered window.

"How's this place?" I ask.

"Well, one's as good as the next," Paul answers without a hint of irony. "The egg salad sandwiches here are quite good."

"You mean they make them on the spot rather than fly them in from Ohio, right?"

"Yes," he confirms. "The food is better than at 7-Eleven."

Inside, we settle at a small table with Styrofoam-flavoured coffee and egg salad sandwiches that at least look salmonella-free. I don't get more than a bite of my sandwich down before Paul pops his opening question: "What are you going to say to people on Saturday night?"

"Well," I say, already feeling an abyss of possibilities yawning before me. "I think I've been asked to speak because I wrote that book about Alexander Mackenzie and it's been taught at the college for a long time, so I guess I ought to tell people what's in it." I don't add that I'm pretty damned sure that if any elected official had read the book, I wouldn't have been invited at all.

Paul gazes at me silently, as if he believes that summarizing an episodic book grounded in a series of connected and but strange premises is a relatively simple matter.

"I'm not sure how to communicate that to an audience as mixed as the one that'll be there."

Paul takes a sip of his coffee, watching me take another bite of my sandwich, chew it around, and swallow. He's not going to help.

"I want to make people angry, but the danger is that I'll only get them pissed off at *me*—some outsider coming around to tell them what's wrong with their lives."

Paul doesn't tell me I'm not an outsider. "Yes," he says. "That might happen."

"The only reserve of anger left in Prince George that hasn't been diluted with business propaganda and fear-mongering about lost incomes and jobs," I say, sounding more firm about this than I feel, "is over the remoteness of the corporations. They just don't give a shit, and people here sense it."

"I think some people are upset about it, yes," Paul concedes.

"But," I lurch on, "what I want to tell people is that this corporate remoteness isn't new. It's been with us since Mackenzie's time. He was a partner in the North West Company, so he was a *corporate* explorer; a shareholder interested in profits rather than places. His curiosity was shaped by his commercial ambition, despite the force of character and the will he backed it up with. I'm going to argue that he's a contemporary guy, and that we ought to be seeing his behaviour as a precursor to the corporate behaviours that have gutted the resource here."

This seems like a fairly exciting insight to me now that I've blurted it out, but Paul appears to think it is either self-evident or so far beyond the pale it doesn't warrant comment. I can't tell which.

"Who would you compare him with in today's world?" he asks.

"Well, remarkable people are as often motivated by crappy impulses as they are by evil or decent ones. Mackenzie was a man who wanted to trade goods, and to trade means to want to have the advantage in whatever transaction is occurring. If we cut out all the noble-explorer crap, Mackenzie wanted to make a large profit so he could go back to Great Britain and live like a gentleman. Sort of like Conrad Black."

That doesn't make Paul flinch, but it gets me reaching. I don't really want Alexander Mackenzie to be Conrad Black even if I don't have a clear notion of who else I'd like him to resemble.

"The Mackenzie we're supposed to be celebrating or commemorating this week was a real person," I say, "not merely the embodiment of a commercial ambition, not a Tourism B.C. slogan, and probably not the Mackenzie depicted by conventional historians, who all seem to think he was made out of iron and hardwood. The Mackenzie I tried to depict in *The Secret Journal* was at least believably human, with much more touchable flesh and blood than the one history has given us. When I flew up to the Arctic Divide with Kent on Monday to meet the commemorative brigade—Hey! where was the *Citizen* that day, anyhow?"

Paul shuffles in his chair. "Well, I was on an assignment," he says. "But the staff cuts essentially mean that there's no one to cover events like that. We cover the economy, and some entertainment, but that's really it, unless someone stabs their wife or something similar. We tend to cover what advertisers can get behind, otherwise."

I'd made my gibe playfully, forgetting that Paul doesn't recognize play when he's in reporter mode. "Anyway," I continue, "when I saw the brigade at the Divide, Mackenzie was there, in a way. If I could have put together two of the men there—Jim Smithers, the Lakehead University professor who led the brigade, and Lyle Dickieson, who organized the contingent of expert canoeists from Prince George that went up there to guide the brigade through James Creek, I'd have a pretty fair approximation of what I think Alexander Mackenzie was like."

Paul stares at me inscrutably, and it births a piece of mischief that for once isn't verbal idiocy. "Oh, wait," I say. "You'd have to toss in a bag boy from Safeway, too. And maybe the chief bonehead accountant at Noranda. Dickieson and Smithers are both better human beings than Mackenzie was. So are you."

Paul is considering who Lyle Dickieson might be, and misses—or ignores—the rest. After a moment he nods, having sorted Dickieson out to his satisfaction. "I know Mr. Dickieson," he says. "I'll see Mr. Smithers on Sunday at the barbecue. I'll have a better idea what you mean at that time."

I've got more. "Mackenzie was a powerful, wilful man with good leadership skills. He was also prone to depressions, some of which were probably intense enough to be considered clinical if there'd been any clinics he could check himself into. But it's very clear that what he found after he crossed the Divide sent him into a very serious depression."

"So you wrote in your book," Paul says, looking momentarily confused. "But what was your evidence for that?"

"Well, he missed the juncture of the Fraser and the Nechako, and given the distinctly different colours of the two streams, that would be difficult."

"Perhaps he was sleeping," Paul says.

"Always possible," I admit. "But don't you think his crew would have been instructed to awaken him if they encountered a big waterway?"

"I suppose." Paul shrugs. "But maybe they wanted to get down-river, and didn't tell him." He stops, as if considering the labour relations consequences.

"But Mackenzie missed it both times—going downriver and again on the way back," I say. "What are the odds on that?"

"I'm not sure," Paul says, and lapses back into his customary stillness. It forces me to pick up my own lead.

"At the time I wrote that book, I believed Mackenzie became depressed because he and his crew had so narrowly escaped drowning in James Creek, and because they lost so many of their trade goods when the canoe broke apart. Traders with little to trade tend to be unhappy.

"But maybe it was more than that. It had to have occurred to Mackenzie—with forest fires burning in the distance even though it was mid-June, with the blackflies and mosquitoes chewing on them, and with the crazy watercourses of James Creek and the McGregor River trying to drown them every 6 metres—that the God he believed in might just have a less-than-thorough attitude toward his job. The disordered firmament Mackenzie was struggling through would have been a convincing argument either that good old God either didn't have his stuff together or that he was deliberately laying the whip to his—Mackenzie's—backside. That's depressing either way, particularly when you're as far up the proverbial creek as Mackenzie was."

Paul ignores the rhetorical flourish. "What do you think this means to people today?"

"I don't know," I say. "Maybe just that it's still hard to convince yourself of God's power and dominion when you live here. Or rather, it's hard to believe in a competent, encompassing God. The world of things here denies it every time you turn around. The streams and rivers don't fit into the landforms. The life forms—the trees, and some of the other flora, and a lot of the animals, like the moose or wolverine, look and act like they were made out of leftover parts or were designed for someplace else. And Prince George, as cities go, sort of follows that model."

Paul looks puzzled by this, so I head deeper into the wilderness inside my head.

"You've seen moose in the winter after a crust forms on the snow? They're miserable, and their shanks are always barked up and bleeding. That's why so many of them are on the roads and rail lines, getting killed. A competent creator would have given moose webbed feet, like caribou have, and made them five hundred pounds lighter. Or wolverines—they're giant weasels on steroids. The reason they're so ornery is that they know they're an evolutionary mistake, and they're out to punish everything they encounter because of it. I think everyone and everything feels a little of that around here—as if we're part of an experiment that somehow got abandoned. It isn't just the sense that everything—like everyone—is merely passing through. Being unsettled and temporary is the way things are."

"I haven't thought of those animals this way," Paul says, maintaining his composure. I suspect he's deciding that I've lost my mind.

"But look," I say, "maybe we're the ones who have to change that temporariness. Our generation, people like you and me. I guess I'm saying that if we're here to stay, maybe it's time to accept that the messing around we've done here is an inevitable part of being human, and that maybe it's even a good thing."

There's alarm in his expression—or at least there *is* an expression, for once—as we both recognize where I seem to be heading. That startles me into a hasty retreat. "What I'm suggesting is that we have to take over, take responsibility. Change our approach. When we cash in, we have to stay around for the aftermath, and give some back in kind. I don't know if it's in human nature to do that now—if it ever was. Capitalism is so ingrained *and* ascendant right now that trying to interpose ideas about reciprocity feels quaint, even to me. But at the same time, common sense tells us we can't simply be on the take indefinitely."

Paul takes a bite of his sandwich and munches on it carefully, back to his neutrality. Oddly, it makes me want to continue on this more reasonable tack.

"So, at very least, we've got to adjust the timber-harvesting formula, even if it is against everything experience has taught us about the way things are. And against everything we know about capitalist economies, which have always traded and exploited without restraint. You know that trading and using up resources that can't be replaced are the only things human beings do that no other animal does."

"Weren't corporations restrained by governments at one time?" Paul asks, managing to make the question sound *not* rhetorical.

"Yes," I answer. "When governments were capable of recognizing that public interest and business interests were different, and could distinguish the differences. Those governments seem to be gone for good, even though it's bloody hard to think of a past B.C. government that knew the difference between public and business interests. But look, Paul. Blaming the corporations is too easy. Whether the corporations stay or not, if the current pattern of exploitation and trade isn't altered, we're going to turn the north into a desert as deep and dead as the Sahara. It'll just be much, much colder. If you're not sure what I'm saying, go out to the Bowron River valley and see what's been done out there. That clearcut is out there, weakening *your* will, undermining *your* ability to believe in the future and to build it. Or rebuild it, because the continuum that we've all been on in the past 200 years—Mackenzie's trajectory—is a terminal one."

Paul nods, but not in a helpful way. I head for deep space again.

"You know that a few of the radical ecologists out there believe the different elements within ecosystems aren't simply connected by academic abstractions and hand-holding circles. They believe that under our forests live giant fungi that organize and feed the system, and distribute genetic and biological feedback. The one under northern B.C., if it exists, starts somewhere just south of Quesnel, extends to the mountains east and west, and to the north, peters out somewhere around Fort Nelson and the Yukon border. It's enormous, in other words—among the biggest in the world. So, the radical ecologists reason, who knows what damaging a chunk of this big mushroom will do to the whole forest. Maybe the trees will stop growing or something. Maybe they'll keel over and die, like they're doing in Europe. Or, maybe they'll just grow 10- or 20-percent more slowly, and be less able to cope with diseases and bug infestations."

"They're not doing too well with insects and diseases just now," Paul observes. "Bugs were the reason given for the cutting on the Bowron."

"Well, this truffle theory may seem fanciful, but I don't think it's completely loony. Mainstream environmentalists believe that the natural world is a complex but fragile organism, sort of like a Local Area Network in computers, or the old NORAD shield against Soviet missile attacks, where a collapse in one part can cause a chain reaction failure throughout, resulting in system crashes or Armageddon. What the truffle theorists are saying about forests is that this isn't just an abstract notion, but a physical entity that actually exists in a quasi-conscious way.

"You dipsticks up here," I continue, again trying to draw Paul into the net of moral opprobrium I'm attempting to weave, "have treated the north like it's a supermarket, a subsystem of a larger project that's to be used for buying and selling goods until it's used up."

"You had a supermarket appear in *The Secret Journal of Alexander Mackenzie*," Paul points out. It's an observation, not a criticism. There's no trace of irritation or disappointment in his tone.

"Yes," I answer. "I was working out the idea of supermarket culture in that book. I've learned a little more about it since. I keep thinking it's going to become more obvious to people, but it doesn't seem to. So it has me wondering if I've been using the wrong approach."

"Calling us dipsticks isn't likely to increase your audience," Paul says.

"No, I suppose not. But I'm one of the dipsticks, too. I mean, I've already admitted that exploitation is necessary, to a degree, if we're to make any kind of living or get anything done. And I'm not suggesting that people can live in a place without leaving marks. I'm a man who has lived to make marks on paper, so I can testify better than most to how consuming this particular impulse can be. Human beings leave marks, willy-nilly, because we are, as a species, makers of marks."

"What about Prince George?" Paul asks. Implicit in his question is the very small accusation that I'm turning Prince George into an abstract metaphor for writing.

"Well," I say, trying to be as thorough in my coverage as he is fastidious in his qualifiers, "around here, mark-making means that we're flatteners of landscapes, gougers of hillsides, polluters of rivers, desecrators of leafy vales, cold executioners of hapless fawns and does, and so on. We push things around, including one another; we bulldoze. Sometimes the marks we make carry meaning, and sometimes our changes are for the better. What we need to do, maybe more around here than anywhere, is to improve the quality of the marks we make. That's a modest enough goal, isn't it?"

"Until you get to the practicalities, perhaps," Paul says. "That's where things seem to break down. So many ways to go."

And so it continues, another half-hour of blather, all of it mine. Everything I say to Paul refluxes; nothing I see or say is unreservedly true, or rather, nothing true is without back-splatter. It is messy, trying to pin down this conspiracy to transform the world into supermarkets and malls and to make clearcuts out of every forest: messy, mucky, sticky, incomplete, unsatisfying. As each verity ripens under the fluorescence of scrutiny, its contrary also becomes visible. Under Paul

Strickland's neutral gaze, each grand pronouncement I make calls forth the negative pole in the inherent equation.

I remember that in the chilly barren of the Bowron River valley, trees are growing, and that the clearcut is really just the south edge of the general repository of human carelessness, heartless greed, government neglect, and corporate myopia and incompetence called Prince George.

Finally, I remember the single political belief I've been able to secure with evidence: Most people, given the facts, the leisure, and some freedom from subsistence, will do the right thing. I have to assume that this rule applies here as much as anywhere else. So maybe instead of hunting for Alexander Mackenzie look-alikes, I ought to be searching for the embodiment of the sort of human being that can move us beyond the limited definitions of human enterprise Mackenzie and his vision represent.

I find myself thinking about Joy's pink petunias, and I forget about the bad coffee and egg salad sandwiches and the faint stink of the pulp mills wafting through the air. All these good people trapped by Alexander Mackenzie's supermarket, not knowing whether it is heaven or hell. Well, what about the ones who don't want out? What about them as an alternative? The thought strikes me dumb, and my monologue—our lunch—ends in silence.

As Paul and I say our goodbyes outside the *Citizen*'s front entrance a few minutes later, an insect begins to buzz me insistently. I assume that it's a yellow jacket or a blowfly, but what lands on my forearm turns out to be an adolescent bumblebee, newborn and with a summer of nectar ahead, intrigued by the blue of my shirt.

17

Kent calls on Friday while Barry and I are enjoying an after-breakfast coffee on the deck with Joy's giant petunias. It's a sweet morning on

Gorse Street, sunlit, about 16 degrees C with more warmth coming by early afternoon. The sky is cloudless, and after years of living in the polluted south, the deep blue overhead reminds me there's nothing above us but space and that this is a planet it might be possible to fall right off.

"The brigade has reached the Huble Homestead," Kent says, "and they're preparing to set out for Prince George. Are you interested in coming out to see them off?"

I am, but I'm foggy about what and where the Huble Homestead is. Since Kent's tone suggests that he expects I should know *exactly* what and where it is, I don't risk either question. My guess is, on the Fraser not very far north and east of Prince George, likely a short way upriver from where the Salmon River joins the Fraser. That isn't much of a guess and I don't have to guess at all that the canoe brigade has successfully navigated the James Creek–McGregor River system with a day to spare and is resting before coming into town. It'll be interesting to see how they came through.

"Ask Barry if he wants to come, too," Kent says. "We can all go in my car."

Surprisingly, Barry *is* interested in coming. Just the suggestion rescues him from his funk. He takes the phone from my hand, and he and Kent confer animatedly before deciding that Barry and I will drive out on our own.

"You're going to have all sorts of shit to take care of," Barry says to him, grinning at me. "And who knows when you'll be free to leave. What if you go out there and the canoeists all want to quit? Fawcett's got a pretty short attention span, and you wouldn't want him tugging at your sleeve whining about going back to town while you're pleading with them to get back into their boats."

They finish their conversation and hang up.

"Tell me about the Huble Homestead," I say to Barry.

"It's on the Fraser, a few kilometres upriver."

I rev my hand to indicate I already know that. Barry pauses for a moment, then continues.

"Well," he says, "let's see. Around the turn of the century, a couple of guys—Al Huble and someone named Seebach—moved in on an old Indian trail from the Fraser across to Summit Lake that had been made into a wagon road during the 1870 gold rush. They cleared a few hectares of land on the north side of the Fraser, knocked together a few buildings, recut the wagon road, and hauled freight across it into the Crooked River system. Apparently the riverboats that used to run up to Tete Jaune Cache before the railroad came through stopped at their place, and a lot of people went through there on their way north and west. They had a trading post, and so on, and until a road was built from Prince to Summit Lake just after the First World War, they had a good business going."

"How'd the freight get there in the first place?" I ask.

"Almost all of it by riverboat," Barry says. The skeptical look on my face—*How does he know that for sure?*—makes him add, "According to Kent, anyway."

"Okay," I say.

"After they stopped using the Giscome Portage, the place fell apart pretty fast, and it had a bunch of different owners before the government bought it back for use as community pasture lands in 1975. Kent and a bunch of others in the Historical Society got $50 grand in the early '80s to restore the main house—it was all that was left—and they've been working on it ever since. I think it's a Regional Park, now. Or will be soon. It's really pretty out there. You'll like it."

"Why was it called the Giscome Portage, when Giscome was 25 kilometres to the south on the other side of the river?"

"The Portage was named first, after a miner and trapper by the name of John Robert Giscome, who was the first, er, non-Native to walk the trail between the Fraser and Summit Lake—that is, between the Arctic and Pacific watersheds. Giscome was a black guy, from Jamaica. He's buried over in Victoria, I hear. Died around 1905 or 1906."

"Does the trail extend south to Giscome?"

"No," Barry says. "There's no connection. Whoever built the sawmill on Eagle Lake needed a name for the bunkhouses he built to house the mill workers. Or maybe the railroad named it. From there, a general store opened up, and the rest sort of evolved on its own until the mill closed and the townsite was bulldozed."

I press him for more details, but there aren't any. The Portage got itself named after a black Jamaican who happened to be the first man to use the trail with commercial intentions. What's more significant is that no one has thought much about it except a few recently coined black history partisans from outside the area. In the early days, a lot of unusual people—eccentrics, exceptional loners, black people— came north because the extremity of the life here bred a kind of indifference toward appearances. People were too busy to care whether you were black, or oddly shaped, or had other features or habits that weren't those of an Anglican clergyman. What mattered to them was what a man could do on the trail or in the bush, and how fast he learned, because that dictated whether or not that man survived—or was safe to work or travel with. Nobody would have gone onto the rivers with the Three Stooges, for instance. But if a man was smart and reasonably amiable, people accepted him, whether he had two heads and 12 fingers or a fetish about postage stamps—except if he happened to be Chinese. The Chinese were treated as less than-human until well into the 20th century.

Barry and I get onto the road around noon, and drive nearly 30 kilometres north on the John Hart Highway past the Salmon River valley. He pulls the truck onto a barely marked road and soon we're bumping along gravel through what he tells me is the old W.M. Ranch. The fields seem familiar to me, but I can't put my finger on why. Was I down this road while I was in the Forest Service, or was it earlier, on one of my family's blueberry-picking expeditions? What's familiar is that the road seems to run through the fields (just now turning golden with the first hay crop) in straight lines, turning by 90-degree angles. For most of a kilometre, we drive along a shallow depression that offers vistas of hayfields meeting the sky: no hills in the distance, no trees looming at the margins of the cleared land. It's like being on the prairies, an illusion that leaves me not quite ready for the return to bushland, or for the descent to the Fraser and the Huble Homestead.

If I've been here before, I don't remember. It's my loss, too. The homestead is a pretty piece of landscape, a cleared meadow several hundred metres long and perhaps 50 to a 100 metres wide. The land is old river bottom, and the significant building on the property is the original one: a square, log, two-storey structure about 7-by-7 metres that looks out over the Fraser River. Immediately behind the main building is a smaller detached building an interpretive placard identifies as a summer kitchen.

I've never heard of a summer kitchen this far north. There are only a few days in July and August that get hot enough to warrant an outdoor kitchen, and I begin asking myself whether Huble and Seebach had other motives for building it. Most likely they were hedging their bets against accidental fires, thinking that if a kitchen built separately went up in smoke, it might not take their entire enterprise with it. A separated kitchen would also keep the hired help and the customers, most of them Indians or slightly addled white men, out of the main house unless they were specifically invited inside.

The house and cook shack have been refurbished with "old things." Some of them are likely authentic, but most, since the homestead was abandoned for several decades, are probably items collected from elsewhere in the region as "representative" of the time. The several outbuildings on the site, some set up as bunkhouses and others as supply stores, have been reconstructed on the sites of original buildings long since burned or collapsed beneath the weight of the winter snowpacks. The virtues of the local lodgepole pine and spruce are that they're light woods to transport and easy to work with. But they're not particularly strong, and they have little resistance to rot. The fact that one building survived the decades of neglect is fortunate.

In one of the new outbuildings near the gate that serves as a reception centre during tourist season, there are maps of the original site and the wider geography of the Portage, along with blow-ups of old photographs depicting life in the north at the turn of the last century. These, and a walk-through of the main house, with its plank beds, straw mattresses, and rusty enamel cookware and lead-soldered tins, give an impression that life at the Giscome Portage came with minimal creature comforts, and even those were probably infested with lice, fleas, and bedbugs.

The sprinkling of formal furniture—dressers, tables, and sideboards mostly—are characterized more by ornateness and weight than by good taste or even practicality. To the people here, civilization meant Europe, and Europe in the 19th century was dark and ornate. What's surprising is how much big furniture got here in the early days, delivered by wagon and pack horse. By the beginning of the 20th century, transport became slightly easier, with river steamers operating in the upper Fraser above Prince George and a short distance to the south. But pianos managed to get to places like Barkerville during the gold rush of 1858, well before the steamers, and the Huble Homestead has some pieces of European walnut and oak nearly as large and heavy as a piano.

The other impression that's hard to avoid at the homestead is that life there was hazardous to health, particularly when it came to diet. The available foods—or rather, the food white people ate—were the kinds that travelled easily and didn't go bad: dried beans, flour for bread, bacon for frying oil. Protein would have been easiest to come by back then because the rivers and lakes were still full of fish and game was plentiful. Keeping it edible was a bigger problem.

The north isn't rich in edible plants, but it isn't without them, either. There is feral onion and garlic, and an assortment of seasonal roots and greens can be eaten if they're cooked carefully or long enough. Berries are more plentiful later in the summer, the best being the blueberries, huckleberries, and alpine strawberries. But you had to compete for them with grizzly and black bear.

There are one or two choice seasonal foods the Indians ate but neglected to tell Europeans about. Their silence wasn't malice but rather a surprisingly common form of Aboriginal civility that involves not offering information to strangers unless they specifically ask for it, and not answering questions that haven't been asked. It is a form of civility I've hankered for from my own culture, actually, but in the past it was a politeness that likely cost a few dumb Europeans their health, and occasionally their lives.

Most of the Europeans who came to this area after Mackenzie believed that Aboriginals were too stupid to know anything useful, and they paid the price for their arrogant presumption. The cultural blind spot survived well into the 20th century, although in an increasingly non-lethal way. My parents, for instance, knew nothing about the local abundance of fiddlehead ferns, which grow in a 100-kilometre east–west envelope that runs through Prince George. The Carrier populations here binged on fiddleheads every spring but said nothing to whites about them, maybe because the whites would have rejected the ferns as Indian food, anyway. Ergo, I picked and ate my first Prince George fiddleheads with Barry and Joy when I was in my mid-thirties. When I'm forced to celebrate spring in the Big City with the shrivelled fiddleheads I pay $5-a-pound for in Toronto's gourmet vegetable markets, I kick myself for not finding the Prince George fiddleheads sooner.

Barry and I make our way through the long grass down to the river and the beached canoes, partly to let Kent know we've arrived and partly because most of the brigade members are milling around by the riverbank. For a moment it seems as if they're on the verge of launching themselves back out onto the river. Kent is there, talking to Lyle Dickieson, when we approach. Dickieson nods at me and goes on with what he's explaining to Kent.

They've lost one of their original canoes—a boat already in weakened condition—coming through James Creek, and now they're wrangling over who will man the remaining canoes and who will be redistributed to the extra canoes they're borrowing for the Prince George leg. They've got celebrity paddlers to fit in amongst them, politicians mostly, along with several private citizens who have offered them help along the way and actually deserve the honour.

Kent sees that I'm interested in these deliberations and politely offers me the chance to join one of the canoes as a celebrity paddler. He's making the half-hearted offer to be polite, and though I'm powerfully tempted, I tell him thanks but my back isn't up to it. I'm sure my back would be fine, but over the past few days I've been feeling increasingly reluctant to celebrate the historical continuum the brigade represents. I'm not aligning myself with the radical environmentalists and eco-feminists, who see the celebration of Mackenzie as an aggrandizement of white male patriarchy, and I'm not completely sympathetic to the humourlessly righteous Indian bands rumbling about stopping the brigade once they leave the Fraser. The truth is, I'm having trouble feeling any sincere pride about Mackenzie and his accomplishments. If we were celebrating human stamina, fine. But Mackenzie was about mercantile ambition, and about having no respect for any other impulse than the one to exploit, get rich, and get out.

I see Barry wandering away from the brigade members toward the meadow, and I detach myself, too. I don't want to bother Barry, who seems occupied with his own thoughts, so I explore upstream along the narrow margin between the riverbank and the water. I need to divorce myself from the logistic wrangling because I really don't want someone else generously deciding I ought to go with the boats. Out of sight, out of mind, I figure.

The Fraser here is close to high water in what is going to be a tame flood season. It's about 200 metres across to the other side of the river, and except for the small eddies that perpetually form and dissipate close to the banks, and some recently uprooted trees—likely wash-down from the McGregor system—and a few derelict sawlogs floated on the high water from God knows where and what instance of crappy logging technique, the murky water is calm. Breezes are playing across it, not strong enough to shill the surfaces, but sufficiently robust to rustle the poplar and cottonwoods along the banks. An even sweeter music comes from the river itself, a background rumble of rolling currents that plays into the sonorous intermittence of bumblebees and songbirds among the trees.

I follow the bank until it peels back at an already dry rivulet, and I sit down on the clay for a few minutes to take the river in. But it's unsatisfying—there's something essential that I'm missing. I get to my feet again, see that the underbrush comes down to the water's edge on the far side of the rivulet, and track away from the river. In a few paces I'm clear of the underbrush and at the meadow's margins, where it breaks open into a profusion of wildflowers I didn't notice on the way in: Indian paintbrushes, fragrant red clover, ox-eye daisy, a species of wild lupines I don't recall ever seeing before, along with clusters of late dandelions and some buttercup. Amongst them, an ecstatic army of buzzy honey- and bumblebees, without a single urban carrion-eating yellow jacket to be seen.

I climb up to the meadow and walk to the middle, where I turn and take in the vista. Grandeur it is not: some scruffy log sheds clustered around a two-storey log house, with a wide, murky river in the background. The only human beings I can see are two of the brigade members shooting souvenir snapshots of one another against the wall of what they'll wander into their futures believing was a summer kitchen.

Then I see the other way of looking at this: *It isn't Stalingrad or the Somme*. No wars of any kind have been fought on these meadows. This cluster of organized and now-historical logs is the only intervention that has ever been perpetrated here, the only human settlement attempted. No Aboriginals massacred one another on these fields, and neither have any Europeans. Aside from a few game animals shot and slaughtered, and a few less-than-lethal fist fights a lifetime ago, this place is free of ghosts of any kind.

And these conditions do not pertain just to this modest little settlement. There are few bones anywhere in these northern woods that aren't simply animal bones gnawed on by other animals, likewise now bones. The comparatively light bone cover is like the soil: thin, sweetened with clover, and not the stuff that invokes nightmares. History's hand rests lightly here, like a butterfly on the wrist or a bumblebee on a blue shirt. There have been some smallpox deaths, some lives ended early by brutal labour and accidents, a few more enriched by ambition, hard work, and sometimes even by passionate commitment. As everywhere, still more lives have been frittered away or lived without moment or consequence. Though not the setting for the next *War and Peace*, it's the only history there is.

But absence of grandeur and the scars of violence don't free anyone from the obligation to understand it, and to make it the basis for a coherent collective life. That can be begun by cataloguing what was built here and why, as Kent Sedgwick and people like him have done at the Huble Homestead. They won't have to make the sombre registration of how many people died for no good reason, and that's to the good. We should be grateful that human beings have trod as lightly here as they have, and maybe we ought to do what's necessary to ensure that our history stays as it is, whether we're Aboriginal or from elsewhere. This isn't a land that can bear heavy human footfalls. It isn't built for a lot of habitation, and it can't stand the sort of abuse and violence most of the rest of the world has seen. The soil is too thin, and if it is wasted, it'll become too thin to sustain even the boreal forests we know today. We could all wake up one morning and discover that we're living in Iraq's deserts along with a lot of blowhard latter-day Gilgameshes looking to have their moment of expressive dominance.

I stop, take a deep breath of brisk northern air, and return to the Huble Homestead. This restored human habitation, and the great forest it is lodged in, has now become a knowable *place*, one among many human inhabitations and a possible rebuke to the fate that every other great forest on the planet has suffered. Equally important, the Homestead's restoration signals that the north might no longer be a mere stopover on the way to somewhere else, that it is more than a temporary eking out of some profits before the wilderness closes in again.

I'm not sure how deep the good side of human civilization runs here. I can testify that my own past has plenty of memories of human decency; of people treating one another fairly—or at least trying to. And it has other memories of violence and myopia, lots of both. Those memories end when my childhood ended because within a few years my family moved on, each one, elsewhere.

But the generation that Barry, Joy, Kent Sedgwick, Harvey, and John Harris are part of isn't like me and my family. They're the first generation that has come here without the general intention of making enough money to go somewhere else. In the past, only a few eccentrics fell in love with the north and settled for good. There weren't many of these, and there was always the feeling that they'd gotten just a little bushed and crazy, and wouldn't be able to survive anywhere else.

Now, it's enough simply to live here, and that makes these new citizens the first true settlers. They may have come here with the same motives that brought earlier generations, but these people have had opportunities to leave and they've stayed on, and settled down without eccentricity. That's really something.

In this context—as new to me as the Huble Homestead—it is a fine thing that the citizens of Prince George are celebrating 200 years of Alexander Mackenzie. I'd be happier if there were more taking part, and if the majority weren't watching television and wishing life was more like it is in Los Angeles. I'd be happier still if everyone was using this occasion to re-examine the effects of Mackenzie's way of looking at the world and his methods for treating people and things, but that's just my party-poop programming. Whining aside, today should be a celebration of this new generation of true settlers, men like Barry and John and Kent and Lyle Dickieson, and maybe—particularly—the people who have reclaimed this homestead from the elements and from the built-in indifference of transients like Alexander Mackenzie, and like me.

18

At 1:00 p.m. on the day of my speech, Barry and I drive down to Other Art, where we're meeting John Harris for lunch. Harris has been at his farm 30 kilometres south of town all week, out of touch and away from comforts like electricity and running water, the way he likes it when he's not teaching. Though he grumbled on the phone, he agreed to come in so I can pick his brain about tonight's event. He'll be introducing me, and I'd like to get a sense of how he plans to do that.

Barry and I leave the house a half-hour early because we're going to gumboot the drag for a few minutes, see what's there. We park the truck in front of Other Art and walk north past Spike Enemark's Downtown Motel and the derelict government liquor store with its ancient glass-brick windows—now fashionable, but in those days installed to prevent children from seeing their parents buying the demon rye—a see-no-evil-drink-no-evil government scheme that failed spectacularly. We circle the block between Fifth and Sixth avenues, past CKPG, the radio and television station. From there we'll walk north a block to the post office and east past the bowling alley and Mosquito Books, the second bookstore the city has ever had and the only one that has taken any interest in local history.

"That's where Brian Spenser's old man died," Barry says, gesturing at a vacant lot next to CKPG.

He doesn't need to say more than that. This is a story everyone here knows. Brian Spenser was a kid from Fort St. James, 160 kilometres north on Stuart Lake, who made it to the NHL with the Toronto Maple Leafs during the 1970s. On ice, Spenser most resembled the Tasmanian Devil from the Bugs Bunny cartoons, and it made him an instant favourite. At the beginning of his first full season with the Leafs, Spenser's father drove down from Fort St. James to demand that CKPG switch from *Hockey Night in Canada*'s regional broadcast of the Vancouver Canucks game  to the broadcast of the Leafs' game being played at the same time. He wanted to see his son play, and he supposed, correctly, that everyone else in northern B.C. did, too. What he didn't have right was taking a rifle into the station to make the demand, and doing his supposing by waving the rifle at the station manager and a few others who happened by. Things went wrong, and the RCMP shot him to death.

After his father's death, Brian Spenser drifted from NHL team to NHL team—always a fan favourite but not talented or smart enough to be popular with the coaches he played for. Eventually the manic energy that made him fun to watch burned out, and he was gone. He moved to Florida, bought a Hummer and an oversized RV, and eventually got himself killed in a drug deal in which he appeared to have been the same combination criminal perpetrator and innocent victim his father was before he wound up dead. True sons of the north, both of them.

Thus, I bow from the waist as Barry and I pass the spot where Spenser Senior was killed. The gesture is respectful but inaccurate, as Barry's raised eyebrow confirms.

"You're bowing to a guy who didn't know that small-town television stations don't control their own programming," he says.

We round the corner, walk a short block north, corner again, and stroll along to the closed-up but "Under New Management" bowling alley. There we pause to debate whether to stop at Mosquito Books. We decide we'll do that later with John, and soon we're back where we started, still 15 minutes early. For two Prince George boys, this has been a long walk, so we open the door of Other Art, find a table, and settle in.

———————

Barry McKinnon has been part of this book from the start, on and off my radar and his own, occasionally depressed and usually complaining about the things in his private life and the city that he can't do anything to change. But John Harris has been mentioned only in passing. So, since the last chapter marked them as among the first true settlers and normal citizens Prince George has had, it's time I explained who these two men are.

Barry McKinnon writes poems. Not for a living, because writing poems for a living isn't something a person can do anywhere in the English-speaking world, not even in London, or New York, and certainly not in Canada. Despite this, Barry is a poet before any other identity he might agree to. He also teaches at a college, has a wife, Joy, who has had a working career of her own and, more importantly, has never played second fiddle to anyone. They have two children, a daughter who recently left home to work in Calgary, and a son at that painful-to-parents age where having a father is an embarrassment.

Barry and Joy own a house, maintain some recreational property they never use, and employ and/or pay for a changing assortment of recreational vehicles and devices like everyone else in Prince George who has a steady job. Barry is also a conscientious if given-to-levity member of the various collectives life has pushed him into, a man prone to scoff and groan at the silliness and the excesses of living in a minor industrial centre. But he is unapologetically without cynicism when it comes to the instruments important to making his poems—

obtuse meanings and resemblances, the complex divisions between human desire and indifference. There, he is like a scientist examining an infinitely fragile formation beneath a powerful microscope: at once tentative, precise, and methodical, and wonderfully careful not to falsify his findings.

Poets are supposed to make everything more interesting. Their characteristic preoccupations are with drawing cognitive and then linguistic parallels between the different levels of human and natural enterprise: the biological, the social, the political, the economic, the interpersonal, the extra-rational, and the cosmic. All the talented poets I've known do this, at least the ones unwounded enough to be relatively reliable as communicative beings. With the *really* good poets these attentions are mated to the kind of mental vigour that breaks through the most solid gloom and misfortune, as their skills recognize the bond between what is cosmological and what is comic. Barry is one of the really good ones.

John Harris is a very different sort of man, even though, like Barry, he too teaches at a college, writes, and has a wife and children. Like Barry he owns some real estate and runs a truck and various pricey recreational machines. But he's not a poet, and what he's about is more fundamentally moral than artistic. John is attempting to live his life without deception or even indirection—to the point of (ostensibly at least) dispensing with the concept and practice of discretion wherever he suspects it might be rooted in fear or moral cowardice.

Barry's natural instinct is to cower under the nearest physical object or cognitive distraction whenever he has to deal with anybody trying to exercise authority. John does pretty much the opposite, confronting everything and anyone foolish enough to get in his face. He isn't this way because he's an aggressive person. I'm pretty certain John has never committed a violent physical act in his life, and very few that violate other people's dignity—unless, of course, they're fools. He plays by the rule book everyone *claims* to play by, in both his private and professional life, and he's developed a sixth sense that tells him when others are faking.

In 1989 he published a book titled *Small Rain*, which systematically obliterated every illusion it confronted, including its author's own illusions about marriage, relationships, labour, and pedagogic relations in higher education. The book does this by delivering its materials with a deadpan as comedically flat as Buster Keaton's. The two books that followed, none of which reached the audiences they deserved, employed the same relentless eye for bullshit.

To say that John writes in order to tell the truth as he sees it is to diminish the complexity of his undertaking. First, his directness is free of artless sincerity. In art, sincerity is merely stupidity that isn't hiding malice within its fog. Harris the writer is like John the citizen. Both seem self-deprecating and egoless, but this quality in Harris's writing masks his unique brand of irony. Since self-involvement and egomania are the usual fuels for writing conventional fiction, that makes for interesting reading.

He's aware, as a literary scholar, that past attempts to create literature free of illusions, like, say, L. F. Celine's *Journey to the End of the Night*, have usually produced bombastic nihilism, fascism, or clinical depression, so he's aware of the difficulty. But that's his mission anyway: telling stories without any formal or private bullshit in them. For him, there's nothing else worth doing.

John and Barry have a symbiotic relationship. It comes naturally from their different temperaments and personalities, which is what made them friends in the first place. It really kicked in when the college they work at began to turn against its liberal arts programs and its other responsibilities that involve civilized behaviour. John's inability to compromise became Barry's proxy courage, enabling him to stand up to the administrators that were chewing at his confidence and will. Barry, in turn, protected John from no-win confrontations with the administrators, usually by reducing him to helpless laughter with whiny but exact descriptions of the unjustness and absurdity of what was being done to them. Barry also talked John through the breakup of his dysfunctional marriage.

During the worst part of their two-decade traverse of labour-relations hell, Barry also talked John—and probably vice versa—into taking some adult education courses, including an industrial first aid course Barry wanted to complete because he decided he didn't want to bleed to death, after slicing open his hand on a discarded beer bottle along a derelict stretch of highway leased from Harvey. It was shortly after the industrial first aid course was completed that John met Vivien Lougheed, the woman he's lived with—when she's in town—ever since.

Vivien is even more plain-spoken than John, and as incapable of compromise. She's what's called "a character"—local code for eccentrics who don't carry concealed weapons. If she'd lived 100 years ago, people would have called her an adventuress. Today, her women friends use her as a prod to get them to places they'd never travel to on their own, and sometimes to do and say things domestically they'd never do or say unless drugged or mortally provoked. John thinks of Vivien—more simply—as the best thing that ever happened to him, or at least he does when she's not trying to bully him into accompanying her to the growing list of countries where he'll be shot for insolence 10 minutes after arrival.

Vivien got her hunger for travel growing up poor in rural Manitoba—one of the few places I can think of that might be closer to the ends of the earth than northern B.C. As she tells it, she started off her career trying to run away from home when she was a child, but it wasn't until she got to Prince George with her first husband, and acquired some training in medical technology that made her broadly employable for the first time, that it occurred to her that she might actually break free. As soon as their collective debts were paid, Vivien dumped the husband and hit the road. Now, after 20 years of more or less constant travel, she's always closer to her next departure from town than her most recent arrival.

This isn't even slight exaggeration. Since she and John began living together, she's been disappearing with very little notice or fanfare and then turning up in spots across the globe where it is less than safe to be a relatively attractive middle-aged WASP woman with a V-8 motor on her mouth and a talent for arguing: rural Mexico and Central America, Tibet, Iran, rural Egypt. For a while John was either bemused or entertained by her brashness and her travelling, but underneath that he was deeply grateful for no longer being under house arrest the way he'd been throughout his marriage. Then she began to explore the isolated rivers and valleys of the northwest tip of British Columbia and the southwestern Yukon, and decided that John ought to tag along.

John agreed to the first trip because he couldn't come up with a good reason why he shouldn't, not because he had any deep urge to be out in the wilderness. After the second or third trip, the chilly vistas and icy rivers of northwestern British Columbia got to him. Now he spends his summers pushing a bicycle along abandoned mining roads enjoying the clear, cold summer air, and hoping the can of pepper spray in his shirt pocket will keep the grizzly bears from eating them. He's become an expert woodsman despite himself, as competent as Vivien and much less likely to end up sitting on a grizzly's knee.

Vivien, meanwhile, has worked her way into a career as a travel writer. She sees the world in terms of travel practicalities, and tends to fill her books with advice for and solutions to travel problems most tourists never have to face. She writes guidebooks to places most people would never set foot in, or about doing things sensible travellers never do, like riding on chicken-buses in Mexico and Central America. She writes books that tell travellers how to behave once they've arrived in a place, but the books aren't very curious about why a traveller would go there to begin with. For Vivien, that's never an issue. In her mind, travel is what any human being worth bothering about does—and why would she write for people who aren't worth bothering about?

John has been dragged into travel writing with her, with predictable adjustments. His last book, *Tungsten John*—the title is a play on the wilderness area in which it is set and the self-promoting mythologizer he is emphatically *not*—is a travel book with a sense of slapstick. The book provides the required how-to information about place and custom, but his real curiosity is about why people—or large, furry animals—are where they are, why they do or don't leave, and why they don't rob or kill defenceless strangers like him. I'm pretty sure he got interested in my book about Mackenzie because it asked questions about why Mackenzie was on the voyage in the first place, and because it raises the possibility that a project memorialized officially as history might contain the same grainy slapstick as ordinary life: things like clinical depressions, mixed motives, second thoughts, and jackasses carping from the back of the boat or bus or faculty meeting.

The new Other Art is more supper club than coffee house. It takes up most of the space the GM dealership used for car and truck repairs. Here it is filled with mostly circular tables, and it can seat 100 people easily. There's a small elevated stage in the southwest side of the room for bands or poetry readings—or Wayne Newton, if Harvey could talk him into coming, which, judging from the decor, he's probably tried.

Harvey has done more than make the place larger. The food, once it comes, is actually decent, and the service is polite and competent if not speedy. Best, there's a sense of community to the place that three years ago would have had Harvey in tears. As before, there are tree-planters, but now I spot five or six business people having late lunches, and a table of arty hosers, Prince George–style, talking loudly in one of the corners about tattooing technique and the sexiest part of a woman on which to find one.

The failures of the place are subtle, and likely in progress. The art gallery angle seems to have withered, possibly because wall space is scarce and the lighting dim, but more likely because Harvey's strange ideas about what constitutes a good painting didn't bring buyers flooding in. The gift shop has been reduced to a more-or-less-abandoned kiosk to the left of the entrance. The only goods for sale are some ugly T-shirts—Harvey's creations; several not-great ceramic bowls, and what may be local Native crafts: leather and beadwork and some flimsy New Age dream-catchers.

The empty gift shop shelves remind me that I received a letter from Harvey two years ago about a plan to feature books by local authors among the other merchandise. That meant stocking his own chapbooks, along with some of my books, Barry's, John's, and whatever he could talk the small presses around B.C. into giving him on consignment. I sent him a box of my books, with the condition that he pay for them before asking for more. I haven't seen any reorders, and I don't see any books in the gift shop, mine or anyone else's. I make a mental note to write the consignment off as a donation.

On the table in front of me is a plastic menu card with a list of upcoming Other Art events. Most are music, but one is a poetry reading. When I ask Barry how Harvey's been doing, he tells me this is the first time he's been here in months, and says Harris doesn't hang out here either. He isn't quite clear why, and when I relate Paul Strickland's view that Other Art is a going concern and mention that Paul has read some of his translations of Argentine poet Julio Machado here, he shrugs.

I can't quite get Barry's indifference or the new location into focus, and Harvey is impossible to read. Maybe that's because he stops only briefly at our table, mumbles a few clichés, and seems reluctant to make eye contact. When he sees Harris arrive, he scuttles into the kitchen without saying hello.

"Harvey owe you money or something?" I ask John as he's settling into his chair.

John grins. "Probably. But it's his problem, not mine."

We waste a few minutes trying to figure out how much Harvey owes each of us, concluding that it's not enough to put us among his major creditors. Other Art may have grown, but so, I gather, has its debt load.

"Nothing wrong with a few debts, I guess," I say, trying to be diplomatic. "No risk, no gain. Or so they say down at the World Bank. Alexander Mackenzie probably carried a few debts he didn't talk about."

Comparing Harvey with Alexander Mackenzie gives Barry the giggles, but John finds the speculation interesting.

"Harvey's the most likely of any of us to have made it onto Mackenzie's crew," he says. "Trouble is, he'd most likely have fallen out of the canoe and drowned long before he got anywhere near Prince George."

Barry watches Harvey glad-handing an incoming customer. "Or been pushed out of the canoe by one of the other crew members he'd borrowed money from," he says.

John is insistent. "At least he'd have made it into the canoe in the first place. We'd all have been clerking in some London counting house."

"Edinborough," Barry says. "My ancestors were from Scotland, remember? What about yours, Fawcett?"

"I've got some in both England and Scotland," I say. "One of my English uncles used to claim we're related to Henry VIII, until everyone else in the family laughed him out of it."

"So tell me," John asks seriously, "why you dragged me into town this afternoon when I'm going to be introducing you to a bunch of politicians in a few hours."

I tell him I'd like to know where he'll be coming from when he introduces me tonight.

He stares at me neutrally. "What difference does it make what I tell them about you? They'll all think of me as some stuffy prof from the college, anyway. If you want to influence them, you should have Harvey introducing you."

"I want to know how receptive they'll be. Or how hostile."

"Well," he says slowly, "I'd tell you, but I don't have my notes with me. Besides, it's better if it's a surprise. I mean, I'm not going to tell everybody that you're a big-city bozo who doesn't know Connaught Hill from his own asshole. If I said that, I'd have to find another book to teach, wouldn't I?"

For a second I wonder if he's going to tell Prince George that I really am a big-city bozo who doesn't know Connaught Hill from my asshole, but then I remember that John doesn't do things that way. He's simply being truthful again—as far as he's willing to say what he thinks. And I'm going to have to trust him.

A couple of young RCMP constables clank into Other Art and stand in the doorway looking over the patrons. Instinctively, Barry ducks.

"Wonder what those guys are looking for?" John says, as Harvey appears from the kitchen and advances toward them, smiling.

The three men confer for a moment, and then Harvey seats them at a table close to the door.

All they're looking for is lunch.

19

I get through the lecture just fine. After John Harris brings me on with wonderfully witty introduction, I try to tell the audience of about 80 people what I understand of Mackenzie's strengths as an individual and as a leader of men—and of his weaknesses as an entrepreneur and philosopher. A few listen attentively, more find what I'm saying funny, others look vaguely disappointed that I'm not drenching them in rhapsodic images couched in Robert W. Service–grade rhyme and metre. After an hour and a bit, the occasion is ready for crossing off the calendar of festival events: *done, let's move on to something a little more fun*. For everyone here but me and one or two others, this was supposed to be a light-hearted and hopefully boozy celebration of Alexander Mackenzie's historic moment, with an intellectual back-pat applied to themselves for following his way of doing things: make money, do it fast, party hard later and mostly elsewhere.

I don't have any urge to congratulate myself about the impact I've made, but John administers the antidote anyway. As we're crossing the parking lot to his truck, he reminds me how many people didn't show up, the thousands at home watching television with a beer and a bag of Cheezies, or simply going about their business, out and about, shopping, eating, working in the yard, or trying to make some money so the ends will come somewhere close to meeting. It's his way of suggesting that those who did give enough of a damn to show up ought to be forgiven any lapses of attention even when they fell asleep and began to snore. At least they came.

He's right, but I wasn't feeling cheated. Between Harris and me, we provided a decently interesting hour, and I'd been able to say some strange things to an audience that seemed to have an inkling I wasn't merely being squash-bug serious and negative. That's worthwhile. And so is the fact—not to be undervalued here—that nobody offered to beat me up for it after.

Among the strange things I'd said was that Mackenzie's voyage of discovery had been a failure on *his* terms. He proved that it was *possible* to come overland to the Pacific along northerly waterways, sure. But it had been just barely possible. His routes, comparatively, were arduous, slow, and excessively risky-to-product. The proof is that none of his technologies or his routes are currently in use for anything but recreational purposes, and then only for the slightly crazy or, in the case of Professor Smithers and the Lakehead University kids, those bent on re-enacting the past to secure it as Official History. The Finlay River valley that leads to the Arctic Divide is now under the waters of Williston Lake; the only use anyone has ever found for the James Creek/McGregor River country has been to log it and get the hell out; and the overland route to the Pacific that Mackenzie took after he left the Fraser south of Prince George is now a wilderness trail nobody takes because the Native peoples in the area aren't fond of white intruders, even those wearing hiking shorts made from relatives of marijuana plants and travelling on dried vegetarian rations you couldn't force-feed to a sensible human being—or to the bears.

Right at the end of my speech I revealed to the audience another rarely noted anomaly in Mackenzie's voyage that conventional historians have studiously ignored in their effort to keep the explorer heroic. Toward the end of the overland trail Mackenzie's Native guides took Mackenzie over the snow-packed 1,800-metre Rainbow Range rather than the long-established trails that lead to what is now the Dean River valley. I wasn't sure, I said, whether this was one of the elaborate practical jokes for which the Native peoples of northern B.C. are famous, or if it might have been the first stirrings of their instinct for self-preservation. I concluded by suggesting that even without Mackenzie to set them off, Europeans and Natives were squabbling over land rights and tenure in 1793, just as they are today. One hundred and twenty kilometres to the west of where Mackenzie reached the Pacific, at what is now Bella Bella, George Vancouver spent part of that same summer repairing his two ships and firing muskets at the Natives, who kept on showing up to wave farewell before he was ready to leave. Those disclosures get me the only laugh I'm sure I've induced on my own: one loud guffaw from below the podium. It came from a middle-aged man with broad shoulders and a beard. I thought it was accompanied by a few knowing snickers from mid-audience, but that might have been wishful thinking.

In the end, none of it mattered because I'd been paid for my time and effort in that brief moment at the Arctic Divide where the glassy lake let me see the world through Alexander Mackenzie's eyes. A few days later I was paid double by the bumblebees muzzing the wild lupines and Indian paintbrushes at the Huble Homestead, by the soughing of the breeze over the Fraser River, by the river's rumble in the midsummer sunlight. I was paid a third time in the clearcut on the Bowron, where I understood for the first time in my life that nothing here is permanent and that any wish for permanence contradicts the way things are here, in the deepest possible sense.

In yet another way, I've been paid off by the way John Harris introduced me to the audience. He made them see the humour in what I think and write before I opened my mouth. He did it so subtly that there was a moment just before I launched into my speech where I considered passing up the opportunity to pontificate and instead to start a conversation with the audience. That I delivered my speech without much humour didn't screw up the effect of his introduction. The audience was amused at most of the zingers I tossed at them, and they hit their cues like pros even if the cues were set up by Harris's introduction. At the end I had the uneasy feeling I was the only one who wasn't clear about what got said and what got a hearing.

But the biggest payoff comes when I leave town a couple of days later to fly back to Toronto: I have the most cheerful sense of Prince George and its people I've had since I packed my belongings into a Volkswagen Beetle at age 21 and left for good. This time I've left a city with a history and some permanent residents. John and Barry and Joy and Vivien and Kent are just the ones I know about.

As the 737 lifts me above the bright green poplars north of the runway and circles above the Fraser River before the altitude obliterates detail, I have a vision of the bees and the birds and the bears at the margins of the clearcut on the Bowron. They are massing for a resumption of normality, which will not resemble the Golden Mean or a State of Perfected Bliss, but the condition in which what is alive strives to remain alive and grow larger and older and—unlikely, but possible—wiser. I understand that some of the people now living in Prince George are doing the same, but they have the added responsibility of caring about the conditions of life beyond the impulses and dictates of the moment.

That's what I imagine, and that's what I hope. In spite of the evidence, but also because of it.

THE BUDDY SYSTEM, 1996

20

Two months after the Alexander Mackenzie re-enactment brigade was prevented from following Mackenzie's route to Bella Bella and the Pacific by one of the Native bands, I returned to Prince George, this time for my 30-year high school reunion. I'd missed the 10- and 20-year reunions, busy with what I imagined were the important parts of life—marriage, children, breakups. Without recognizing it, I'd slipped into the practice, peculiar to my generation, of treating the private stagings of an individual life as if they were the "real world," and of thinking I was free to ignore the political, social, and economic continuums everyone is part of. Those collective continuums had been shifting in relative importance most of my life, but it was becoming clear that the economic one was now dominating all the others, including the private ones—and it was chewing up Prince George in ways so raw and visible that, well, it was visible from outer space.

I'd changed, too. I was getting persistent inklings that life—including my own—wasn't always all about me.

I'd missed the 20-year reunion for an additional reason. The two high school friends I'd have most wanted to hang out with, Don White and someone I'll call "Jim" to protect his privacy, weren't accessible. Don and I weren't talking to one another, and Jim, well, Jim hadn't gone to any of the reunions, and he wasn't about to come to the thirtieth. It wasn't the usual excuse—that he wasn't a success in any of the normative terms established by high school reunion organizer. Jim couldn't show up. Jim was no longer Jim.

No one ever had much more than a theory about the causes and extent of his breakdown, and it wasn't because his family went out of their way to suppress information. They didn't. Jim didn't collapse in a dramatic or diagnosable way. It was gradual, and progressive, and he was never fractious or manic. But somewhere in the progression, Jim simply wasn't there any more. He'd walked away from himself, and maybe from normal life itself.

I mean this in a specific sense. In the mid-1960s, Jim began to walk. It wasn't a Forrest Gump routine motivated by inner simplicity, and it wasn't the "mad traveller" syndrome that ran wild in the last decades of the 19th century when the advent of popular tourism allowed the working classes to widen their perspective beyond the city and village societies they were born into. Jim was a middle-class kid from northern British Columbia, which is at the far edge of European civilization: there was nothing beyond it to discover except a few forests. The frontier was gone. His walking began innocently enough while he was in Vancouver, taking creative writing classes at the University of British Columbia, where he got into the habit of taking regular walks across the Granville and Burrard Street bridges into downtown Vancouver from his Kitsilano lodgings. Then he began walking out to the UBC campus, a noticeably longer distance. It relaxed him, he said.

But he dropped out of university for no apparent reason halfway through the year and returned to Prince George, where people spotted him walking from one side of town to the other. Soon he was walking from one town to the next, 100 or more kilometres at a stretch. At first, those who knew him stopped to offer him rides, and were met with replies that grew increasingly strange: "I'm in no hurry." "One place is as good as another." "This is where I am." That kind of thing.

During the next few years he spent time in most of the lock-ups across northern B.C. and Alberta because the way he explained his presence and behaviour wasn't satisfactory to peace officers, who found him vagrant and potentially criminal. About 1975, I asked why he walked so much, and so far. His answer was more complaint than explanation. "I feel restless," he said, his eyes shifting from wall to ceiling and back. When I asked what "restless" meant, his eyes went blank.

Reluctantly, the people who knew him, me included, acknowledged that something serious had gone wrong. One wiseass joked that

Jim had lost his mind and was trying to find it along the road. Since I was as puzzled as anyone, the notion that he'd lost some necessary part of his sanity and was walking to find it stuck with me. I began to think of him as a one-man, landlocked Ship of Fools. The truth is probably, as we now know—or think we know—much less romantic: a genetic absence of an obscure neural chemical, or the wrong balance.

I'm aware that all explanations of how the human brain operates are theoretical and metaphoric, but the chemical theory now in vogue strikes me as more limiting than the diagnostic metaphors that preceded it. I'm not happy to think that human beings are merely associations of chemical components held together in leaky, imperfect bags. The human mind, in particular, is both a mystery and a miracle. Jim's mind had been a fine and singular one, a miracle of *particular* association, a remarkable device for the calculation of moral and physical obstacles and opportunities. My guess is that it was a little *too* finely tuned, and that it overloaded on what it was taking in— what he read and thought, measured against what was around him. The overload damaged some circuits that turned out to be unreachable and irreparable. And by 1993, it had kept Jim literally lost in thought for a quarter of a century, and barely able to relate to the day-to-day world evolving and devolving around him.

While we were in high school, Jim was an energetic reader. By the time he was 16, he'd been reading—and understanding—books I couldn't crack code on until I was in my thirties. Pretty well everything I read before I was 20 that hadn't come from Bill Morris came from Jim's reading: I followed him to Dostoyevski, Albert Camus, Louis Ferdinand Celine, Jack Kerouac, and the loony discursive edges of Norman Mailer and other American writers I'd thought, up to then, merely wrote novels.

Jim's reading had an agenda, somewhere, but one that was indecipherable to a stunningly normal high school boy like me. I couldn't match his brilliance or penetration, and I didn't try. But I did have the good instinct to hook on and let myself be carried along. When he talked about Dostoyevski and Camus in particular, his eyes lit up. Despair and alienation were Jim's mental chocolate, and what he found in those two writers was the rich, dark variety. I was happy to follow him into the chocolate, even though, for me, the darkness of it was usually dispelled by the next sentence I read, the next sunny day, and the endless possibilities of ideas to think about and more books to read. I could read my way through the world—that was a plan. And who knows? Maybe I could one day *write* something worth reading.

Whenever I talked to Jim in the years after he returned to Prince George, he would seem to focus for a few minutes or a few ideas, but then he'd drift off into memories of the handful of years when things had made sense to him. That would leave him repeating, virtually verbatim, his part of conversations we'd had as he pondered the imponderables of his—our—late adolescence, reifying, for a little while, the petrified organics of a lost world.

In 1993 we were nearing 50, and I wanted to see if anything had changed for the better, if he'd escaped the trap his big brain had led him into. We'd been friends, and I didn't want to let that, or him, go. So I didn't go north merely for a sentimental reunion to dance with my now-wrinkled high school crushes and measure pecker sizes with old antagonists. The Reunion was special in another way, too. I was making the trip out of Vancouver in a rented van together with Don White, his wife Georgina, and two other girls from my graduating class, now middle-aged women. One had flown in from London, England, for the trip. I hadn't seen either since I was 20 years old. By the time we were halfway to Prince George, Don and I had settled the differences that had separated us.

The events of that reunion don't matter to this book. There were amusing confrontations with former teachers, a few ugly ducklings turned to aging swans, and an abundance of pork on the hoof. Many of those who came had succeeded in various ways; most of the disappointed stayed away; one or two had died of disease and a few others had been killed in car accidents or other violent misadventures. A profile of a normal small-town reunion, I guess, with a slightly higher mortality rate.

The hoped-for meeting with Jim took place, but it wasn't uplifting or enlightening. The five of us met him in downtown Prince George, and we took him for a car ride the afternoon of the Reunion banquet. He'd grown a ZZ Top beard since I last saw him, and he'd developed a very strange kind of pot-belly, one that, since he seemed to have gained little weight elsewhere, made him look like he'd swallowed a basketball. At first, he seemed almost normal, if unresponsive. Since the collective occasion of our being there was patently sentimental and nostalgic, Jim fit in easily be-cause he remembered the past better than we did. But when one of us asked him a question about his pres-ent life, his answers were vague. He drove taxi, sometimes. He lived here, maybe he lived there. He didn't read much anymore. He wasn't sure. Since the occasion was also polite, no one pursued any question that made him uncomfortable.

I *had* to let it, and Jim, go. I told myself that he was still alive, and there would be another time to get it straight, maybe. Meanwhile, the Reunion made me remember how much I liked Don White, and why. We discovered that most of our high school class-mates and teachers really did think of us as a joined-at-the-brain-stem menace to public order, and that pleased the part of us that was still 17 years old. For a few days, we became a middle-aged version of that same symbiotic menace.

I made another discovery at the Reunion. It is this: Most people, me included, are so blinded by consciousness of self that they do not recognize that nearly everyone else is blinded in the same way. I'd been tormented, as an adolescent and young adult, by the belief that I was transparent to everyone around me. I believed that everyone could see through my know-it-all, sarcastic outward persona to the clumsy, uncertain pretender I knew myself to be. I was wrong. The people around me were sufficiently involved in trying to maintain *their* personae and hide their own perceived inadequacies that they'd either taken my act at face value—or, maybe more often—didn't care one way or another. This insight didn't come in a blinding flash. It was more like the confirmation of a long-held suspicion, illuminated by an onslaught of sudden data and context provided by the people I was now among, once familiar but mostly absent from my life for 30 years.

The inability to see beyond oneself isn't confined to high school kids. As far as I can tell, it is a nearly universal human characteristic. The exceptions, I've since concluded, seem to be the very stupid and a small fraction of the very brilliant among us. And how are we, blinded as we are by persona maintenance, to tell who is brilliant, who is stupid, and who is normal and blinded? I also came away from that Reunion with a private puzzle. The only one there who seemed aware of what I was discovering was Don White, the person among them I'd been closest to, both while I was in high school, and since. We didn't talk about any of this during the Reunion, because our renewed symbiosis took care of it. I was seeing through his eyes, and I had a feeling he was seeing through mine. That's what this part of the story is about: what friendship permits people to see, and what blindness it inflicts, if any, in the country of the blinded. And because I'm not a foolish sociologist or a pre-mortality archaeologist pretending to empty objectivities and tropes, that will make this an inquiry into the things that steal our ability to see others, and what might restore that ability.

21

That takes me to 1996, the second week of September. I'm gazing across the Bowron River valley through the windshield of a 1980 Volkswagen Vanagon. The first warnings of winter are already in the air, though it isn't yet officially fall. The leaf edges of the poplars are yellowing in the upper branches; the fireweed foliage is turning black and maroon as the night temperatures sink to freezing, the recently profuse mauve flower stems empty and broken, their seeds already dispersed. The overcast sky in the distance is purple where rain threatens, silver where it doesn't.

"Jesus," a voice beside me mutters. It's Don White.

"It's pretty horrible, isn't it," I say.

Don glances at me distractedly. "I'm talking about the sky," he says. "I've always hated this kind of weather."

Let me go back as far as I can with Don White, which is to the fall of 1953. That was when he moved with his parents to Prince George. His father had purchased some land and the rights to a block of timber 35 kilometres south of town, and set out to build a new sawmill with the most advanced equipment then available: an automated carriage to carry logs into a huge circular saw, and a partially automated green chain that made sorting the sawn lumber easier and less costly. The family moved into a bungalow on Patricia Boulevard, a few blocks from my parents' house, and Don started school at Connaught Elementary in the same grade as me, but not the same class.

His first teacher was a young woman named Miss Knott, who gave the impression that she called herself that even when she was putting on her makeup in the morning. She was fresh out of teachers college, and believed in encouraging pupils to learn by making school a positive academic experience. She gave Don 56 O's that year, each of them for being outstanding. I remember the exact number because it was an instant school legend.

My teacher, Miss Mowat, had also just graduated, but she hadn't brought any fresh ideas with her. She didn't like Prince George and she didn't much like children. She liked being in stern control, which meant keeping the spirited, energetic children in her class in check by making them write lines after school about how they ought to become more orderly and obedient. She didn't appear to care in the least if her students were having positive academic experiences, and I wasn't. I amused myself and my fellow line-writers by mumbling her first name, "Yvonne," while I wrote my lines. Doing so was the most shocking defiance of her authority I could imagine.

I don't recall if I was the smartest kid in the class, just that it took me until the year's last report card to get an O out of her—I'd gotten my first pair of glasses shortly after Christmas and could now see the blackboard. My improved performance didn't earn me fewer lines to write, and "Yvonne" let me know the good grade she'd given up was strictly relative. To her, Prince George was a town filled with morons, and so, as an ill-behaved offspring of local morons, standing out didn't amount to much.

During that year and most of the next I saw Don mainly in the schoolyard—at that age another class is as far away as another country—and it didn't go very well. He sneered, mostly, and I sneered back. When I beat him in the grade five marble tournament, he retaliated by asking me how many O's I'd gotten on my report card.

Grade five also happened to be the year that a new kind of clear-glass marble—called a "petal"—was introduced. Most of the kids I played against thought the marbles were pretty and bought petals by the bag. But over a noon-hour game a few weeks after the tournament, Don and I agreed that petals were ruining the game—they were as pretty as the clear-glass shooters we used, but as common and cheap as the opaque dakes we anted into games to win or lose. Agreeing on this didn't make us friends, but we had seen eye to eye on something, and we found ourselves drifting together at recess and lunchtime to compare complaints about other things. For grade six we were put in the same class. He still got a few more O's than I did—part of the natural order by then—but two weeks into the school year we were inseparable.

I think it was a common turbulence that we recognized in one another. Mine came from a couple of contradictory personality traits. One of them, inherited from my mother's side of the family, is a mild sort of heedlessness. Mine isn't as wild as it was in past generations, probably because my mother didn't get an iota of it herself, and because she did what she could to stomp it when she saw it in me. I hid it at home, but elsewhere it made me slightly careless of peer judgment, and helplessly insolent toward authority. A few generations ago, it would have gotten me into big and possibly life-threatening trouble—low-born insolence didn't go over well back then. But in my world, it has merely had lots of tasty materials to chew on. Caution and circumspection haven't ruled my life, in other words, because they haven't been imperative.

From my father I acquired a serious streak of xenophobia. It renders me uncomfortable with strangers, particularly when there are a lot of them in one place. My father compensated for his xenophobia by becoming a salesman, deploying his considerable charm in a life-long stream of pitches—if you've got a product to flog, you never have to engage with strangers because you've turned everyone into a customer. You don't really have to listen to what the other guy is about.

By the time I reached high school, I'd heard enough sales pitches to last a lifetime, and I've since become a man who never does sales pitches. The small portion of my father's charm that I got translated as a smart mouth, and I've been tagged as a wiseass since I was a toddler. Eventually, I overcame enough of my fears to make it outdoors on a regular basis, and eventually I stopped yapping long enough to discover that strangers aren't so bad. Now I listen a lot, but only to one person at a time, and never while they're standing on a podium with one hand on their wallet explaining why things are the way they are.

Don had his own, and very different, personality conflicts. They came from the dourness of his Presbyterian ancestors, the sort of dumb, muttering English and Scottish peasants who, from centuries of having their faces pushed into mud, learned to disbelieve everything but the tactical protections of God, convention, and keeping whatever cards one had close to one's chest. Their shadows didn't quite make Don God-fearing, but they did make him respectfully wary of authority, and he rarely let anyone see what he was thinking. Running against this, and usually over it, was an intelligence, an affability, and a self-confidence that melded with the close-held cards to make him a charmer who could hold nearly any pose and see through everyone else's. He was a near genius at bluffing, even when we were kids. At the tender age of 18 and in Europe, he talked his way into a job as a mechanic at a Canadian Army base in West Germany, and by 20 and back home, he'd bluffed his way into selling cars at one of Prince George's most prestigious dealerships. Others rarely saw through his bluffs. When I did, which was rarely, I usually got to watch him make good on them once he learned the territory, and that never seemed to take long. But when he got away with something, I caught occasional glimpses of his contempt for himself and others.

When my conflicting traits weren't rendering me dangerously oblivious, they conspired to make me cynical, lippy, and uncooperative. Ignoring the rules is easy when you don't see the logic behind them, and breaking them easier still if you're pretty well convinced there isn't any logic. But on the street, the illogical practicalities constantly ran over me. Don's competence and social confidence, meanwhile, made navigating the rules dead easy. Breaking them was harder.

Those personality differences—my gormlessness and his broody smoothness—were the cement for our odd friendship. My merry disrespect for convention and authority often pushed him from the hot introspection that was natural to him, and his nervy smoothness got me to places I wouldn't have dared on my own. Where he took me wasn't always safe, but once there, he made a point of keeping me from getting my head bashed in.

All very balanced and psychological, yes? Not quite. What made and kept us friends was a simple, very supple thing: we made each other laugh. We were usually the only ones who knew where our laughter came from, and we were *always* the only ones who could see what it would land on next.

The friendship had some conventional aids, of course. As mothers do, mine decided Don was a bad influence. His mother thought the same of me. Disapproval is one of the essential cements for childhood friendships: anyone your mother doesn't approve of must be okay. In addition, we each had workaholic fathers that we had trouble getting the time of day from—unless we didn't want it—so we had similar domestic wrangles to complain about.

After we finished high school, Don, Jim, and I took off to Europe together with some other Prince George kids, slingshotting out of northern B.C. with the vaguest of itineraries, little money, and a clueless hunger for adventure that got us into minor trouble in most of the countries we stumbled through. Whenever I got myself in a fix, it always seemed to be Don bailing me out, usually without my having to ask.

We survived Europe; I went into the Forest Service and he worked in town. Eventually we landed up at university in Vancouver, where I wrote poetry while he got a useful degree. I got married, had my first son Jesse, and screwed up frequently enough to cause a divorce. Don was more cautious with personal commitments, but he was otherwise much more adventurous, travelling to various parts of the world and working at new trades he wasn't trained for. Eventually he turned to writing and producing documentary films, and made a decent living at it.

There was a reason for his domestic caution. In the early 1960s, Don's father lost his right leg when a slipped log carriage dragged him into the big circular saw he'd installed at his mill. In the summer of 1966 he died suddenly, leaving Don as the reluctant head-of-household for his family. Don did what he had to, and competently, but it stewed the frustration he'd always carried around into a rage that resulted in a series of self-destructive incidents. The worst one was a 150-kilometre-per-hour late-night spin in his mother's car off the end of a road at the outskirts of town. He was lucky to walk away from the accident, and it was the final straw. Soon after, he left Prince George for good. And not long after that, he moved his mother into a small house in one of the Okanagan Valley's retirement communities.

I didn't fully understand this new anger of his, despite my instinct that its fuel was his father's death. The sense of injustice we'd shared since adolescence didn't seem to apply now that he was faced with "real life" and its responsibilities. I was still merely refusing to co-operate with any part of the adult world I could feel leaning on me to conform, and even though by now no one could stop me, I felt like a child playing in a sandbox. Once I got to university the world seemed like a pretty good place, and the future much more open than I'd anticipated.

Don, I sensed, was going in the opposite direction. He seemed to feel thwarted—or more precisely, without some sort of abstract licence he believed was essential to do what he wanted, which I still assumed, without asking, was to be a writer. I didn't know *why* he felt thwarted, or how to get him to the licence-free world I'd discovered, but I was keenly aware of his frustration.

I'd missed a clue that might have explained some of it. In our own version of the blood-brother ceremonies common at the end of high school, Don, Jim, and I swore to become writers or to die trying. For me this was, as usual, an easy promise: I would write what I could, and someday far in the future, I might acquire both the skills to write well and experiences enough to write about.

None of this was simple or easy for Don. I got a glimmer of just how oppressive his promise had become when, one sunny fall afternoon in 1965, Jim and I drove over to his house, wanting to talk or play or both. Don appeared at the door, glowering.

No, he couldn't come out with us.

"Why not?" Jim and I chorused. "Come on."

"I'm making my last stand as a writer," he said, and closed the door.

Jim and I left him to his crisis. It was serious stuff, we agreed respectfully. But it puzzled me. There was Don at his basement writing desk, staring at his portable typewriter and measuring himself against the writers we admired: Ernest Hemingway, Albert Camus, and the portions of Shelley, Keats, and Byron we'd dragged along from our high school literature classes. I could imagine this because I'd been there myself. These were writers with demons, writers who'd died young, or romantically. To me, they were a promise—or threat—to be faced somewhere in the distant future. But they were down there in the basement with Don, their weight on his shoulders as heavy as the other responsibilities he was soon to acquire, challenging him to match them now, or never.

"I don't get how Don can make his last stand this soon," I said to Jim. "I'm not ready to make my first stand."

Jim, who often had answers to such questions, shrugged it off. "Maybe he knows something we don't."

I let it go. I decided that Don had handled his crisis, because I'd always believed he was capable of handling everything. I'd never quite forgotten the 56 O's from grade four, and there'd been plenty to corroborate them since. He was smart and he was fast, and he was better than I was when it came to any sort of fight, even the kind against demons. He got things done. Of course he'd be fine. So the next time I saw him I didn't ask how the stand had gone, and he didn't offer an explanation. But the moment, and its mysteriousness, stayed with me: yet another difference between us had emerged.

———————

Because Don kept his cards up so high, I never had a clear notion of what he thought I did that was useful to him. We weren't really equals, but that didn't seem to matter. What mattered was that we each recognized, without having to talk about it, that we were better off when the other was in the picture. It made us friends who used one another to make ourselves larger and stronger, and that is the best kind of friendship. Along the way, and by some miracle of happenstance, we became permanent parts of the other's mind, able to see what the other could see. If we had been more similar we'd likely have drifted away as most childhood companions do, or spent our lives feeding one another's sentimentality or weakness.

That was the well-lit part. Off in the Darwinian murk, we were competitors, and we competed more ferociously as we grew older. While we were boys, we had a game that consisted of seeing which of us could kick the legs out from under the other. For a few months, our bouts could—and did—break out anywhere: on a street corner, in the school hallways, on the way home from school. We must have looked as if we were seriously intent on injuring one another, because adults sometimes stopped their cars to watch, and once or twice, climbed out to put the collar on us. That was never needed, because we knew when and where the line was with one another. The purpose of that game—and dozens of other, more complicated if less physical ones that followed—was to instruct me about where the lines were, or ought to be, with others. For Don, I think it was about how to stretch those small rules he had inside his head.

As we got older the competition grew obscure and clandestine—adult intimacy being as often served by what isn't declared or done openly as by what is. I was content to let Don be the social alpha—he took most of the risks and suffered most of the bruises—and I kept scrupulously clear of the women he was interested in. He seemed to do the same for me.

But by 1973 (to keep things symmetrical) we'd crossed some boundaries with one another, mostly involving the women in our lives. That created an uneasiness between us that took us most of the next 20 years to get through. The Darwinian explanation, I suppose, was that we'd gone after one another for the reason young male lions —or hyenas—do: too much testosterone. Common sense now suggests a more simple explanation: young men behave badly unless they've accepted some superior authority like God or (today) the Center for Disease Control to keep their appetites in check. We'd grown up in that brief period of history where fundamental beliefs were in decline and bacteria-based diseases seemed conquerable, and so we had absolutely nothing constraining us.

Lots of things happen in people's lives that they can't or won't articulate. Sometimes it's a matter of insufficient courage, but other times, it is discretion and common sense: sleeping dogs best left to lie. As a husband, parent, friend, and lover, I've had to live with those blanks more often than I care to admit. But as a *writer*, which for me means being a student of the human condition, they are an insult and a humiliation. That said, I'm not going to detail what happened between Don and me in this story because my affection for him is undiminished after 40 years, and I'm not going to sacrifice our understanding of the Buddy System to scratch a literary itch.

The Buddy System itself is another matter. It is, like all interactions between human males in Western culture, under deserved scrutiny by those who are dedicated to human betterment. It is also under blanket censure by Feminists, who see it as among the most barbaric and violent elements of a patriarchal system of social, political, and economic relationships.

The Feminist criticism of the male behaviours that give flesh to the Buddy System are justified, mostly. The clearcut that lies across the Bowron River valley could not, for instance, have been created without it. That doesn't mean I'm positing an organized, conscious, and clandestine conspiracy to over-cut the valley or, more generally, to abuse the public's trust. The Buddy System is more subtle than that. Corporate executives help out like-minded government officials, and vice versa. Lumber workers talk to independent loggers and suppliers, and they do it the same way that the executives and the officials do. Forest Service personnel talk to fallers and truckers over Thermoses of coffee in the bush. What makes the system work are two things. First, these men are in agreement that life depends on carrying out the orders-of-the-day, whatever they are. Things get done because men agree to get them done, willy-nilly. Second, they're offering mutual support to one another's *sincerity*, not to their beliefs or their points of ideological agreement. Beliefs are private, and matter only in the bar or around the barbecue.

The essential transactions of this Buddy System may happen in the office, over breakfast, or socially. Just below the surface specifics is the constant, casual affirmation of a tacit agreement that they're all virtuous people, working hard and working within the rules as they understand them. This affirmation of sincerity goes up and down the scale of authority, back and forth from practicalities to principles, without bribes or immoral promises, and—most important—without very much cynicism. In Prince George, the collusion is sometimes indistinguishable from the practical co-operation that is a necessary part of living in the Canadian north, but I don't see it as fundamentally different from the coded and tacit co-operation that occurs anywhere else where men aren't at each other's throats on a daily basis. For most men, biologically and culturally, the nearest alternative is violence, not thoughtfulness, and it is their fear of violence that makes it work.

A powerful—and affective—proportion of this collusion is sentimental and tribal, which is where the abuses take root: our gang against the other gang, the further away and more abstract the better. The other gang can be tariff-wielding Americans, petition-waving environmentalists, tax-sucking federal bureaucrats, criminal money-laundering Asian entrepreneurs. It can be advantage-seeking Feminists, language-crazed Québécois, or tenure-seeking professors. It can even be Koran-thumping Islamic fundamentalists who can't see that globalization's goal is the continuance of the cheap energy prices that keep the system getting things done, and not the humiliation of Allah, or the removal of their right to oppress women with forced illiteracy and burkas.

Since this book has a nearly all-male cast, it had better acknowledge the dysfunctions of the global Buddy System that builds clearcuts and steals the livelihoods and dignity of good people. But if you're looking for a blanket condemnation of male socialization, don't be holding your breath. Beneath the entropy of partisan nonsense we often mistake for meaning, undercurrents of light glimmer, even in the deep, dark, and polluted waters that flow beneath every bridge in northern British Columbia. This is one of those subcurrents of light, and I would like to use it to illuminate the clearcut on the Bowron River, the globalized Buddy System—and some humane alternatives.

22

Don and I spend a full day in Vancouver checking equipment and packing the Vanagon for the trip into northern B.C.—and getting used to one another again. I spend a second day with my son Max, who's in his last year of high school, nearly grown to full size and so jammed by his hormones it's hard to get through a conversation with him without seeing his hackles rise. He's amazed that I'm still interested in the clearcut on the Bowron River after seeing it with me in 1990, but he seems willing to file it under the fluid-to-him categories of writers, fathers, and old people's strangeness.

Don and I have made a very basic plan for the trip. We'll drive to the clearcut, camp there, and take photographs until we've got our heads around it—or until we can't stand being there any longer. Then we'll drive to town—Prince George—see a few friends and acquaintances, and try to get a sense of how badly our old stomping ground has been stomped. Don has another item on his agenda. His 24-year-old daughter Bryn has moved to Prince George to take a degree in Environmental Studies at the University of Northern British Columbia. He wants to make sure she's settled in okay, and that the apartment she's rented is livable.

I've got something of my own that's making me feel old and strange, but vanity prevents me from mentioning it to Max, and I'm not going to talk about it with Don, who'll tease me mercilessly. One of my front lower bicuspids is loose. Twenty years ago, I was lying on my back on my living room carpet, roughhousing with my eldest son Jesse, who was then about four years old. I'd bought him a child's carpentry set, with hammer and saw made from metal and wood so he could saw and bang for real, instead of making believe with safely rounded plastic approximations. While we were roughhousing, he picked up his hammer and gave my front teeth an experimental but less-than-tentative *whack*. Likely he thought I was invulnerable. I still did.

We were both wrong. He hit me hard enough to loosen the bicuspid that took the main force of the blow. Two decades later, the full proof that I'm not invulnerable is here, front and centre and about to drop into my lap. I'm trying my best to ignore the proof, even though I can now tilt the tooth 45 degrees in its socket and it is intermittently as painful as when it first got hammered.

The fine weather—clear and cool—almost lets me forget about the throbbing as we leave Vancouver to begin the 800-kilometre drive to northern B.C. We're taking the TransCanada Highway through the Fraser Valley and up to Cache Creek, and north from there on Highway 97. It's a route we've each driven a hundred times, and more than a few times, together.

We're on the highway early enough to see the golden morning light climb above the blue Rockies at the eastern end of the Fraser Valley, but we're not in any hurry. Good thing. The Vanagon vibrates as soon as it nears the speed limit, and Don keeps it at around 90 kilometres per hour. We've agreed to stop wherever there's an attraction that we've been in too much of a hurry for in the past, but the only one we find worth our time until we're beyond Clinton is the retired bridge over the Fraser at Alexandria, deep in the heart of the Fraser Canyon. It's now a Tourism B.C. site, and the attraction, other than the bridge itself, is a patchwork of the original precarious roadbeds that were hacked and dynamited into the rock alongside the river 60 or 70 years ago, and which now seem incredibly narrow and precarious, almost archaeological. We scramble down a steep path from the highway, stroll across the bridge, take a few snapshots of one another at each end, and are soon on the road again.

At 100 Mile House, which is roughly halfway, we blow nearly an hour trying to get in touch with an old friend—closer to Don than to me—but can't make the connection. He's around, but he's working too far back in the bush to drive in for a cup of coffee with two people he hasn't seen in 30 years. Don's disappointed. I'm relieved.

By five in the afternoon we're in Quesnel, 50 kilometres southwest of the clearcut. We stop for groceries, then lose another hour eating steak sandwiches at a hotel café, the Billy Barker Inn, before we head northward once more. We're not going much further. Darkness is falling, and we're going to camp along the Cottonwood River, a few kilometres north. It is dark by the time we stop, and given

the overcast, that means it is pitch dark. When I duck outside the van for a smoke, the only way I can see my hands is by the glow from the cigarette. For creature comfort before breaking out the sleeping bags Don boils some water for herbal tea. I'd prefer coffee, but Don stopped drinking it years ago.

When I crawl out of my sleeping bag the next morning, the air inside the Vanagon is chilly enough that my breath looks like smoke, without my morning cigarette, and my body feels as if it's crusted in rust. I dress as quietly as I can— not quietly enough, because I awaken Don—and wander down to the river for a smoke. It hasn't rained during the night, but the dew-fall is heavy enough that my runners are soaked through before I reach the riverbank 30 metres away. I try to uncoil myself by throwing a few rocks. The first four or five land midstream, but it helps. I finish the first smoke, light another, and toss a few more rocks. The last one lands on the bank across the river, and I head back, satisfied. Don is already frying eggs for breakfast.

So far, we're getting along fine. It helps that I don't smoke inside the Vanagon, and don't whine about not being able to. But there's more to this than my good behaviour. I'm trying hard to make this work. There's a slight but palpable tension between us, and I can see that Don is working as hard as I am to keep it in check. It occurs to me that there's a lot at stake here, and it isn't just the health of a friendship between two grumpy old men who've known each other forever. Who we *were* to one another is up for grabs, as is how valuable and affective our friendship really was. Don isn't any more sentimental than I am, so the test is a real one.

We decide on a quick side trip into the 1850s gold mining town and current tourist destination at Barkerville. It's been restored without the knife fights and shootings, but it manages to make weathered wood feel like plastic. The most interesting thing is a patch of brilliant blue delphiniums in blossom, a full two months out of season. From Barkerville, we drive to the provincial park at the headwaters of the Bowron River, which neither of us has seen. The park is a series of connected lakes well regarded for canoeing, but we're more interested in the off chance that there's a road open into the clearcut from the south.

After the plastic of Barkerville and the dinginess and pulp-mill stink of Quesnel, the well-kept provincial park and its lodge is oddly urban, and so are the people we see wandering around the grounds. Nearly all are young, blond, and dressed in expensive outdoor duds that show the grime of camping in cold weather as a badge of honour. The blond canoeists look as if they'd prefer vegetarian quiche to the steak sandwiches we settled for in Quesnel, and we look and feel as out of place as they would at the Billy Barker Inn.

There's no road north into the clearcut, and the raised eyebrows we get when we ask about it let us know that this isn't a query they often hear. Several of the youthful blonds we talk to aren't even aware that a very large clearcut begins a few kilometres north of the park boundaries. Their upstream obliviousness—I can't tell if it's studied —is oddly disturbing, and we don't stay long, doubling back the way we came until we roll back onto Highway 97. We follow the highway to Dunkley, where we head northeast on the Willow River forestry road that will take us to the edge of the clearcut. It's close to mid-afternoon when we reach its western edge, and we drive straight down to the Bowron River Bridge, which is what I've come to think of as the clearcut epicentre even though the patch of blow-down that triggered the bug infestation is several kilometres to the southeast.

This is the first time I've seen the clearcut this late in the year. The season and the dark overcast adds some muted reds and purples to the palette of greens, blacks, and muddy grey and brown, but at first it seems little different than I recall it. It is desolate and it is silent, with the only new sounds those of Don muttering under his breath. I still can't tell if he's muttering about the clearcut or the weather.

When we park the Vanagon near the river, a more familiar part of his character takes over. He busies himself with the cameras, cleaning the lens and fussing over the right film to load. I follow his lead. On the drive up we decided to use black-and-white at first, so we can see

the clearcut detail without the distraction of colour. Yet from the moment we start shooting pictures, we both find our eyes drawn from the detail into the far view. Because I've shot a half-dozen rolls here in years past, I have the advantage of knowing this will happen, but it doesn't help. My eye is drawn away from the monotonous foreground to the now-whitened snags at the hilltops and in the draws. I see Don's eye scanning the same way. It's impossible not to be drawn to the spectacular atrocity of this place.

That isn't what we're here for, and we soon correct our focus. Crowding along the margins of the forestry road are small evergreens, lodgepole pine, and spruce. Some are just beginning to poke their crowns above the brush, but others are a metre or taller, particularly in the draws. It's the downwash of nutrients from the hillsides above that makes them grow so vigorously, not the shelter from the wind. On one hillside we see a sharp line separating a symmetrical thicket of bright green pines from another of darker, shorter spruce. There are thousands of small trees growing here—millions. More than 50 million, if we accept the Forest Service claims.

I spot evidence of wildlife that wasn't here in 1990 or 1993—most noticeably bear scat, always at the edges of the road or in the still-barren log skids and landings. The scat is filled with salmon and blackberry pits, and the mounds are of two distinct colours. The larger deposits are muddy brown, but the smaller, more numerous leavings are purple from the berry's pigment. We deduce from this that grizzly digestion must be slightly more efficient than that of black bear.

"There wasn't any scat here in 1993," I tell Don as he pokes a stick through a mound of grizzly scat. "I guess the berry bushes have had time to mature. Good sign."

He's not paying attention because he's laughing.

"What?"

"Well," he says, "the Pope may be a Catholic, but bears don't shit in these woods. Not if there's a forestry road anywhere near."

It takes me a few seconds to get it: the bush here, with its cover of nettles and devil's club spines, must be very hard on a squatting bear's notoriously tender sphincter. So they've made a sensible adaptation, safe in an abandoned area like this. They deposit their scat on the roadways where there is no underbrush. So much for conventional wisdom.

As we work, we talk. The question about the clearcut Don formulates startles me. *What entitles human beings to do something like this?* That's interesting because I see how different my own questions are: *Can we get away with this? If so, for how long?*

Gradually, we settle into a low-grade argument that lasts several days. Each of us keeps coming back to it, clarifying an element of our thinking, adjusting another term, pulling back from an earlier disquisition that turns out to be merely a digression.

My basic position is that the mess we're in—in the Bowron River valley and generally—exists because we appeal to the laws of nature for our working models, which aren't exactly efficient and are frequently stupid and wasteful. Instead, we should be using the specific knowledge that we've accumulated over the past two or three hundred generations of living together in numbers larger than tribes or troops. Not shitting in one's own dwelling is, for instance, common sense for us and for some other larger mammals, but it isn't a universal law of nature. Birds do it all the time, but they survive because they don't stay in the nest long enough for the diseases for which they're creating a breeding ground to kill them. If human beings defecate in their own dwellings and leave it lying around, there's a cholera epidemic in three months, and civilized life ends.

I've stopped believing that the human species can safely use nature as a model, and that we've overpopulated the planet, for good or bad, with our own species to such a degree that we have to create alternative systems—most of them technological—that improve on nature. If we stopped placing a value on human consciousness and the avoidance of human suffering, we could, of course, reduce the population to nature's limits within a couple of generations. But we'd also cease to be remotely human in the process, and we'd give up all the things that make us marvellous creatures.

When nature proposes to treat me and my kids the same way as it treats an amoeba on the grounds that any single individual or even group of individuals doesn't matter, it makes sense to start looking

around for something better. If you and I and our kids don't make it, nature simply restarts the process, and in a few million years you'll have six-foot cockroaches wandering around making stupid mistakes and eating everything in sight, just like we do. At least we're pleasant to look at, and we don't smell as bad.

Don takes it in a different direction. He says he doesn't necessarily buy into either the concept that nature has laws, or the concept that human beings, en masse, possess "common sense." In his view, laws of nature are rare, at least in the way I'm using the term to describe behaviour. There are mainly genetic traits or experiential predispositions to act in certain ways given certain circumstances. The predispositions which tend, over the long haul, to put offspring on the ground with a reasonable chance of survival tend to be reproduced because, and when, they're successful. Predispositions that don't produce successful offspring don't reappear, for the same reasons. Any behaviour that neither increases nor decreases the chance of producing successful offspring will continue or die out according to chance, if, for example, it happens to be partnered with another advantageous or disadvantageous trait. In his view, common sense, in the "best" instances, consists merely of cultural articulations of similar values. Otherwise, the term describes just about any kind of preconception people have that justifies their actions after the fact.

Don believes the problem we face is that for 5,000 years a segment of human culture has attempted to behave as if human beings aren't part of nature, when, in fact, they are. The dichotomy that places what is human against nature just isn't valid for him, and his distaste is extreme. We may be a species behaving in self-destructive ways, but we are still doing it "naturally." There's little difference, in his mind, between what I've described as human overpopulation and a jar of budding yeast.

I argue that there is a fundamental difference. We're bigger, and we consume more of everything. If a yeast culture overflows its medium, it either spills onto the next surface and dies, or starts transforming other things into different chemical forms. The issue of scale isn't one that can be swept away as if human culture and yeast culture are analogous. Logically they are. Effectually, they aren't. For good or ill, the human species has the means to eradicate practically every life form on the planet, either gradually, by destroying their habitats, or in a hurry, with a thermonuclear cataclysm. Yeast can make a few loaves of bread, or some wine, or it can make our private parts itchy. Or even more simply put, *we* can control or stop yeast and most other species from growing and thriving, but *they* can't control or stop us—or, at least, they haven't yet. We alter and manipulate our environment to a degree and on a scale that's unprecedented in nature.

When it gets right down to it, the idea of nature is like the idea of God: it's too far away and too abstract for me to place any faith in it. I'll trade God and everything in heaven if my kids get to grow up healthy, sane, and educated well enough that they can make their way in the world without joining a cult or living on lies and corporate entertainment. If we weren't being romantic we'd admit that nature's main operating model is the pyramid scheme.

Don is skeptical about this, so I argue that every species starts off with a few individuals who reproduce themselves, and so on, until there are 6 billion, or 6 trillion of them. If they don't bump into all the other pyramid schemes, that is, and get themselves eaten, or contract the plague, or lose their habitat to a more aggressive species.

Nature has rules that are consequential, not predictive. The rule that always seems present is to eat or be eaten; to push and shove or be pushed and shoved. But it seems to me that human beings have too many powerful instruments for that to work much longer. Further, there's little compassion in nature—and there's none of the common sense that occasionally keeps human compassion from being suicidal. Most important, the rules don't add up to a master plan. Human beings invented common sense and planning to get around the slowness and the brutishness of natural models. We're not doing very well with any of it, but at least we've trying.

Don insists that species don't behave as pyramid schemes. Species may increase exponentially, but a pyramid scheme is a self-contained model in which everything flows from the inverted base down toward the few that start it. Organisms flow outward, through time and space. There is no recycling or balance with pyramid schemes, while life on this planet has been maintaining a balance for a few billion years, and that's what matters.

I counter that this is only so in the abstract and on the macro scale. From an individual's point of view, the balance is a wasteful and violent mess, with feedback loops so elliptical and indirect they might as well stretch around the far side of Jupiter. When it can take thousands of years before corrections are reintroduced to the system, they're not much help to individuals. Human beings live 80 years if they're lucky, so a slow correction isn't much help.

But Don doesn't believe that the absence of any master plan in nature is a flaw. To demand that, for him, is simplistic, and a problem only for those trying to manipulate or control nature. He argues that the real danger is the notion that human understanding is or will ever be comprehensive enough to invent a successful alternative—and that we will ever be sufficiently magnanimous to allow other species to exercise *their* agendas. "If you really want to know when you should get alarmed," he says at one point, "it's when someone uses the term 'stewardship.'"

I'd prefer to step back and think this all through a few dozen more times, but we're here, in the middle of a vast tract of evidence for human incompetence. My instinct is to accuse him of being an animal-rights nut and turn it all into a joke, but I'm pretty sure he's not simply being misanthropic. Rather, he's carefully refusing to be anthropocentric. And it's not as if I think human beings have the right to mess around the way we've been doing for the past 3,000 years. But we're in charge of this planet even if we're doing a thoroughly lousy job. This clearcut is perfect proof of both his points and mine.

We move the conversation along these parallel tracks, Don building a theory around whatever principles that support it, me working more anecdotally, looking for the fox dens. Yet we're not quite slapping speeches at one another. We're working the material, never completely agreeing on anything, steering clear of confrontational disagreements that will stop the forward motion. I catch myself relaxing, and the uneasiness I'd felt for the past several days evaporates: hey, we *can* still do this.

For Don more than for me, the camera work starts to be of interest, and, as always, his concentration is better than mine: he can walk and chew gum *and* shoot photographs at the same time. Technical questions, or simply getting technology to do what he wants, free him from issues of judgment, which he's always taken more seriously than I have. I'm more comfortable nibbling at the edges, flaking around, sneaking up behind whatever I'm supposed to be thinking about and hoping I'll get lucky by trying four or five different things. Okay, this all fits.

Ah, but maybe, it occurs to me as I look out over the wasted land-scape, there's something more defining here. Precise technical tasks have been Don's alternative to the empty white page, the moment where you have to slap your licence on the cultural table, know everything that's necessary even though you know damned well you can't, and get down to the obsolete occupation of inventing a world with mere words. Don has written, but he's preferred to do so as an adjunct to forms of expression where the technology plays a major role or leads, and the sentences are not so open-ended: film, television, journalism. Well, I've never liked facing the empty white page, either. My way has been to invent methods of writing that avoided it: coloured paper, backlined engineering pads, strangely coloured pens, coding systems as a before-writing act. Where that fails, I write in public places—cafés, train stations, in the midst of other jobs—along with a dozen other lesser tricks. I'm resourceful in a different way, I guess. And maybe I got that way to avoid a terror he revealed to me before it came at me on its own.

Yet for all our chattering and our differences in method, on this first day we stick to what we've agreed on, and have both shot a roll of film and are into a second by the time the light begins to fail. And we've penetrated the desolation and are able to zero in on the details. The question now is, do we camp inside the clearcut, or drive a few kilometres and camp at Narrow Lake, where Barry and I camped with our sons in 1990? There's no difference of opinion this time. Maybe it's the bear scat everywhere, and maybe it's the desolation and the silence. We'll come back tomorrow, but right now, we want out.

23

It has taken us four days together to settle into a domestic routine for the mornings. The routine is pretty simple: we don't talk until after breakfast. Getting to it hasn't required negotiation. It has evolved from body language and eye contact. Even the division of labour was worked out mainly with shrugs, pointing, and one or two grunts. So it isn't until after a breakfast of eggs and bread that we sit at the campsite's picnic table over mugs of herbal tea to examine the aerial photos and forestry map of the clearcut and plan our day. The overcast has lifted slightly, and behind the screen of young evergreens, Narrow Lake is still and frigid, waiting for the morning breezes from the warming hills above us to disperse a thin layer of fog resting just above the water.

The map tells us there are two roads that leave the clearcut at the south end, but the detail in my photocopied aerial photo is less certain. I'm interested in the south end because I've never seen it, and because I'm pretty sure that if the loggers who were cutting in here did any serious screwing around, that's where we'll find it. I don't even want to think about what the screwing around will amount to—hard to imagine anything more than what was done with the Forest Service's approval. There's also a small body of water identified as "Slender Lake" on the southwest side that isn't visible on the aerial photo. The creek that runs out of it flows into Stony Lake, a few kilometres outside the clearcut, and eventually empties into the Willow River. I'm curious to see how that creek was treated by the loggers, and how much replanting was done around the lake.

We haven't built a campfire, preferring to cook inside on the Vanagon's propane stove, so it doesn't take us long to break camp. We wash the dishes together with lake water heated on the stove, I roll the sleeping bags while Don drops the Vanagon's top and re-ties the spare tire and water can, and we're off.

We drive back to a crossroads close to the centre of the clearcut and stop there to take in the silence and recheck our maps. The main forestry road runs northeast down to the Bowron River where we were yesterday, but the map shows two roads to the south. One of them crosses the river and, just before threading east into the valley of Haggen Creek, forks south along the river's east bank to Indian-point Creek, one of those names that sounds like it was invented by an advertising agency and ought to feature a shopping centre or subdivision.

If there's a shopping centre, we don't get to see it, because the road hasn't been kept up and the bridge, once we get to it, is closed, blocked by several loads of gravel dumped across the approaches. That leaves us to backtrack several kilometres to another road on the west side of the river that appears to run past the mouth of Eighteen Mile Creek, presumably so named because it is either 18 miles long, or 18 miles from the mouth of the Bowron. We've been discovering that the further south we travel the more ratty and overgrown the roads are—and the less accurate the Forest Service's map becomes.

The road we go south on also has a name: Frontier Road. It's now-you're-on-it/now-you're-not-so-sure, because haul-roads constructed during logging branch off every 200 or 300 metres and there's little to distinguish Frontier Road's seedy disrepair from the weedy side roads. We're lost in less than an hour. The Forest Service map is useless because few of the haul-roads are marked, and to orient ourselves we have to rely on proximity to the river and what little the aerial photo reveals about elevation and the boundary between cut and uncut forest.

The condition of all these roads is bad enough that I'm worried about the Vanagon, but Don seems untroubled until we encounter a bridge over what we determine is Eighteen Mile Creek. The creek isn't much: the bridge span is no more than 4 metres and the creek barely a metre's width of stagnant murk and undergrowth. But the planking on the bridge is unsound, several boards are missing, and others shredded or possibly rotten. No one has crossed this span for months.

Don stops the Vanagon atop the slight slope down to the bridge, jams on the emergency brake, and climbs out to have a look. He stands there for a moment, chin in hand, head cocked slightly as if he's listening to instructions. I cross the bridge for a snapshot, in case this is as far as we get. Most of the planking, when I test it, is rotten only at the edges. That's encouraging, but in several spots there are gaps wider than the Vanagon's tires. If we drop or break through while we're crossing, we'll be toast: in need of a tow truck or power winch at best, needing a new axle at worst.

Don roots around in a pile of logging debris on the far side of the bridge, lifts out a metre-long pine log, and jams it into one of the holes created by the missing planks. I find a similar piece of log and jam that into another gap, and that gives us a clear if slightly cross-angled route across the bridge.

"Let's do it," he says. "Guide me across and don't make a mistake."

We get across easily, and don't stop to gloat. He pushes open the passenger door, I jump in, and we're off again without completely coming to a stop.

It's early afternoon when we reach the clearcut's south edge. Neither of us is sure exactly where we are—maybe this is Frontier Road, maybe it isn't. But we're no longer lost, and the ratty roads and encroaching underbrush seem normal. Several of the roads we follow are impassable, or simply peter out at a log landing. Wherever that happens, we get out, walk around to check the replanting, and snap a few pictures. We find spots where, far from easy supervision, the replanting is spotty, or the regeneration rates are minimal, but there's nothing spectacular or grossly negligent.

At the south edge the old-growth trees seem remarkably dark and dense, and the air has an acrid redolence that is bracing after the sweeter and milder scent of new vegetation and burn. And something else: a short distance before we reach the edge, the road widens and its bed sits higher than in the cut areas. That tells us it was built recently, possibly while the cutting was going on, and likely with the intention of cutting further south than was done.

We decide to explore as far as we can, but 100 metres beyond the line of trees, a tree has fallen across the road. We climb out, saw a few metres off the top with the small saw Don pulls out of the Vanagon, and drag the top to the side of the road. That allows us to edge the Vanagon around the rest of the tree, and we drive on. The road may be relatively new, but that's more disadvantage than help because the bed hasn't been packed down by logging trucks. Rivulet  washdown has leached far into it, sometimes nearly to the midpoint.

Two hundred metres after the first blown-down tree, there are a dozen bigger trees down, some full across the road. We'd need a 24-inch chainsaw to cut through these ones, along with a power winch and a much heavier truck to pull them out of the way. Beyond these I can see still more trees down. This is as far as we're going.

"You know," I say to Don, "this road is the first evidence I've seen that the Forest Service did *anything* to stop the companies from logging."

"Maybe it was built as an alternative route to the Bowron Lakes Provincial Park," he says. "It's on the map that way, sort of."

"I suppose. Someone must have thought better of letting tourists drive through here and see this. I wonder how far it goes."

"We're not going to find out," he says, backing the Vanagon's rear wheels to the edge of the gravel.

He turns the Vanagon around and we return the way we came, this time veering off each time the road branches to the west, trying to find the route that takes us out of the clearcut along Slender Lake. After a half-dozen more dead ends and a few roads that are too far gone even for Don, we get close enough to glimpse the lake in the distance, but a washed-out bridge on the upper reaches of Eighteen Mile Creek halts us. It's getting late, anyway, we're tired and slightly frustrated, and the weather is closing in again. Time to backtrack— we'll try driving in from the other side tomorrow morning. The map shows the road coming from the west with a solid line until just before the lake, so it ought to be passable.

We stop at the main crossroads, where Don checks the map once more while I stand around outside smoking in the spitting rain.

"I don't want to go back to where we spent last night," he says.

"Narrow Lake? What's wrong with it?"

"Nothing. There's a camp marked at Stony Lake. Ever been there?"

"Nope," I say. "Let's try it. All these forestry camps are basically the same. Better, anyway, than spending the night in this godforsaken place."

24

All Forest Service campsites are not equal. The campsite at Stony Lake is very different from the one we've passed up at Narrow Lake. The lake is larger, the site more open, and the campsite better equipped. The shoreline at the campsite runs straight and flat for almost 200 metres, which is fine so long as the wind doesn't start blowing. Every 15 or 20 metres along the shore stands a wooden picnic table, a boulder-enclosed firepit, and a neat stack of firewood, some of it chopped for kindling. We park the Vanagon at the edge of a site close to the mid-point of the shoreline, climb out, and walk to the water. It is clean, very cold, and still. We're the only ones here.

We set up our camp, but now there's none of this morning's silent co-operation, maybe because we've been out together all day having everything we try lead to a dead end. We're soon into a playful wrangle, both of us trying to give the orders while ignoring the ones coming back. Since it's Don's van and equipment, I do most of the deferring, staying just this side of non-cooperation. We've brought some pork chops to fry, and some fresh vegetables—onions, potatoes, carrots. We argue over who'll cook what and how, and eventually agree that I'll cook the pork chops while Don gets to wrap the veggies in tinfoil with some seasoning salt and put them at the edge of the small grill someone has left behind. The chops are ready well before the veggies, but we eat them together even though the potatoes are bony and most of the carrots like small pieces of rock. That's a mistake.

While I'm chewing the half-cooked veggies, I bite too hard on a chunk of uncooked carrot. It catches my wobbly tooth the wrong way and the nagging claim against my vanity instantly becomes acutely terminal. (The tooth will fall right out three weeks later in Orlando, Florida, while I'm filming a CBC television segment on Disney's sur-real model community, *Celebration*, and we'll have to find a dentist to epoxy it back in place so I don't look like a gap-toothed hillbilly on camera.) Don spots my expression and asks what's wrong.

"Dental problems," I answer, not wanting to give him something to rag on me with. "Nothing serious."

He turns back to the campfire, picks up the hatchet, and pushes one of the smoking logs at the edge closer to the firepit. "I'll bet," he says. "You should quit smoking before you lose them all."

What I'm experiencing at this moment is a version of what Don and I longed for years ago: a life with some undeniable consequences. That we'd grown up with the permanent threat of nuclear bombers bringing the annihilation of the world made us want something we could get our hands on—or our teeth into. But locally, all we saw coming at us was self deluding business slogans stuck together with sentimentality or booster-brained optimism. We wanted consequences we could inhabit, learn from, have proprietorship in, even—prefer-ably—if they involved a little pain and hardship.

We were young, but we weren't being airy-fairy or romantic about this. The enchantment of living on a frontier that had energized our parents' generation was dissipating, and wisps of the consumerist continuum that has since replaced it were already in the air. The range of product choices around us was widening, but we could sense that as life grew easier and more filled with entertainments and distractions, the opportunities were going to be fewer, more technical, and more obtuse. Now the choices seem to be between things like VCR or DVD, wide-screen or digital. How about building software for a market that might not exist when you learn its rules, or manipulating currencies for an offshore financial corporation that might vanish as mysteriously as it appeared?

Now, in this shattered physical parcel of wilderness, I'm getting the full force of a tangible, slow-moving down-to-the-roots consequence of living, even though it is writ about as small and specific as they get: Teeth break if you hit them with hammers, and then they fall out.

There's something else, and it's almost as compelling. As twilight approaches, the landscape around us grows eerily still. The breezes, already light, die, and the shifting overcast, as it darkens from grey and silver to a steely purple that transforms the dark green of the surrounding forests to black, suspends every turmoil. The lake is a mirror of the sky, unbroken by wind or leaping fish. Even the pillar of slash-burning smoke at the far end of the lake is motionless above the crewcut of trees that hides an adjoining clearcut. There are no birds flying, and none singing; no jets overhead, no trucks rumbling along the distant roads. Nothing.

I call Don's attention to it, and he picks up his camera as acknowledgement, hands me mine, and we crunch our way across the smooth gravel to the lake. This isn't the silence we experienced in the clearcut earlier, which was that of subtraction and damage, like a city—or world—after it has been bombed. This is a teeming silence, a respite, the full-flight world taking a breather. The loudest sound is the snapping of our camera shutters, our blood coursing through arteries and veins, the crackle of campfire embers audible 10 metres away.

As twilight fails, the moment ends. A chilly breeze shills across the water, and behind us in the trees another breeze raises a low, complex harmonic from the branches. When we turn back to our camp, I spot a coyote at the edge of the trees. Used to having the place to itself, it begins to yip and yowl. As we walk, it begins to run, side to side at first, but then growing bolder; moving closer, stopping to yowl, then moving closer again. I toss several rocks in its direction, but that only deters it a little. Five minutes later, it is back, and this time, less than 100 metres away. It takes a couple of my deep wolf howls—I was taught to howl years ago in Vancouver by a full-blooded timber wolf a friend of mine kept—to send it scurrying. It reappears only at day-break, when we hear it scratching around in the garbage.

After Don and I talked each other out, I spent an hour rereading the set of brochures I'd received in the mail, just before I left Toronto, from the pro-industry organiza-tion Forests Forever. I got them from the Council of Forest Indus-tries (COFI), a well-heeled coalition of the industry's major players across B.C. The president is a man named Jack Munro, who was once the provincial head of the Inter-national Woodworkers of America, the largest trade union associ-ated with the forest industry—which says something about both the politics of the union and the slickness of the industry. The brochures they've sent are expensively produced, the language used loaded with environmental buzz-phrases about "sustainability," "husbandry," "biodiversity." In general, the brochures propose that the forestry corporations have learned their lessons, and are now committed to scrupulous regeneration of the forests the government gives them to cut, to rehabilitating lost forestlands, and to carefully farming the old-growth forests that remain. Their argument is agree-able and soothing, and nothing they claim is unequivocally *untrue*. Yet it isn't true, either. I have to remind myself that a corporation has a pre-emptive mission to satisfy the requirement of shareholder profits and that any other moral (or legal) tenets it may profess are secondary. These are facts of life not worth whining about, but they still shouldn't be swept under the rug. If the tactics inherent in con-temporary pro-industry programs like Forests Forever had been used 2,000 years ago, would North Africa be as barren as it is today? I suspect so.

That's because Forests Forever isn't aimed at protecting old-growth forests or planting trees in the ones cut down. It's a public relations exercise mounted by the forestry corporations to counteract the bad publicity their lousy behaviour in the B.C. woods has earned them over the years, and it should be seen for what it is—one of the new costs of doing business. The companies got serious about public relations only because European environmentalists have squawked loudly enough about our forestry practices that the EU's trade bureaucrats have been alerted to the possibility that attacking North American wood harvesting might be a useful smokescreen to protect their own agricultural subsidies. The environmentalists on this side of the Atlantic are, in turn, using the EU sanction threats as levers to get the federal and provincial governments to protect a few tracts—most of them small—of old-growth glamour forests along the Coast. The Americans sit on their hands, because they have agricultural subsidies of their own to hide—or they impose self-serving trade sanctions and tariffs on B.C. wood products, even though their forestry practices are as bad as, or worse than, the ones used in B.C. Outside of Prince George, and a few other forestry-dependent towns around the province, the biggest victims of this geopolitical pushing and shoving, ironically, are Canada's grain farmers, thousands of kilometres east.

On my maps and on the mid-1980s LandSat photo I have, the clearcut looks like a vast, mutilated starfish draped across the mountain ridges and valleys of the Bowron; a mass of reds and browns amid the dark green of the remaining patches of old growth and the brighter green of lands replanted or regrown on their own.

But in the decade since, the clearcut on the Bowron has been transformed, in the minds of those in the forest industry, from an industrial disaster into an industrial model, a showpiece for how forest reclamation should be done. That isn't what it is, but when you've seen other clearcut areas that are under less scrutiny, you understand why they're yapping about this one as if it's a triumph. For them, that's what it is.

Like everyone else, they're not wrong. But they're not right, either.

25

We drive into town across the Fraser River on the still-new-to-us bridge. To the north, the pulp mills are pumping clouds of fluffy vapour into the sky, and it tinges the purple with the faintest trace of yellow. We drive along First Avenue to the Alexander Mackenzie cairn, turn left onto George Street and right onto Third Avenue. Since we were last here, Zellers has closed and part of its building — once the Hudson's Bay Company store and the commercial heart of downtown—has been taken over by The Brick furniture outlet. The other half houses something called Liquidation World, another franchise that seems to be exclusively devoted to selling cheap knockoffs of expensive brand-name merchandise.

Don doesn't say a word until we reach Victoria Street. I can't think of much to talk about, either. We're home, sort of, and it's dumbfounding.

"So," he says. "What's to do first?"

He has his daughter to check on and see how she's making the adjustment to Prince George. She's bought a pickup truck, rented a basement suite apartment, and is already attending classes. The apartment is Don's main worry. When he talked to her on the phone before we left Vancouver, she'd complained about scary light switches, chintzy locks, and trouble with the telephone. But we'll have to tread lightly, he says, because she's ferociously independent. I suggest that he can distract her and I'll do the fixing, but he doesn't think that's funny. Does he think I can't fix things? Probably. When we were kids, I was much better at walking into doors than at fixing them.

"Let's start at the Mr. PeeGee phone booth," I say, "if it's still there. We can make some calls."

He shrugs and flips the signal lever for a left turn.

The phone booth is intact, although there are a few more dents and the colours are more washed out than last time. But the telephone still has a dial tone, and there's even a tattered phone book attached to a metal cord. Don pulls a slip of paper from his wallet—Bryn's number —and calls her. They talk for a minute or two, and he hangs up.

"We're supposed to meet her at the apartment around four," he says. "We'll probably have to put on some doorknobs and light switches, so be ready."

I nod. Okay with me. "We should phone Jack Butcher, no?"

He's already looking for the number in the phone book. He makes the call, and his frown tells me it isn't Jack who answers. There's a polite and very short exchange with whoever he's talking to—likely Jack's wife—and he hangs up.

"Jack's in the doghouse," Don says as he leafs through the phone book again. "What's the name of his restaurant?"

"China Bob, I think. Or Pickle Pete. He was managing two of them last time we were there."

"I heard he lost the Pickle Pete franchise," Don says. "I'll try China Bob's."

He finds the number and punches in the digits. He gets Jack on the second ring. They talk briefly, and he hangs up again. "He wants us to come up for lunch. Billy Walsh is going to be there."

"Oh, good. May as well see them at once."

"Actually," Don says, "you might want to talk to Billy. He's worked on and off in logging for most of his life. And I'm pretty sure he's been involved in creating a lot of the equipment they're now using around here to get trees out of the bush."

"Billy? I thought he was selling real estate. I remember some stories about him working for Ben Ginter years ago, driving scrapers and that sort of thing. But I always thought most of his stories were bull-shit."

"Not really. Billy may talk loud, but he doesn't puff himself. It's usually the other way around."

"I'll bring the tape recorder."

I take my turn with Mr. PeeGee, using it to call Barry McKinnon, whom I've warned, by letter, that we're going to be here and that we might need to park in front of his house some night. No one is home and there's no answering service. I'll have to call again later.

We've got 45 minutes to kill, so we drive down to the Nechako River and cruise along what used to be Planer Mill Row. The road is paved now, and only two of the original dozen or more mills remain. One is derelict, its beehive burner rusted and silent. Aside from John Brink's finger-joint operation, this is now a vast log-sorting yard, half empty because breakup has just ended and the back roads are only now sufficiently hardened to take logging trucks. We stop to photograph the one long row of logs we find. They're nearly all spruce, and no smaller, as far as I can see, than 30 years ago.

We're at Pine Centre before noon despite ourselves, so we take the long route to China Bob's through Sears and along the mall's concourse. This is now the heart of Prince George's retail shopping, but it doesn't do its job very well. 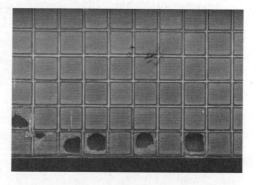 Nearly all the stores are franchise outlets, and they crowd closed-in hallways instead of lining streets, most of them offering merchandise chosen by corporate profilers and head buyers instead of goods that people in Prince George actually need to live their lives in a harsh climate. Nearly all the adult shoppers are overweight and out of shape, and the mall's shiny surfaces manage to make them seem more down-market than they'd be if we were to see them on the streets or in the bush. On the way in, I had spotted a middle-aged man in a baseball cap parking a pickup truck with the usual 45-gallon barrel of diesel in back. I watched him slink into the Sears store like an animal with its tail between its legs, as if the sheer abundance of merchandise were declaring him too eager to buy, his income level too low, the dirt beneath his fingernails a reminder that he's slipping every day, his hard-won Ski-Doos and motocross bikes and RV all showing rust through the coating of mud the way his pickup does.

Now he's standing in front of the Sony store, staring through the window at a bank of television sets, all displaying *CNN Headline News.*

At the centre's rotunda we stumble across a dozen or so flimsy kiosks displaying the wares of local cultural and social organizations. It's about as far from the universe of CNN and Sony as imaginable. The displays are rudimentary and the people manning them are mostly women. They seem tentative about being there, to the point of being apologetic, not quite like beggars outside church, but close. Don notices that there are a lot of small children wandering around. We decide they must belong to the women at the kiosks. These aren't mothers who can afford nannies while they do volunteer work.

But China Bob's is doing fine—more than half filled with diners, and it takes us a moment to spot Jack and Billy sitting at the bar. They're both large men, noticeably larger than we are. Billy's over-weight, balding, red-faced. He's dressed in blue jeans, cowboy boots, blue windbreaker, blue houndstooth shirt. Jack has a short-sleeved golf shirt with a loud brown-on-brown pattern, dark slacks, and Gucci loafers. His hair is as silver as mine, and he hasn't lost any of it—except to the barber who gives him his crewcut. He looks like a retired army drill-sergeant, one that's still in good enough shape to mean business.

Jack begins to rag on us even while he's settling us into a booth and gesturing at one of the waitresses to bring us menus. Billy, playing Ed McMahon to Jack as he has for as long as I can remember, grins broadly, enjoying the play. I let Jack work me over for my long hair and the summer goatee I've left uncut for this trip, only half-listening because I know the harangue by heart and I'm busy priming the tape recorder. He's soon onto Don, patting his belly and checking his hair-line, but Don isn't so tolerant. He deflects the jibes with a question he knows Jack isn't going to enjoy.

"So, what's going on with you at home?" Don asks, tapping the table in front of him and then looking straight into Jack's eyes. "When I called there, my ear damned near got frostbite."

Jack leans back, stretching his arms in the air. "Dough-mess-tick problems," he says, spitting out the first word as if he's said it so often it hurts his mouth.

That gets a loud laugh from Billy. "Take a number," he says. "Jack's where I've been for the last 10 years."

Don doesn't relent. "What do you mean?"

"It means I've been living in the basement most of the time," Jack says. "And talking to the wife only when the kids are around. And only about the kids."

Billy grunts, and the two of them launch into a litany of their domestic woes. It doesn't matter that the woes are mostly self-inflicted —and both men are willing to concede that they are. And it doesn't make them any less pissed off. Yet they're both decent men. They take care of their domestic responsibilities: they pay the household expenses and the mortgages, and if it's about their kids, they're generous to a fault. Billy has three kids, two girls and a boy, and Jack has one of each. They're willing to pay alimony, too, if it comes to that.

Don and I aren't saying so, but we each have some idea about why Jack is in trouble at home. Ever since his mother died when he was still a teenager, Jack has been taking care of people as a kind of freelance big brother. He isn't a mother substitute and he's not paternal, but a lot of people have gladly accepted his chiding, over-the-top concern. It isn't always fun to be on the business end of it, but no one has ever had reason to doubt Jack's good  intentions. He shows up every day ready to make himself available, and he doesn't back away when the bad-smelling stuff gets into the fan. It's no accident he runs a restaurant, and that there are usually one or two of his long-time friends perched on the bar stools.

It hasn't helped Jack that the woman he married is extremely shy, or that his favourite way of helping friends get their heads straight is to take them out for dinner or drinks and let them air out their troubles with enough alcohol splashed about to pickle everything in sight,including the rawest trouble. It's pretty certain Jack's out most evenings, and it's likely he often comes home later than late.

Chances are that's the main reason he's in trouble, even if it isn't the official one. He's good with everyone's problems but his own.

When Billy's and Jack's complaints begin to wind down, I pull out my recorder and explain why we're in town. Jack sensibly concludes that taking photographs in a clearcut and camping there means that we're nuts, but Billy quiets down and seems interested. I begin dumping general questions at them both about the clearcut and about what's going on in the forests around Prince George, and just as Don predicted, it's Billy who responds.

He answers a few of the simple questions with simple answers: Are we running out of trees? *Yes.* Is the industry in trouble? *Yes.* But then he raises his hand and stops me. "Let me tell you a few things," he says. "I don't know if making that clearcut out there as big as it got was right or wrong. I don't think we'll ever know for sure. But you've got to understand that these are spaghetti forests we're looking at here."

"Okay," I say. "Explain."

"I mean, they're only good for 2x4's: structure wood. Pine or spruce wood, you see, is light and soft and strong, and you can drive a spike through it without it cracking or splintering the way a harder wood like fir would do. But the price you get for it isn't great, so you have to take it out of the forest as efficiently as you can, cut it up, and get it to market without a lot of hooh-ha. And believe me, they do that around here about as efficiently as anywhere in the world."

While I'm calculating how to turn that single-pole explanation around, his cell phone rings. He fishes it out of his pocket, grins at us, and says, "I gotta talk on my shoe-phone here. Somebody wants to buy some dirt." He answers it, turns his back on us, and strolls out into the mall where the reception is better.

By the time he returns, all I've come up with is what Don and I were chewing over while we were in the clearcut. The local community isn't getting much of a share in the profits, most of the dollar value is being whisked out of town, and if Prince George doesn't get any benefit from its resources, isn't there an argument for not allowing the forests to be cut at all?

Billy waves that away with a sneer. "You can't stop the companies from logging, and you can't stop them from shipping out the profits.

That's just the way things have gone. There's still a fair bit of money flowing back to town—at least from the logging side of it, which is still done by independents. It's only when you get the logs into town and into those big motherfucker mills that the jobs dry up. But you can't argue against efficiency, and that's what those mills are about."

Don has been looking distinctly bored until Billy gets into this, but here he repeats what I've told him about how the Bowron was logged, and the flimsy excuse of a bug infestation. Billy listens carefully until he's finished, and sweeps that away, too.

"Look," he says. "All this hoity-toity stuff is just wrong. The laws of nature are pretty simple: eat everything you can, kick everyone's ass you can, and crap wherever you like. After that, you get out or you go to sleep until the stink fades. Look at birds and bears."

"You're saying that the forest industry has been much more in tune with nature than the environmentalists are," I say.

Billy ignores me. "Mother Nature has a plan for these forests: everything grows, and you can't stop it. But when the trees are 200 years old, the bugs come in and start eating. Then one lightning strike will burn the whole place up and kill them all. And then the thing regens, and gets on with it. But today the forests aren't allowed to burn, because these tree-huggers get smoke up their asses, or whatever. And the weather isn't cold enough to kill the bugs any more. So, now, you can't log these forests fast enough to get ahead of the bugs. They're just going to keep eating us up. The Forest Service claims we've got about a 100-year supply of wood, but that's a joke because the bugs are eating it and no one does anything about it."

"Wait a minute, Bill," Don says. "Aren't the bugs always there?"

"Oh, sure. They're always around. But the only sure way to get rid of them is to burn it all up. They were hoping that cold weather would slow them down or kill them off—40 to 50 below C for two or three weeks like we used to have in the old days. But that's not going to happen any more with Williston Lake softening everything up. So there's bug-kill out there as far as the eye can see, and there's nothing to stop it, except to log it or let it burn. You can see what happened down in Yoho, where they wouldn't let them log the bug-kill. That monster fire was what they got.

"What they now do, where they burn it after they log it, that's a good idea. But then, the way things are, every time a government gets around to acting, it's already too late. They're dumping their own nuclear waste into the ocean, but there's not a level playing field for the loggers to work with. You can't even put a groove in the bush without some bureaucrat finding it and regulating it to death. So you tell me who scrapes the bush the worst? The logger or the politician?"

I ask him about the increased amounts of money the government is sinking into reforestation.

"Oh, sure," he says, his face reddening at the thought. "The government's got $900 million for reforestation, all right. But they're putting it into general revenue so they can finance the welfare system and send their bureaucrats to some Commie school in Portugal or Sweden."

"Seems to me," I say, trying to move back to the issue of the local community not getting adequate value for the use of its resources, "that the main difference between today and the old days is that the profits are all getting sucked out of town and into the bank accounts of offshore corporate shareholders. In the old days, when there were hundreds of independents, the owners at least put their profits back into the community."

"No," Billy replies. "You've got that backward. The people coming out here now are different. In the old days, as soon as anyone had enough money, they'd sell out and leave. They'd go to the Okanagan, or to Vancouver Island, and they'd sit around with one foot on the porch and the other foot in the grave and piss on Prince George. I think we've got a better deck of cards nowadays. The people who're coming here now are educated, and they stay—and they're more community-minded too, starting up different societies for history and recreation and that sort of crap. They're good people."

Billy's cell phone fires again, and he's off to the mall to sell more dirt. I glance over at Don. He shrugs and jerks his head in the direction of the door to signal he's ready to go. Jack would keep us here all afternoon if he could, and Don wants out before Jack comes up with a plan. The two men are virtual opposites now, it occurs to me. Jack runs on coffee and booze—and people—while Don's cleared himself and his life of every stimulant and most of the human distractions he can jettison. He's got caller ID on his office phone, and he doesn't answer the door unless he's expecting someone.

At this point in his life, Jack strikes me as a man who's simply trying to hold it together, and having a hard time succeeding. Don's been on his present program for a long time, reducing his life to dimensions manageable enough to give him the time and privacy to live a careful, deliberate life and—now it comes to me—to write without distractions.

I glance over at him, to confirm visually that I've got him straight, but he's busy putting on his coat. I pack up, but not before snapping a couple of pictures of Jack, who mugs for each one, getting close enough to the camera to throw off the focus. The snapshot I take of Don shows someone who simply wants to be elsewhere. Before we leave, Jack shows us a large colour photograph framed on the restaurant wall that clearly makes him proud. The photo seems innocuous enough: a group of people standing around at some forgotten occasion. Then you notice, at its centre, that someone is mooning the camera. It's Jack.

Billy and Jack want us to meet them for dinner, which we both know means dinner and too many drinks. Don tries to evade the issue, telling Jack we've got a lot scheduled—his daughter to help, photos to shoot, and so on. They're all real things, but it sounds like he's making excuses. Eventually Don agrees that we'll call in the late afternoon and set it up then. I stay out of it.

Where Don wants to be, it turns out, is behind his camera. He's got his eye working, and wants to exercise it. We spend a few hours shooting the city's grainiest details, along with some of its visual ironies. I catch a white stretch limousine with blackened windows whizzing along Fourth Avenue. Later I see a rectangular yellow-and-black "Share B.C." sign in a derelict Third Avenue storefront announcing that "We Support the Timber Industry" with the *i* in the word *timber* replaced by a stylized Christmas tree.

Don sticks with the black-and-white, and his eye is much sharper than mine: a row of boarded-up trailers in a vacant industrial tract; the city's 1950s bowling alley with the bottom edge of its glass-brick facade kicked in, the city's first medical building—its "Professional Centre"—with a large "For Lease" sign plastered across the wall and one of its two mailboxes about to tip over; a graveyard of worn-out and pirated logging trucks piled one askance the next. Next to the town's roughest stripper bar, he finds a rooming-house window with peeling trim, prim organza curtains, and a vase of plastic tulips on the windowsill. Across the parking lot, he photographs the badly drawn stripper-bar mural depicting George Street in the 1920s. The only human being in the scene is a man carrying beer kegs into the long since burned-down Astoria Hotel, and the mural itself is reflected eerily in a large mud puddle that somehow makes the ill-drawn buildings seem more realistic. The best photo he takes is of a large portable signboard that someone has parked beside an abandoned building near the rail yards. Along the 2-metre length of its top edge, the signboard has an arrow that points slightly upward. There is no message, and the arrow is pointing nowhere.

26

Bryn is waiting on the porch when we arrive. She's an attractive young woman, red-haired like her mother, not quite as tall, and athletic rather than statuesque. She's been brought up to be self-confident and direct, and that's what she is. Careful not to appear like we're parents taking over, we help her with the things in her new apartment that she hasn't yet figured out—the buzzy telephone, a couple of faulty light switches, an entrance door that doesn't close easily and won't lock. We also tease her about her pickup truck, which is a long way from being new and which Don thinks is going to be trouble, and she teases us right back for our skanky appearance after four days in the bush.

This is only the third time I've met Bryn, but she treats me as if she's known me all her life, probably because she's been hearing silly stories about me for most of it. She's busy, too, has class to go to, and has books to read later. But she wants our itinerary, which we really don't have.

"What the hell are we doing tonight and tomorrow?" Don asks.

"I don't know. See if we can find Jim, sack in at Barry McKinnon's place tonight, drink some beer, shoot some pictures tomorrow. If we can, I'd like to visit Bill Morris's grave before we take off."

Bryn wants to know who Bill Morris was, and I explain that he was an older friend who recently died of liver cancer. She decides she'd like to come with us, not because she likes graveyards, but to be with her father. It's clear that she likes him as much as he likes her.

I call Barry once Don has the phone working. He's home from the college, and tells us to come over whenever we like. He sounds cheerful and relaxed, happy to be back teaching. Don's still fiddling with the locks, so I ask Barry about John Harris and a few others. The only real news is not that Other Art has gone bankrupt, which I'd heard already, but that Harvey left town under a cloud and is now living in Texas trying to drum up money so he can take a kitsch art car on tour.

It's time to visit Jim, or at least try. Don makes another call, this time to Jim's sister, and gets the address. Jim is living in a rooming house not far from Barry's place, so it isn't out of our way. Don is more apprehensive about this visit than I am. When I ask why, he explains that the only times he's seen Jim willing to talk in the past 15 years have been when Georgina is there. That makes sense; Georgina could make a pile of rocks talkative. My best hope is that the sight of the two of us, grubby as we are, will lift Jim out of wherever he is, at least for a few moments.

The rooming house is more halfway house than anything else. Most of the men we see are tattooed and missing teeth, and probably just got out of jail. We ask one of them—a skinny old guy with no teeth who's likely younger than we are—which room belongs to Jim, and he points down the hall and then crooks his finger: last room, turn left.

Our knocks get us nothing until we're ready to give up. Then the door opens a crack, and a husky voice asks who it is.

"White, and Fawcett," I say. "Come out and talk to us for a few minutes."

There's a pause. "Uh, okay. Give me a minute."

When he appears he's yawning, but it's wariness rather than recent sleep. "Hey," he says, as if he'd last us last week. "What's shaking?"

As we're walking outside, Don explains why we're in town, and then pops a question at him: "So," he says. "How are *you*?"

Jim turns his back on us. "Oh, fine, I guess. Not much I can tell you."

"What have you been up to?"

"Not a whole lot, really. I drive a little taxi, but they keep taking my driver's licence away. And I keep having to move. You know how it is."

The conversation struggles along, more dead ends than the clearcut. Jim doesn't ask questions about us. I find myself unconsciously but literally stepping back, examining the porch, a parked car, my shoes: giving up. But Don stays with him, trying to make some sort of contact.

He fails, and after a few more minutes we say our goodbyes and leave. As we drive off, I watch Jim return to the rooming house. He doesn't look back. Later, Don will tell me that he's always been slightly uncomfortable around Jim, even in high school. He wasn't, he says, ever sure Jim liked or cared about him.

"Jim was always talking about what he was reading or thinking," I answer, feeling my way to something I wasn't aware of knowing. "He never really talked *with* us, not the way you and I talked to one another. I never thought he gave a shit about me, either, but somehow it never bothered me. I sort of accepted that to him we were just two guys he could talk to without us going "huh" all the time. It was just the way he was. Funny, eh?"

"No," Don says. "Not funny. I was always frustrated by it. Still am, I guess."

Barry McKinnon and Don haven't met before. That means we're abruptly on my social turf, and the identities Don and I have slipped into over the past days shift as I'm making the introduction. It isn't that Don becomes my drooling Igor, but a veil drops and he becomes a reserved, almost shy man feeling his way, not presuming anything. When Joy comes home from work a few minutes later, the veil drops again, more opaquely still, as he finds ways to make her comfortable with his presence. He isn't uncomfortable, merely careful to make a good or neutral impression. This is how he must be in his own world, the one he inhabits without me or without the small circle of people he trusts. I've never seen this side of him before, and it startles me.

I know Barry has warmed to him when he suggests that we park the Vanagon in the backyard overnight instead of on the street, and a few seconds later, invites us to come up to the university to hear the jazz band he plays drums in. Joy interrupts before either of us can respond, telling Barry he ought to unlock the gate now so he doesn't forget. Barry offers us a beer, cracks open one for himself, and disappears. I flip the tab on mine, and Don, who stopped drinking completely a few years back, settles for a Coke.

"I suppose you smelly buggers will be wanting to clean up," Joy says in her cheerful way. "I'll get you some towels."

I let Don clean up first—I'm barely a guest in this household—and by the time I come down, showered and shaved, Don's sitting at the kitchen table making conversation with Joy, asking her about how long they've had the house, and how she likes Prince George. Eventually we all settle around the backyard fire, just as Don and I would be doing if we were still out in the clearcut. The air is cool, but it's warmer in town than in the clearcut, and the skies have cleared. It's the best weather we've seen since we left Vancouver.

After Joy has gone inside to make dinner and Barry has gone for another beer, I ask Don if he really wants to go hear Barry play.

"Sure," he says. "Why not? I want to see the university, anyway."

I can't read him on this. It means we're dumping Jack and Billy for a dinner and dance date with Barry, so he's either forgotten about them, or he's agreeing to forget because he doesn't want to deal with Jack's sea of troubles.

Later, while we're sitting in a darkened lounge at UNBC halfway through Barry's second set, Bryn appears.

"I've got Jack and Billy outside," she whispers to Don. "They're really steamed. They wouldn't even come in."

"Oh, shit," Don says. "We didn't call them. How did you find us? How did they find you?"

"Jack called me—I guess he got the number out of information—wanting to know where you guys were. I heard you say something about staying with Barry McKinnon, so I phoned there, and his wife said you were all up here. So I called Jack back and here we are."

It takes a while, but we get Jack and Billy calmed down enough to come in and listen to the rest of the gig. But we're in for it, obliged to go wherever they want to go afterward. Bryn is enjoying herself, watching her father and me weasel our way out of the mess we've created—and into something else we don't want to deal with, either.

The something else turns out to be Earles, where the six of us sit and drink at the bar until midnight. Bryn tries to help us out by turning the conversation to the kinds of forestry questions Billy and I had chewed on at lunch. With the alcohol, it's a much louder question-and-answer this time around, with the biggest loud coming from Bryn. She's not having any of *their* reactionary nonsense.

"You know what people like me are doing here?" she says, after Jack winds down a tirade about half-assed environmentalists who've never had to face the difficulties of raising a family or making a living. "We're waiting for dinosaurs like you to die off."

It's a pretty amusing shot-to-the-ribs, and it doesn't seem to bother Jack and Billy. It brings me back to something Billy had said at the beginning of our conversation at China Bob's earlier in the day.

"I don't know what's out there in that clearcut that could interest guys like you two," he'd said. *"There's nothing there."*

He was right, but not quite in the way he thinks. What he doesn't know, because we can't quite explain it even to ourselves, is that we've been out in the clearcut trying to find its meaning by documenting details. The details are sparse, and they're repetitive: 50 million little trees growing; a fractured and invisible ecological system broken in the name of an economic juggernaut that no one has an alternative to, except holding hands and hoping the coyotes won't devour the helpless. Jack and Billy, at least, know what the coyotes will do, even if they can't defend themselves against the vicious corporate pack circling Prince George. But 50 million specimens of two unspectacular kinds of coniferous trees planted with the less-than-uplifting hope that a future generation of corporate loggers can come back in 75 or 100 years to do the same thing they did in the 1980s with even less gravy spilled on the local community is the sort of future that will demoralize anyone.

For all their practical common sense, Jack and Billy are demoralized men. This isn't the way they thought life was going to be. That their marriages fall apart and their business lives don't rocket toward unlimited wealth the way their parents' did isn't something they're able to connect to what happened out in the Bowron River valley. I can't make that connection detailed or convincing enough to turn them, because the fine detail doesn't exist and isn't even remotely objective. Every datum is ideologically loaded, and the largest detail —the money trail—is quickly morphed into inscrutable corporate accounting systems and then obliterated by mergers. We all agree that it happens, but it is impossible to object to without rejecting our knowledge of the way things are.

I suspect, despite our differences, we'd all agree that at the end of this continuum we'll likely end up facing one gigantic corporation that covers and controls every life and runs every activity—and that if it goes that way, there will be no forests left in northern British Columbia. Jack and Billy aren't dinosaurs, and they're not stupid. They're men facing difficulties that literally have no solution. They're the small fish in this evolution, and the muddy water in their pond is telling them just how small. But Don and I are small fish, too, and so is Bryn. The difference is that the ponds we're from are still large enough to delude us into believing they aren't connected to the one in which Jack and Billy are struggling.

27

No one in Barry and Joy's house is up bright and early the next morning, and when Don and I do get moving, we're feeling a lot less than bright. I've got a hangover, and Don has a headache from all the cigarette smoke at the bar. The skies match our mood, returning to the overcast of the first few days. Yet by 10:00 we're downtown, and shooting enough pictures that I need more colour film. While we're in Wally West Studios stocking up on ASA 400, a second-hand Pentax catches Don's eye. By the time I've got one of the rolls I've bought out of the box and loaded into my camera, he's bartered down the price of the Pentax far enough to convince himself it's a deal, and is buying it. Another camera won't hurt.

As we pass the Columbus Hotel I spot two middle-aged loggers giving us and our dangling cameras the evil eye. To them, we're outsiders, fucking tourists. They're in summer duds, basketball shoes, and jeans, T-shirts stretched across their potbellies, with baseball caps clicked tight at the back. They probably think that to us, they're "local colour," and it pisses them off.

They're not local colour to us. They're the guys we've spent our lives eluding, on these streets as kids, and inside our own heads since. We're not going to shoot photos of them and we won't stare them down. Why would we? These men are engraved inside our skulls, the way Michelangelo's painted angels inhabit the Sistine Chapel.

Don glances at me, and we both grin even though it isn't exactly prudent. For a moment, we're again what we once were: outsiders, together against it. Smartassing men like these two was one of our survival mechanisms when we were teenagers, and here we're doing it again, conducting a conversation we've had so many times we can run its lengthy codes inside a shrug. Here's those guys, here's the addled ironies of town life matched against our disrespect and laughter. The tensions produced served to drive us out of town once upon a time, but today they only move us down the street, and the only cost is a couple of never-to-be-taken photographs that no one but us would understand.

All but a tiny minority of the photographs we do take are documentary, and as documentaries go, it's a depressing one that wears on us the same way that the clearcut did. In part, it's the light. The overcast is dense without being heavy, the skies so solid a grey that they draw the colour from everything the light falls on, erasing shadow and texture at the same time. It masks any beauty hidden here, but not the fact the place is falling apart.

Things do fall apart when they're built on the cheap. Yet there's something more corrosive than simple decay in this grey light—it accentuates the run-down buildings, the peeling paint, the chipped gutters, the seediness of the street wanderers. Pretty well everything that might have supported a sense of permanence and culture has been sacrificed in this part of town so that no one will have to walk more than 50 metres from their vehicle to their commercial destination. And so no one does, unless they're drunk or lost.

We break for lunch early at the local White Spot, which isn't local and doesn't serve quite the same quality food it does in Vancouver, where the franchise originates. We get a window table, order without looking at the menu—Triple "O" burgers and fries—and while we're waiting for our orders to come, we talk.

"You know," Don says, "I hate this place. I hate this light. It always made me nuts, and it still does."

I follow his gaze out the window, and see, maybe for the first time in our long friendship, the exact difference between what he sees here and what I see. He sees the flat grey light, the sparse greenery, the muddied pickup trucks and their doe-eyed occupants absorbed by walking—or driving—up and down and back and forth without being absorbed by life itself. So unlike the Point Grey Vancouver of his early childhood: leafy green, civilized, damp but unmuddied. For Don, these are the conditions of hell. It was hell when he was 10 years old, and it is hell now that he's 50.

The insight asks me to study exactly what it is *I'm* seeing. It isn't pretty, either. The light isn't tinged with brimstone, it's just a flatness that diminishes everything. For me this is a desecrated paradise, which isn't the same thing as hell.

Ridiculous theologizing? It doesn't feel that way, sitting in the White Spot. Notions of paradise aren't something we import from the Bible or the Koran. Everyone has them, and they're specific—constructed from elements of wherever we draw those first thoughts that are uniquely our own. Before we go very far from our initial awarenesses these elements send powerful roots into everyday perception, and paradise grows: the way things are supposed to be.

My paradise was made up of the things of Prince George during the mid-1950s, a place that wasn't so very different from what we're seeing out this window in 1996. When I was very young, the drab temporariness I see today was filtered through my limited experience and understanding—this was the way the world was, and I had nothing else from which to build paradise. It contained a white clapboard house in a stable neighbourhood, was informed by a loving mother, and circumscribed by a family order it hadn't yet occurred to me to challenge. All around me was the spare bounty of the north, the things from which I took intense pleasure: the cool brilliance of the summer sunlight, the dark, snowbound winters, a vegetable garden in our backyard, a family that seemed normally loud and loving, a widening circle of others who seemed interestingly different from my family. I was dimly aware of a larger world beyond the wilderness of green forests, with exotic orchards, prairies, modern and ancient cities, oceans and other continents. I was given—and this might be the most important gift parents can offer any child—the expectation that the world was, all of it, mine to explore and exploit as I wished. But Don's paradise was wholly elsewhere: *down* there, among the mossy trees of the coast and Vancouver, the clean, paved streets, the rich greenery, the ocean within scent and sight.

As I remember paradise, our common experiential burden floods in, and we're both 18 again, feeling the town on our necks, a fog of irrelevant purposes impossible to lift or blow off without giving up the obligations to family and friends we each accept as part of life's order. We can stand aside, we can ridicule this place, but somehow we're beginning to realize, in our different ways, that we're about done here. The difference is that Don has no regrets about going, save for leaving behind his father's bones and broken dream. For him, leaving Prince George is escaping from hell.

At this moment, I see Prince George as he sees it, and it is painful. I've used his way of seeing things since I was 12 years old as a survival mechanism and as a growth medium, and he's been able to use my eyes—but this is different. We did that to make ourselves stronger, able to see and do and be more. But until this moment, I've *never* looked out through his eyes on his terms. That was the unspoken discretion we've had—or was it that I was too self-centred? Has he looked out through my eyes this way? I honestly don't know, but I suspect he has, and more often than I recognize. If he has, he'd never have told me. He'd have used what he saw to do what he thought was necessary and right, and he'd have said nothing.

So this is what our plan for this trip had in store for us—its true purpose. For me, it began with his camera, watching what it was he was seeing differently than I did, and how differently he framed things. Then this, which seems like a miracle and a humiliation at the same time.

"Was there anything good about this place?" I ask.

He thinks this one through carefully before answering. "There are things I'm grateful for," he says. "The biggest one is that I had to deal with *everyone*. In a small town, that's just what you do."

"That's pretty much," I say, "the opposite of how multiculturalism is working in the big cities, where you're supposed to 'celebrate' all the diversity."

"How so? What's wrong with diversity?"

"It's not the diversity that's the problem, it's that the only obligation involved is to celebrate it. We know how things go at parties. You never really engage with people—you shout pleasantries at them over the background din, and then go home with the people you *really* feel comfortable around. In Prince George, you couldn't separate yourself that way. So the range of things and people you're comfortable being around is much wider."

He frowns, and we drop back into the lifelong disquisition that is our friendship.

———————

It isn't until we arrive at the Prince George and District cemetery that I understand why Bryn is there—and that I'm the fifth wheel. She and Don are there to visit the grave of Don's father, not to find Bill Morris. Don's father's grave is down at the far end of the cemetery, and I don't tag along. This is a private, bittersweet piece of family business, and none of mine. I wander about the grounds for a few minutes—it's completely deserted—hunting among the recent burial plots, but I don't find Bill. I haven't phoned ahead for information, and there's no on-site index. I don't even know if I'm looking for a cremation plaque or a plot with a headstone, and I'm not smart enough to remember he's likely buried with his parents, or that after just four months, the gravestone may not yet have been laid. So I lean against a stone cairn not very different from the Alexander Mackenzie cairn at the bottom of First Avenue, light up a smoke, and relax.

When I catch sight of Don and Bryn walking toward me along the asphalt pathway, she has her head on his shoulder and her eyes are wet with tears. Don is dry-eyed—or maybe not. I can't tell because I don't look. It isn't lack of curiosity, but a version of the discretion I've practised for 40 years. We get into the Vanagon without talking, and leave. The silence isn't about emptiness or absence, or not knowing what needs to be said. This one is theirs, and it is full of lovely, complex human indeterminates.

———————

Don and I leave town the next morning, early, and drive back out to the clearcut, this time from the north end. We shoot photographs all day, methodically, but Don's focus has altered. He is after what he's detected in town: it's more than mere compositional coherence. He's looking for the spots along the river where the landforms reveal both the original forest and what's been done to it: the present, in its momentary complexity, the spectacular ugliness of what we've done to ourselves.

We camp that night at a small lake without a name, a few kilometres south of Stony Lake. It's another forestry camp, but this time, it's barely adequate. We have to park the truck at the edge of the forest, and the parking bay is sloped enough that we need to level the truck with rocks and pieces of firewood. Late that night, with the wind blowing and the spruce trees all around us creaking and groaning and my wobbling tooth hurting, I write this passage in my notebook:

A clearcut is silent. It is not the stillness of a northern lake when the components of the world suddenly cease to contend, like the interval between notes in a piece of music when the composition of duelling vibrations rests and becomes a bridge to something larger and sweeter. The silence of clearcut forests is exhaustion, a void in which the world comes to recognize that it is being broken, misused, betrayed, and it ceases to struggle. I've grown fearful that this silence now resides in the minds of people here, and that it is sapping their vitality as it spreads and consumes the integrity of the materials they live by. I wish I could make this silence visible and audible, so that it can be understood, and so it can end.

ELM TREES, 2001

28

On the five-hour flight to Vancouver, I watch a movie while the plane plows the jetstream at 800 kilometres per hour. The movie is a silly American production about a young man with what used to be called a "zest for living," which has come to mean, in the 21st century, excessive entrepreneurial energy without any moral constrictions. In the movie's first half-hour, the young entrepreneur beds the two sisters of the woman he's about to marry, behaving like a self-involved jerk and occasionally winking at the camera to make the audience his accomplice. That's amusing, because on this plane his accomplices are mostly bemused Chinese tourists on the way home from a visit to Niagara Falls.

Eventually I pull off the earphones, sure that by the end of the movie the entrepreneur will have a Hollywood change of heart, grow mushy and sentimental and transform himself into a caring and faithful-to-his-wife entrepreneur—ho-hum—even though such transformations are rarer than planes that cross continents in a few hours and forests that have been obliterated in a few months of cutting. I edge the window shade up to scan the prairies 11,000 metres below. Most of the lakes and reservoirs are expanses of dried white alkali even though the cultivated fields are green. That's what it's like now: technologies deplete resources and serve production instead of quality of life, while all of us stumble along the edge of environmental calamities that leave every breath we take acrid with their threats. In other words, it's so much like the last half of the 20th century that everyone mistakes it for normality.

I doze fitfully, but long and deep enough to get me past the movie's conclusion. When I come to and glance at the movie screen, a pitch-man named Dave Chalk is touting electronic books: for $500 consumers can read print on a bad pixel matrix and store what they read on a medium that'll begin to decay in about 10 years. Progress, apparently. My attentions drift away to a harassed-looking woman in a Tommy Girl shirt-dress a few seats ahead of me. She's shepherding a three- or four-year-old, evidently her daughter, up and down the aisles of the half-empty plane. The child is dark-haired and pretty, but not as pretty as my own daughter, who will be four years old in a few weeks.

I wake up fully as the flight crosses the Okanagan Valley south of Kelowna, B.C. I last flew into that city in December after my 90-year-old mother suffered a stroke that, a few weeks later, resulted in her death. In a sense, that's also why I'm on this plane. I've been working on this book for 10 years, and I need to make some conclusions about it and a lot of other things in my life. The book I thought I had 10 years ago—an exposé of an environmental atrocity with a clear moral and ideological track—has evaporated. I honestly don't know what I think about the clearcut in the Bowron River valley now, so I'm heading back to find out. The death of a parent makes some people sentimental. It has made me ruthless—slightly impatient to look the past, present, and future in the eye.

West of Kelowna, for instance, I begin to spot the tighter patching of cuts that signal the effect of B.C.'s new *Forest Protections Act*: 50 percent cut, 50 percent leave. But as we close in on the Coast Range, the fabric of the forest looks more threadbare, with entire valleys and mountain ridges denuded. It is curiously *not* shocking, any of it. I ask myself if I've grown inured to clearcuts, and can't come up with a clear answer. Suppose I am? So what?

Maybe this, for one: British Columbia's government has just changed. The government that was tossed out was a social democratic regime riddled with minor corruption, and suffering a strange failure of will that made it ineffective on anyone's political terms. It was unable to pursue changes that really serve the interests of lower income groups, but it still angered the wealthy and the corporations on a near-daily basis. The incoming government is a right-wing coalition more in sync with the globalist program of smaller governments, lower taxes for businesses, and user fees for social and government services to make up the revenue shortfall. It has self-mandated itself to punish and exterminate any and all residual communist tendencies left by the previous regime by treating social entitlements and equity programs as character-corrupting crutches. Most British Columbians I've talked to since the election have predicted that every business project, mega or minor, that the social democrats put on hold will now get a green light, and every social program will find itself under a spotlight—and sooner rather than later, a boning knife. This sort of turning-of-the-wheel has happened before in B.C., but this government is saying it wants to take the wheel off the hub, and it has the kind of majority to make good on the threats.

South of the border the U.S. Commerce Department, with the support of American lumber producers, has imposed a punitive series of tariffs on Canadian softwood lumber that threatens to cripple the forest industry across British Columbia. Behind the U.S. tariffs is the intention to force British Columbia to sell off its forests to the private sector—not forgetting the profit windfall the lumber producers will enjoy as the tariffs drive prices for structure wood higher—thus "harmonizing" a little more of Canada with American business procedures. Curiously, no one on either side of the border seems interested in pointing out that this exposes the true intentions of the "free trade" initiatives that resulted in the 1989 Canada–U.S. Free Trade Agreement and 1994's NAFTA. Free trade was never aimed at eradicating tariff barriers or at making goods cheaper to consumers. Both agreements were designed to create uniform commercial and financial practices in North America, ones that would always be based on the terms set by the United States.

The plane lands safely in Vancouver, the Chinese tourists file off slightly more bewildered about North American values than they were five hours ago, and I get off with them, no smarter than I was. The flight is on schedule, which means I have an hour to kill in the Vancouver terminal before I have to catch my connection to Prince George. I call my son Max, almost 22 and living on his own. He's already out and about—or still sleeping. When the canned greeting comes on his service, I don't leave a message. We'd had a long conversation the night before about baseball, and about the family's plans to scatter my mother's ashes in July, so we're temporarily talked out. He's working a summer job, busboying at an urban chain restaurant in Vancouver, finishing a Political Science degree at the University of British Columbia, and hinting that he'd like to come to Toronto for graduate school. I call Don White, but he's out, too.

The Prince George plane is a Fokker F-28 turboprop that carries about 60 people. It is full, I notice, mostly with elderly people. While I'm rummaging through the seat pouch to check the aircraft's specs, the man sitting next to me pulls the spec sheet from the pouch in front of him, points to the name, and grins.

"Right sort of plane for Prince George," he says, mouthing the word "Fokker" in case I don't get it. "You live there, or just going up for business?"

"Little of both," I say. "Grew up there, but haven't lived there for years."

He grunts, losing interest when I don't mention what business I'm in—or he spots the small silver hoop in my left ear. I busy myself with the Vancouver newspaper I've brought while the luggage loaders rock the plane gently back and forth.

It's an uneventful flight north, silver overcast above and below the plane until we're north of Williams Lake, where the bruised purple of the distant Rockies becomes intermittently visible. I ask the flight attendant about our altitude: "15,000 feet," she says, and then translates it into metres in case I'm not as old as I look.

I'm able to pick out most of the familiar landmarks because the flight path parallels the Fraser River: Kerseley, Alexandria, Quesnel, Cottonwood Canyon, Hixon. As we begin to drop down for the landing at Prince George, I spot, off to the west, a distinct yellow haze. It isn't Prince George, so it has to be a forest fire.

I remind myself that I'm flying into this silver-grey world on the longest day of the year. It is the 21st day of June, and it is also the 21st

century. The slate isn't clean, but at least there is open space on it.
Still, as the plane touches down on the runway, I feel no sense of
event. Prince George doesn't look or feel any different than it did in
the 20th century. The strained trajectories the north has been on all
my life are present and visible and unresolved. The 20th century isn't
over, not here. At least, not for me. That's another reason why I'm
back.

———————

Barry McKinnon is waiting inside the terminal, and we do a half-
handshake half-hug greeting. He looks older and skinnier, but he's
pretty much as he always is when he picks me up—distracted, anxious
to get out of the terminal, clear of my schedules and priorities, and
back to his own life. We've zoomed through the mandatory small talk
before the bags start to roll inside: weather's good, Joy's fine, son Jesse
is in Vancouver working for a plant nursery. He's driving a minivan
now, inherited from his father who died several years ago. The only
thing he's enthusiastic about is his two-year-old grandson in Calgary.
They're going off to visit him in a week.

When I ask him how things are going around town—the question
I'll be asking everyone—I get a surprise.

"I don't pay much attention," he says. "I'm thinking of getting
out of here as soon as we can. Retire, you know?"

"Where to?" I ask.

He rubs his chin, leans down to check the name tag on a bag.
"Well, not Vancouver. Maybe New York."

Barry has a standing joke that the only two cities he's comfortable
in are Prince George and New York, so I'm surprised by what he says
next.

"The only other place I'd want to leave here for is Tumbler Ridge."

"You're serious about moving up there?"

Barry makes eye contact for the first time. "Damned right," he
says. "Tumbler Ridge has all the good things that have been screwed
out of this place."

As we drive, I tune out Barry for a moment and go over the plan I
have for this trip. It's reasonably elementary: Get what I need to finish

the book without imposing myself or my own dopey prejudices. I'm going to listen and I'm going to look, and whatever is here, *that's* the conclusion. Barry has just given me as good a place as any to begin. "Tell me why you're thinking about Tumbler Ridge."

Barry has been on about Tumbler Ridge for nearly a year now. At first I thought it was a lark, but late last summer he and Joy bought a half-share in a three-bedroom house in the townsite for a ridiculously small amount of money, with the plan of eventually using it to open up a writing school.

Tumbler Ridge was the name given to the residential community built to house the employees of several huge and heavily subsidized coal mines opened up on the eastern edge of the Rockies in north-eastern B.C. at the end of the 1970s. To keep employee turnover at manageable levels, Tumbler Ridge was built as a fully serviced community, with different kinds of family-oriented accommodation, schools, a library, a fully equipped recreational centre, and so on. At its peak, the town's population reached 2,600. It is now somewhere around 1,100 because after 1998 the various governments and corporations involved pulled the plug on the mines. By that time they'd poured well over a billion in public money into the initial construction costs and, later, when the price of coal began to plummet, into price subsidies. Probably the single biggest ticket item was the extension of B.C. Rail under the Rockies to transport the coal out.

The curiosity was that the North East Coal Venture—as it was called by business people—was carefully planned and skillfully executed. The fatal mistake was made before the first dollar was spent: grossly overestimating the global demand for coal, which the planners and politicians got wrong every which way. Compounding the overestimated demand was a second mistake: setting up North East Coal to compete with the large coal mines in the southeast corner of the province, which had vast inventories of similar grades of coal, and already had rail access and secured markets. To the extreme embarrassment of the Canadian governments involved, this allowed offshore buyers, once the market glut became apparent, to ratchet the price down by playing the two sets of B.C. producers against one another.

Two other miscalculations—more abstract but possibly more profound—involved assuming that manufacturing technologies would not evolve, and that energy markets would maintain the trajectories established by the energy crisis OPEC created in 1973. Before the adjacent Bullmoose and Quintette mines were shipping their first trainloads to market, the international price structure for coal was collapsing, and the Far East customers who weren't disappearing (or failing to appear in the first place) were aggressively renegotiating contracts. By 1990 the jig was up, even though the Quintette mine didn't close until 2000 and the other, Bullmoose, is still running—at much diminished capacity, and mainly to spare the governments the humiliation of having to admit they were complete bunglers. Since the first closure, the companies involved have been selling off Tumbler Ridge's assets.

While Barry talks about his plans for the house they've bought, we take the leisurely route into town, across the Fraser River below what was once Fort George, then east and north along the river into the Millar Addition. Next thing I know we're parking beneath the conical elms that line the boulevard in front of his house. Since the last time I was here, they've grown, and now form a graceful canopy over the street.

These trees are now as beautiful as they are unique. They're unique because there are few mature elms left in North America. Dutch elm disease has killed off the rest. Their beauty lies in their nearly perfect shape and size, along with their numbers. Finally, a government did something good for Prince George. But this good is so incongruous and fragile that I laugh out loud: they planted beautiful trees that were doomed before they were planted.

Joy McKinnon is on the porch with Buddy, their springer spaniel. She lets him loose as I open the door of the van, and he darts away from her, not to greet us but into the backyard. There are shadows back there, and he wants to capture them for us: his way of saying hello, I recall. Joy doesn't try to stop him. She stays where she is, hands on hips, watching me. She doesn't ask what I'm laughing about, either. She asks how I'm doing, I compliment her on not looking a day older, and she tells me I'm full of bullshit. We've danced this one before, but it doesn't feel stale, possibly because she really *doesn't* look any older.

"Your boulevard trees have grown," I say to her as we embrace.

"Damned right they have," she agrees. "They're pretty neat, aren't they?"

"Better than that," I say. "They're probably the most beautiful elms in North America."

"They're the *only* elms in North America," Barry says.

"Actually, that might not be true much longer," Joy says. "I heard somewhere they've found a cure for what was killing them, so they're growing them again in other places."

"I'd heard that, too." I say. "But I suspect what that really means is that they've discovered a resistant subspecies that'll grow at least three metres tall."

"No," she says. "It's got some sort of patriotic American name down in the States. 'Liberty,' I think. The trees are the same size as the ones that died off. Like these ones here, I guess, only younger."

I think about that for a moment, and bet against it. This is Prince George prime here, whacking me between the eyes as it always does —sometimes with its beauty, usually with its stupidity, and always because it has proceeded as if Prince George is a special case where normal rules don't apply. This time it has produced the largest concentration of elm trees on the continent, and they're definitely on the beautiful side of the scale. Where planting these elms stands on the stupid scale hasn't been decided. If the virus shows up here next week, this neighbourhood will be littered with stumps in two years, just like the Bowron River valley.

I remind myself that God doesn't have coherent plans when it comes to Prince George. This is easier than admitting that on the basis of the available evidence, there's no Grand Plan to life, and no God, period. Elsewhere, there's occasional evidence of design, enough to corrupt serious people with the idea that some sort of benevolent order persists and that goodness can occasionally triumph. Around here, that's very hard to find evidence for. Much easier to back your pickup over every obstruction to personal profit and declare the Dictatorship of the Shoppers Proletariat, even though that strategy doesn't appear to have done much for the locals lately.

This much I'm sure about: the City of Prince George didn't plant elms in the Millar Addition because it found a disease-resistant species. It happened the way most things happen in Prince George. Somebody took a flyer on common sense. A City Hall bureaucrat thought, Hey! Elms are cheap, grow big and grow quickly, and maybe Dutch elm disease won't reach us, or maybe there'll be a cure for it by the time it does. Equally likely, the bureaucrat who made the decision hadn't heard about what happened to the other elm trees in North America. Or more likely still, he or she knew about it and decided to ignore the facts: the cheap price made the risk acceptable. "Let's go for it" is a revered and much-used slogan around here. What it means is that if a decision is bad, someone else will pay the price.

Later—after those who made the decision are long gone.

But it has worked this time, even if it might end with a whole lot of ugly stumps. The elms have grown, their branches have arched over every street, and as a consequence the quality of people's lives in this neighbourhood depends more heavily on them than on being able to shop at Costco or, soon, Wal-Mart.

29

The 21st century is a crazy place. I've crossed most of the North American continent and it isn't yet noon. Am I raving about life in the fast lane? No. I've dropped into Barry and Joy's domestic groove and we're talking about how thick we want the pork chops we're having for dinner, and where we'll get them. Joy says she has a butcher who'll not only stuff them, he'll cut them thick enough to be properly stuffed.

In a town where meats are often prepackaged 1,000 kilometres away, locally stuffed thick-cut chops are worth more conversation than crossing a continent before midday.

Not that Barry and Joy are considering 21st-century insanities. Our discussion of the chops is a ploy to avoid eating lunch, a banal preoccupation of the middle-aged. We're working it because, miracle or curse, we've reached the unglamorous part of our lives where eating is best avoided unless we're willing to make it an occasion. Otherwise, we're stuffing fat hogs, pushing sticky platelets into our arteries, inviting indigestion, heartburn, gout, and other discomforts of gluttony, not to mention the tut-tuts from the federal agency trying to make us live a few years longer.

Once the pork chop question is settled, I unpack my bags. That's when I remember that my sleeping accommodations at Barry and Joy's will be in the basement, their son Jesse's now-unused bedroom filled with discarded teenager-tech and the overflow of Barry's drum collection. The room has no window, and I'll be awakening to darkness whether it's at 2:30 in the morning or 2:30 in the afternoon. Damn. I wanted to see the sun come up.

Well, there's an open invitation to stay at the home of John Harris and Vivien Lougheed, who'll be hiking in the Stikine Valley for most of my stay. I'll have early-morning light there, but it'll take me out of the neighbourhood where I grew up.

While I'm trying to think my way through this, I set up my laptop under the desk lamp in the basement bedroom. Barry, suddenly attentive, comes down the stairs and asks what I've got planned for the afternoon.

"Plug in the laptop to recharge, then gumboot the drag," I answer.

"I'll walk down there with you if you want."

For Barry to suggest walking downtown is between unthinkable and unspeakable. I don't remember the two of us ever doing it before, although I'm sure we have. But, hey, why not today? The air is warm, the sky clear and free from the stink of pulp mills, and it *is* midsummer.

The southeast part of downtown, along George Street, seems healthier than when I last saw it. There's a new restaurant in the old Chrysler dealership building, and several boutiques have opened further along, one of them selling Native spiritual merchandise.

"More of these on Fourth Avenue," Barry says, as I peer through the window of the Native boutique at the dream-catchers and the stencilled T-shirts with idealized wolves and grizzly bears, probably packaged in Taiwan or Korea. Canada's Native peoples have globalized their culture just like everyone else, and with a similar attention to detail.

"According to the downtown planners," Barry says, "these boutiques are supposed to be a draw for the lawyers and court workers. But they don't seem to buy enough to keep them in business for long. The Native boutiques seem to last longer, but that's probably because they're getting federal grant money to buy their product. Either way, it turns out lawyers prefer to shop at Costco."

We stop to look at the new courthouse square at Third Avenue and George Street, which is well designed and clean but utterly deserted, then walk west on Third Avenue. Things quickly get dismal. Pawnshops and second-hand stores alternate with empty storefronts and dingy government-funded NGO offices, many of them involved with Native initiatives. Cynics call the funding for these programs pretreaty money. They're not far wrong. Most of the programs have been generated by good intentions, but another way of looking at good intentions is to recognize that they're attempts to cover up the bunglings of previous generations and their not-even-faintly good intentions. Or to understand that good intentions tend to operate as accurately as missiles fired without guidance systems.

Third Avenue has deteriorated further since 1996, when I last walked it with Don White. Many of the storefronts that were sliding down-market five years ago are now derelict. Even the Royal Bank, once a downtown mainstay, has closed its branch and moved local operations to one of the shopping centres. Only a few things are unchanged: the Columbus Hotel, now the local biker bar, still wafts fumes of stale beer from its glass-free facade, and as we pass Dominion Street I see an elderly woman go into the Flamingo Beauty Salon, where my mother spent Friday afternoons in the 1950s having her hair done.

The Northern Hardware remains a going concern, too, but that's not a surprise. "If that place goes down," Barry reminds me, "they can bulldoze the rest."

The Northern *is* under threat. Among the local issues I've been tracking along with the latest plan for downtown renewal is whether Wal-Mart will be permitted to open an outlet in Prince George—or rather, where.

Wal-Mart is everything the Northern Hardware isn't, and vice versa—despite their superficial similarity in offering both hardware and furnishings. At the Northern Hardware, customers come to purchase something specific: a bolt, an axe handle, a saw blade, a piece of fishing tackle, a cooking pot, an item of furniture. The store usually has the item, but if it doesn't, it arranges to obtain it—usually sooner rather than later. At Wal-Mart, the transaction energies are reversed: customers arrive with money to spend and a need to shop, and even if they've come looking for something specific, Wal-Mart isn't interested. For Wal-Mart, service means having its employees smile while they try to substitute what the customer wants with whatever the corporation has brought in on a mass purchase at a better price than customers would be able to get elsewhere—if they wanted it in the first place.

If there's a telling divide in the economic culture of the late 20th century and early 21st, it isn't between rich and poor, capitalism and communism, but between Wal-Mart and places like the Northern Hardware. Wal-Mart and other remotely based commercial merchandising corporations have turned life into serial shopping experiences through which individuals make successive choices between commodities that are an end in themselves. The Northern Hardware leaves human beings within the Lockean universe, where one's consumer choices are secondary to other choices about what is valuable: you obtain things so you can live, instead of living to consume products.

The block immediately west of the Northern Hardware seems to be the current ground zero of the downtown's decay. S. S. Kresge's is empty, gone the way of the smaller McLeods and Woolworth stores it defeated in the local marketplace a decade ago. A few doors west of the Kresge building, two clothes boutiques are having a sidewalk sale no one is taking the slightest interest in. The proprietors are doing their best to hide the fact that they're holding a bankruptcy sale, but no one is fooled. Just beyond those stores we stumble onto the closing-out sale at Wendt and Phillips.

At the time I left town in the mid-1960s, Wendt and Phillips was still called Patterson's Men's Wear and was run by Neil Patterson, the plane-crash–prone son of the city's long-time mayor, A. M. Patterson. Back then, the store was on the same block that houses the now-closed Royal Bank, and I was a recent ex-employee of Neil's, having worked in the store part-time for a couple of years at the end of high school. The business moved two blocks up the street around 1970, after Neil sold it to two recently arrived young Turks from the coast. One of the them, Dave Close, is sitting with his feet propped up on an empty display fixture when Barry and I enter. He's not so young any more, and the Turk is long tamed.

All that's left for sale in his store are some fixtures, a few dozen pastel-coloured tuxedos, wide-lapelled, bell-bottom trousered relics from the bad taste of the 1970s in shades of pale blue, green, and purple. On one of the other display cases are 10 or 15 pairs of equally out-of-fashion tuxedo shoes in white imitation patent leather that is old enough to reveal itself as cracked white plastic.

As soon as we're inside, I wish we hadn't come in at all, but Barry doesn't seem shy and begins to chat up Close. I've met Dave Close before, in better days. He'd struck me as a proud man: proud of being a respected businessman, proud that he was bringing a better grade of men's clothing to the city as he phased out the lines of work clothes that had been Neil Patterson's bread-and-butter. Close had a progressive eye for men's fashion then, despite the pastel tuxedos he's left with, and I'd made a point of dropping a few bucks in the store whenever I was in town.

Dave remembers me, sort of, because he starts into a story about Neil and one of his float plane crashes. But the conversation flags after we're done with the reminiscences. That's when I glimpse the pain in his eyes. It occurs to me that he's humiliated that I'm here to witness the end of his working life.

"How come this happened to you?" I ask, trying to make it clear that I see him as a victim of circumstances and not a failure.

Close's eyes sweep the empty store, as if he's considering the physical implications of where he is and what's happened to him for the first time. "The street died," he says. "And no one did anything about it. There was a chance about 10 years ago, but City Council wouldn't bite the bullet and the businesses weren't willing to shell out any cash of their own. The shopping centres already had City Council in their pockets, I think. Now there's Costco and the other big-boxes . . ."

"This time," Barry says, "even the Northern is vulnerable."

Close shrugs. "Yeah," he says. "Ain't that a shame."

I can't tell whether he's being ironic or not. "What are you going to do after this?" I ask.

Another shrug. "I'm going to wait around here for the bank to call me," he answers, sounding bitter for the first time. "The foreclosure papers are supposed to be ready by three. When those arrive, I'll lock her down and it's over."

I glance at my watch: it's 2:30.

"What about this new downtown renewal plan I've been hearing about?" I ask after a respectful silence.

"It's nice enough. It makes all the right gestures. But it's too late. The retail base outside the downtown is bigger and a lot more powerful than what's left here, and bringing this"—Close gestures at the empty streets outside the window—"back to life is against *their* economic interests. So . . ."

Outside again, the desolation feels more oppressive. I've just seen the cold abstraction of "failed investment" clothed in human flesh, and that transforms it into failed livelihoods, defeated aspirations, financial and social humiliation.

"Dave Close didn't do anything wrong," Barry says. "He ran a good shop here for a lot of years, and he played by the rules. He just landed in the wrong place at the wrong time, and he didn't see it coming until it was too late. A lot of people in this town are in the same position."

We stand on the corner of Third Avenue and Victoria Street for a few minutes to catalogue the failed businesses we've seen, then cross the street to have a late lunch in a deli constructed from the back end of the old Woolworth. Inside, I discover that among the deli's amenities is the perfectly preserved  and spotless 1950s washroom from the Woolworth store, complete with a bank of green-tiled urinals.

"I'll bet," I say to Barry, as we dig into the cranberry-carrot muffins and coffee we've ordered, "that there are more washrooms than buying customers downtown this afternoon."

Barry grimaces. "You'd win that bet easy," he says.

We walk back the way we came, stopping in at the Northern Hardware to see if Peggy Neilsen is around and, if so, what she can tell me about Butch. She isn't working today, so we return to the thrift shop, retrieve our purchases, and walk home. All that's left to do before dinner is pick up the stuffed pork chops at the butcher shop on First Avenue.

"We'll drive down," Barry says, even though we're only a few blocks away. "The truckers run over any pedestrians they catch walking that stretch."

My brain is too crammed for me to even wonder whether he's speaking literally. In a few hours I'll conclude that properly stuffed local pork chops aren't worth risking life and limb for, but with a decent bottle of wine and Barry and Joy's company, they're enough to ward off jet lag.

30

The next day Barry and I get down to some serious shopping. It isn't exactly the spiritual approach, but Barry's into it, and it's what people do here even when they don't have money to spend. That makes it the most efficient way of finding out what people in Prince George are up to, this side of stopping cars on the bypass to conduct a survey.

Barry has a cleaner-than-usual motive for wanting to shop. He's building a library for his writing school in Tumbler Ridge, and he wants to cruise the thrift and junk shops. If nothing else, Tumbler Ridge has allowed him to resume his book collecting, something Joy put the brakes on years ago because their house was, in her terms, "too full of bloody books."

We start downtown, where he says the best shops are. We've barely parked the van before he zooms into one of the thrift shops—the best one, he says—and within 30 seconds uncovers a cloth-bound edition of *The Divine Comedy* illustrated by Gustave Doré. Though not a fine edition and not in fine condition, it would cost him $25 in any antiquarian bookstore I've ever been in. Barry gets it for 25 cents, along with a half-dozen other books of lesser but substantial value— total cost: $1.75. I'd like the Doré-illustrated Dante for my daughter, but Barry isn't about to give it up. I leave him to the book piles and wander over to the clothing section, where I pick out a nylon windbreaker I can use for the trip into the Bowron. It's a discarded size-large club jacket, royal blue, from a local swim club named the Prince George Barracudas, with the name "Jennifer" on one arm and "Mr. G." on the other. I cheerfully hand over $4 to the elderly but bright-eyed woman at the cash register. Barry settles up his purchases, and because the staff know him they offer to let us stow our things under the counter while we continue shopping. The jacket is spacious even for a large, and it's several days before I find out that "Mr. G" is a convenience store chain—and that the jacket was discarded by a very large swimmer named Jennifer.

"Never know what you'll find these days," Barry says cheerfully, as we wander up to the next stop. There are, he says, almost as many of these stores outside the downtown as in it. The phenomenon—and that's what it is—seems hard to account for, until Barry and I do the math together: 1) This is a town with a falling population and long-term high unemployment that was once seasonal but is now structural; 2) The unemployed here aren't young and/or untrained minimum-wagers who can leave town or live in their parents' basement when they crash. They're from the high-wage industrial sector, long-time loggers mostly, or those associated with the industry. Some are leaving, but many more are merely trying to hold on, cascading down-market as consumers, and jettisoning the property they've accumulated as they descend.

The way those people have lived here used to translate into carports bulging with recreational devices and living spaces similarly festooned with soon-to-be-obsolete electronics and cheap furniture. As a consequence, inexpensive ghetto-blasters and Walkmans clutter the thrift shops, 486 computers and VGA monitors fill the pawnshops, rows of worn-out Ski-Doos and ATVs litter the service station lots and RV yards.

We talk about this devolution on the way to our second round of shopping, Costco. Along with the other big-box retail outlets, it's located on the highway to Vanderhoof. Beyond Costco, the giant foot-in-the-door that arrived in the early 1990s, there's the Great Canadian Superstore, an about-to-open Future Shop, and several furniture chain stores.

The Prince George Costco is identical to the hundreds of other Costco outlets across North America. It is a cavernous Butler building with 10-metre ceilings and rows of gigantic metal utility shelves that hold merchandise pallet-stacked far above your head—to give you, I suppose, the illusion of infinite product. The concept claim is that it is merchandise at wholesale prices, for which customers pay a membership fee of between $40 and $50 annually. But if you strip away the dodge and bullshit, this is bag-your-own volume-discount merchandise, in which the savings come as much from not providing service and keeping employee overheads to a minimum as from volume buying. The store sells a variety of basic products, like quantity-packaged disposal diapers and mega-bags and -boxes of life semi-necessities like bottled water, potato chips, Cheezies, and Froot Loops. Most of the time the prices are cheaper than elsewhere, but not always. Except for the optical and photo departments, the only time you see live help is when you stop for a food sample at one of the dozen or so product demonstrators, and at the checkout, which is where they put their surliest employees.

Barry tells me, and I've heard this elsewhere, that the Prince George Costco has the highest ratio of floor space to volume sales in the chain. It's one of those factoids of civic pride similar to the claim, in the 1950s, that Prince George had the highest per capita birth rate of any city over 10,000 people outside of Bombay, India. The Costco claim is a proof-of-vulgarity and almost as certainly untrue as the birth-rate claim was—the informational equivalent of an urban myth.

We cruise the aisles together for nearly an hour, doing what everyone else does once they're inside the doors and thus inside Costco's artificial reality: we convince ourselves to buy things that we find temporarily attractive by telling ourselves they're necessary, and very cheap. How did we live without them before this moment?

I purchase a pair of jeans I don't need, and a pound of pine nuts I need even less but which are half the normal price per pound. Barry discovers some colour-illustrated naturalist manuals recently published by an obscure B.C. publisher. There's one for native flowers and scrubs, another for resident trees, a third for mammals, and another for birds. It doesn't occur to either of us until we're out the door that our Costco deep discounts likely deprived the publisher of any profits, and that the margin on the five manuals bought between us will be whisked outside the province and country to wherever Costco's big shareholders clip their coupons—just like the profits from cutting the Bowron.

No matter. We played the game, and were played by Costco's merchandising system. We got some things at good value and came out feeling like accomplished bargain hunters and—because we're intellectuals—like we've pushed the world a few steps closer to the boundary of, let's see, a condition where intellectuals will matter even less than they do today.

We've got a few minutes to kill before we're to meet Joy for lunch at a deli downtown, so we cruise the boutiques along Fourth Avenue that are supposed to be the jewel of the Downtown Renewal Proposals, the lungs of its mercantile future. We don't buy anything because the minivan is already full of our Costco bargains.

The deli is a decently clean little place with about 10 tables, the weekday hangout for Joy and her fellow Employment Insurance counsellors. I get the impression Barry and Joy both eat here often, and the lunch-bucket serial intrigues that are part of this are sort of charming as far as I can follow them. The café owner and cook, like Barry, is a part-time musician, so the two of them discuss the behaviour of a third musician they're suspicious is trying to screw each of them. Because they're both sensible men, they're forced to conclude that musician number three is probably just looking out for number one, and thus, no offence. They make this judgment quickly and without bitterness, and as they do, I recognize that they're, well, just shooting the breeze.

Joy's sense of social nuances has always been more direct than Barry's. To her, people are either assholes—her term, not mine—or they're not. Since she lives in a small town, she has to put up with everyone, whatever their designation, and once she's judged someone an asshole, she doesn't seem to have any particular stake in cementing them there. Over lunch, she and one of her colleagues—a slim, short-haired woman in her forties whose features track between vulnerable and hard, one sentence to the next—discuss the antics of the official office jerk. But they're more interested in thinking up ways to manipulate him into behaving like a decent human being ought to, a notion which, like those of "jerk" or "asshole," they define on a purely situational basis. I get the sense from both of them that if the office jerk were to lighten up and buy the right RV for his family, they'd think well of him.

It's hard not to admire Joy's non-judgmental attitude toward the office jerk. Her usual sense of how things are and what people are about is more axe-to-the-neck, but today she's generous to a fault. After her colleague leaves, Joy mentions that the woman's son isn't, as she puts it, exactly the Easter Bunny. He's been in and out of jail, and in and out of several psychiatric institutions. So have other members of the woman's immediate family, she adds with a shrug. They're a family that regularly self-destructs, usually taking along some major piece of technology or property to cushion the fall.

After lunch, Barry and I drive Joy back to the house—she has the afternoon off—and head out to the Pine Centre to buy a tape recorder. A few weeks earlier in Toronto, I'd purchased an expensive digital machine so I could record interviews in Prince George and be able to transcribe them on my laptop on the plane home. The salesperson assured me that digital is the wave of future recording, and I fell for it. The gizmo, a shiny silver Samsung about the size of a disposable cigarette lighter, promised both improved sound quality and the equivalent of five hours' tape capacity. It even came with a software CD that would allow me to use any computer as a transcribing machine.

I should have been paying closer attention. The recorder turned out to be yet another technological advance put onto the market before its time. Sure, I can download the interviews into my laptop. I can even listen to them—but only the way I can listen to a music file on a computer: from start to finish. When I phoned Samsung so see if I could return the recorder for a refund, a technician told me the software needed to allow a machine of this price to rewind and fast-forward within an MPG file is years away, and, anyway, why would I want to do any of this in the first place? His advice, if I insisted on meddling with what I'd recorded, was to make a line transfer of the digital recording to a conventional tape system. Or I could hold my breath. No refund.

Barry and I agree that the Pine Centre is the place to check out the relative cost of conventional tape recorders, because it has both a Sony store and a RadioShack. For him, it's a kill-two-birds-with-one-stone sort of trip. There's a nest of second-hand stores nearby.

"The other thing, you know, is that half the stores still open up there are featuring sales," Barry says, then laughs. "Pre-close-out Sales, I figure, but they're not admitting that."

The Pine Centre is fine by me. I can stop in at China Bob's and talk to Jack Butcher, and I can test the general flavour of the place—which means the mix of franchise outlets and how it has suffered since the prestige retail focus shifted to the rebuilt Parkwood Centre closer to downtown, and to the big-boxes out on the highways.

We park and enter through Sears, which is deserted and doesn't have anything other than vacuum cleaners on sale. That sets Barry to window-shopping for something better, and I have to drag him to

China Bob's. There's no sign of Jack, but I go in anyway, and ask the cashier if Jack has been in today.

That gets me a disapproving stare.

"Mr. Butcher hasn't been around for over a year," she says. "If you want to talk to the manager, he's in the back."

I don't. Barry and I retreat, ambling along the storefronts toward the Sony store. The mall is in trouble, although aside from the several empty units, it is hard to pinpoint how. Then it comes to me: the colours of the merchandise in the windows, and the signage. The dominant colours are bright, hot pink, royal blue, electric shades of purple, teal, and orange. The signage has a similar palate, screaming of "Giant Reductions" that aren't giant, and "Deep Discounts" that rarely get above 20 percent. It isn't quite the bankruptcy sales—covert or open—we found downtown. Instead, the sale merchandise here is slightly out-of-fashion or out-of-season, and every store conveys a sense that whatever sales they make are based on deceiving customers about what they're getting for their money. Pine Centre is turning into a discount mall. The prestige retailers that were present a decade ago are gone, and the ones that ought to be replacing them aren't coming to Prince George. There's no Gap, no Harry Rosen, no French Connection here, and they're not locating elsewhere in town. That constitutes something of a broken promise.

The promise? Once the "enhanced democracy" lie of the Global Village was recognized as a cruel joke, it seemed at least reasonable to expect that the corporations would bring consumer democracy—equal retail shopping opportunities—that would make whatever was in New York or Toronto available to people everywhere. Towns like Prince George are proof that this was another cruel joke. Toronto and Vancouver get Banana Republic and Holt Renfrew. Out here at the margins it is Zellers, BiWay, Wal-Mart—or fly to Vancouver and shop there.

At least there's still a Sony store. Yet even here, the moment we walk in the door and explain what we want, it starts to screw up. The lone sales clerk is one of Barry's ex-students, and he does a hard sell on a tape recorder that's $50 more than I want to pay and has special features that aren't special, like stereo playback and voice activation, the latter of which merely annoys me when he explains how it works.

When he sees me backing away, the salesman shifts his ground and tries to sell me a television set.

"Sell him one of those flat-panel jobs," Barry advises his ex-student. "He can take it back to Toronto in his suitcase."

I tell the sales clerk I'd like to think about his voice-activated stereo model, and Barry and I leave.

RadioShack is better. Unlike the Sony store, which was empty of customers until we arrived, it is bubbling with activity. One of the two sales clerks is another ex-student, but judging from the way he and Barry exchange greetings, this one was a bigger star than the one at Sony. At the counter an overweight woman in her early twenties is trying to decide whether she wants her defective telephone-answering machine repaired or exchanged. When she isn't changing her mind about what to do, she's changing her story about where the answering machine came from. First it's a gift, then it's a pickup at a garage sale. The consistent point is, no, she doesn't have a sales slip for it. Barry's student confides that this is the fifth time she's been in with the machine.

"If it's a gift," he says, "she must have gotten it for her twelfth birthday, because we haven't carried that model for at least 10 years. And she's got enough 'bombers' in her system that the last thing she probably remembers clearly is her twelfth birthday."

He's joking about her, but no one is laughing to her face, and, more interesting, no one is suggesting that her quandary isn't real to her. The sales clerk at the desk explains, patiently and not for the first time, that they can't send the machine in for repair without a sales slip, because the sales slip constitutes the warrantee. Maybe she can look around and find that, and *then* they can get it fixed for her. This renews her confusion about where she got it in the first place, and the rigamarole begins again.

I ask Barry's student what he's got in tape recorders. He shows me two models, one of them a RadioShack model, the other an Acme brand that's $20 cheaper but slightly larger. It's $60 cheaper than its Sony equivalent.

"Listen," he says. "Between you and me, the cheaper machine has a better mechanism. More reliable. So save your bucks. It isn't as if you're buying a rocket ship. This'll do everything you want."

With that out of the way, Barry questions him about the state of things in the mall.

"We're doing okay," he says. "But that's because of what we're selling. Everybody wants electronics, and our prices are decent. A lot of other stores are in big trouble. Costco is kicking the shit out of this place."

"What about Wal-Mart?" I ask. "What's that going to do?"

The other clerk appears to have convinced the young woman with the answering machine to go home and look for her sales slip, and he joins us.

"Wal-Mart won't make any difference here," he says. "The quality of the crap they've got in these stores is too poor to compete with the crap Wal-Mart will be flogging. And anyway, Wal-Mart's here to kill the Northern, not this mall. Everybody knows that."

I take the cheaper of the two tape recorders, on which they give me a further $10 discount because it's the floor model and the last one they've got. I haven't asked for the discount. They give it to me because it's good business, part of their professional pride—or maybe because the clerk is Barry's ex-student. We stay on for another 10 minutes. Both clerks are well informed about local and provincial politics. They're not happy with the state of affairs, but they're not ready to whine, either.

"Prince George is going to get it in the ear over the next few years," one of them says as we're about to leave. "But, shit, you know, this place has it coming. A lot of people here made bad decisions. And they didn't have the backbone to stand up against the bad decisions other people were making for them."

"What can you guys do about it?" Barry says.

"Well," one of them says, "we just sell as many tape recorders as we can and hope the store doesn't close. When you're getting screwed, it's usually a good idea to act like you're having fun until you can think up some way to stop it."

He stops to consider that for a second, and then continues. "The thing about all this globalization we're hearing so much about is that it really isn't about us. It's about rich guys in big cities making so much money it'd make our heads spin. But it isn't malicious, you know. Those guys don't give a shit about people like us, one way or another. To the guys making the world happen, we're invisible."

31

Barry and I spend the afternoon cruising the out-of-downtown thrift stores for books. There are bargains to be had, but nothing matches the Dante-Doré find. I have to remind myself that this *isn't* the everyday reality that occupies Barry. I've taken him away from his routines, and what he's showing me is a worrisome part of living in Prince George, one that alternately attracts and depresses him. He's addicted to the bargains, but understands a little too much about the conditions that create them to take them at face value.

We make a side trip to a music store whose proprietor scouts drum sets for him. It's a very good store, with a range of new and used instruments that rivals those of shops in Toronto and Vancouver. The proprietor, Mark, is another of Barry's ex-students, but like the others, he doesn't talk about the college. He shows Barry the repairs he made to a stereo Barry traded in for some drums, and half-heartedly tries to sell it back to him. When he follows us outside as we're leaving, we get into a complicated discussion of the oversized sign he's just installed. It's a 3-metre tall guitar outlined in red neon, and he's proud of it. He knows the sign doesn't make economic sense, but he damned well likes the thing.

"Why not?" he says. "The town needs more interesting landmarks, and the government isn't building any. Someday, people will appreciate this—if some drunk-ass yoyo doesn't take a sledgehammer to it to impress his buddies."

While we're standing there, a young, wrecked-looking 20-year-old from the transmission shop next door wanders out to chat with us. I know this kid—not personally, but historically. The Styrofoam cup he's holding is shaking a little, not quite enough to spill the coffee but enough to make an adventure out of drinking it.

"What's with you?" Mark asks.

"Out last night," he says.

Barry laughs, knowing what's coming. "What's the story?"

"I wish I knew," answers the kid. "All I remember is the two strippers and the two bottles of tequila."

He remembers more than that, but he's teasing us. It doesn't matter that Barry and I are strangers: an audience is an audience. It probably isn't going to be all tall tale, either, and that gets the three of us, in different ways, on his hook. Under the stubble and the bleary eyes, he's fit and good-looking, and he's as big as a house—about six foot five. He also knows how to string out a story. It's pretty basic stuff: he closed the bar, he picked up the stripper, they went to her place with the two bottles of tequila, and there was her roommate, also a stripper. He leaves the juicy details for us to imagine. What's attractive about this kid is that he has no malice in him toward anyone. He's 21, and life is a comedy he'll play until he can't, or until more serious things intervene.

"Aw, we could have done all that," Mark says when he's done.

"I couldn't have," Barry says. "I'd have puked inside my jacket by midnight."

I don't think I'd have gotten that far, but I don't say so.

We ransack another thrift store on the way home, a huge one that occupies a former supermarket building. I buy two T-shirts, a black one from the Rotary Club of Mombasa and a green one from the Two Rivers Canoe Club. Then we cross to the supermarket, which has been rebuilt across the street, and shop for dinner, which I'm supposed to cook. We arrive back at the house with six full plastic bags. Only one of them contains groceries.

———

After the dinner dishes are done, I call John Harris. Viv answers, and reminds me that they're leaving Friday night for the Stikine. This time, she says, she's going in with two others, but John, with his bad knee, is staying at the base camp.

"What's he going to do? Twiddle his thumbs and chat up the grizzlies?"

Viv laughs. "No," she says. "He'll read books, do some writing, and keep the vandals from looting the truck. Or burning it because they're too lazy to make a campfire."

I'd like to see them before they go, but Viv makes it clear how busy they are. They need to pack. "That," she says in a voice that implies that she thinks I want to sit on her knee and distract her, "takes more concentration than you can imagine. If we make a mistake . . ."

I get the point, and without offence because none is intended. She reiterates that the offer of accommodations is for real. They *want* me to stay there while they're gone.

"So long as the lights are going on and off," she says, "we won't get B&E-ed. You'd be doing us a favour."

I tell her I'll stay there the last four days I'm in town, if that's okay. For the morning light, I say, but her laugh tells me she thinks it's because I want to get out from between Barry and Joy. It's a little of both, I guess. Barry and Joy are leaving for Calgary on Wednesday morning, so they'll be anxious to clean up the house and pack—and happy to be rid of me.

Viv explains how to work their complicated alarm system, John comes on the line for a moment, but he doesn't have much to say other than that he'll put the key in the mailbox and that he hasn't made much progress on the next book.

With that out of the way, I fiddle with the questions I'm going to ask Paul Strickland and Bill Walsh tomorrow, prep the new tape recorder, then join Barry and Joy around the backyard fire. Joy and I drink wine, Barry sips the near-beer he's recently switched over to. Just about the time we're running out of things to talk about, the overcast that settled in around mid-afternoon lifts, and the light I came here to see materializes. It's 9:45 p.m., after dark in Toronto, but instead of fading, this light begins to gain depth, infusing the trees around us with gold, as if a thin rain of honey were coating the leaves. The honey, with exquisite slowness, trickles upward leaf by leaf, branch by branch. It reaches the top of the 2.5-metre fence behind us, then lifts onto the roof of the house next door.

"Let's drive down to the river," I say to Barry.

He nods. "Bring your camera. It'll be beautiful this time of day."

Joy joins us, and the three of us climb into their van as if we're teenagers off to bomb the drag—them in the front, me in the back leaning over the seat. As we drive off, I go into a weird sort of time warp, remembering the jumbled sense of anticipation and joy at being alive, going somewhere exotic, seeing something unique. The part of me that is still 19, or 12, or 5 years old has reawakened to this extreme light. I'm no more articulate to its beauty than I was at those ages, but now I'm conscious that it is part and parcel of being at home, and that doubles the thrill.

We drive to the river through the elm-lined streets in a luminous green-to-gold chiaroscuro. To Barry and Joy this light is common stuff the way the aurora borealis is: occasionally present, not always noted. But tonight they get caught up in my pleasure and go with it, part witnesses, part proprietors.

When we arrive at the river, our pleasure recedes for a moment because we have to park and walk: the local traffic-control dwarves have been up to their malicious tricks, sinking wood posts into the roadway to block off the riverbank.

"Another teenager must have driven his father's car into the river," Barry says. "You used to be able to drive straight through."

"In the old days," I say, "at least the kids drove their parents' cars off the cutbanks."

"Just be thankful they didn't put a suicide-prevention screen along here," Joy says. "I hear they're putting one on the Bloor Street Viaduct in Toronto because some schoolkid jumped off."

"A lot of people jump off the Viaduct," I say, and relate a recent incident in which a despondent writer leaped from the railing, landed in some soft mud and had to crawl back up with nothing more than a sprained ankle and a renewed sense of his own futility. He was dragged off before he could try again.

This gets a deep laugh from Barry. "What do you do for an encore after that?" he asks.

We amble along the edge of the Fraser River this way, discussing the best way for a writer to suicide. Barry suggests stabbing oneself in the heart with a fountain pen. I peer over the banks and find them little changed. High up, swallows are nesting where the bank is clay, and further down there's the usual debris, pop and beer cans, candy wrappers. Someone has dumped a broken toilet tank, and it rests a foot above the water level, half-filled with junk. Then there's the river eddying past, already murky with silt from the Fraser now that the Nechako's blue flow is a trickle.

"You know," I tell Barry, "when I was a kid there was a line out near the middle of the river that you could see a kilometre downstream from here."

He shrugs, not interested. "Before my time. All I've ever seen is river silt and sewage mixed with effluent from the pulp mills."

Across the river, the light burnishes the gravel cutbanks, turning the dark spruce trees along the top edge a brilliant green. Where we are, on the north bank, the air is empty, getting chilly, and darkening. On the far bank, the air remains visible, so enriched with light that it is as tangible as the landscape it illuminates.

On the rail tracks sit a half-dozen lumber cars loaded with big, straight spruce logs.

"Still importing our best logs out of here?" I ask Barry.

"I guess so," he says. "There was talk of stopping it a few years back, but then the World Trade Organization bureaucrats or the Americans put a gun in Ottawa's ear, and that was the end of that. So the Americans get to tax us any way they want, but Canada has to play by the rules. Same old shit as always—Prince George gets screwed. The trouble with living this far north is that you never get to see the guys who are doing the screwing."

We talk half-heartedly about whether the true government of Prince George is Canadian Forest Products, the wTo, or the U.S. Government. In between, I snap photographs. After a few moments we just stand and watch the light climb the cutbanks across the river as the sun sinks toward the hilltops west of town. When the light clears the spruce trees and all that's left is a slight luminescence in the air, we drive back to the house, the gracious elms arching over our heads in the deepening gloom. Barry and I restoke the fire and sit until the dew begins to fall, and it is night. It is past 11:30 p.m. before the sky is completely dark. And then?

Then there are stars.

32

This is what I see from here.

Whether we call it the New World Order, globalization, the Global Village, or the Triumph of Capitalism, the results look very different to people in places like Prince George than they do to international bankers or corporate CEOs in their big-city offices. "It" has a foot on the neck of places like Prince George, robbing individuals and communities of competence and confidence by making it impossible for them to control their own destiny. For that lost sense of self and community integrity, people here got an avalanche of entertainment opportunities and a generalized  incitement to believe that technological innovation and ruthless fiscal aggression will be rewarded by wealth and achievement—just like everywhere else. But here, the local trickle-downs, beyond bigger and better television sets and a few people who make a fiscal killing and get out, are drying up.

The truer constants over the past 35 years have been the economic agglomerations and mergers that make the levers of control progressively more remote, and a factionalization of social life that is tolerated and even promoted so long as it has no effect on the flow of financial capital. Life is easier if all you want is to sit at home and watch television, and it is better if your idea of fun is driving a four-by-four deep into the bush so you can shoot up anything that moves. But people don't seem to like one another as much as they once did, and the certainty of mutual help that was once among the deepest securities of living close to the wilderness is no longer something to count on. Life on the frontier is becoming life on the stagnant edge of nothingness.

Hard work and concentration no longer get people where they want to be. You need to get lucky, or, more exactly, you need a gimmick and a tax loophole. A market may shift on the New York Stock Exchange, and you're out of a job or you're bankrupt; a tariff ruling a continent away, designed to steer an equally remote-from-you government to or from some policy that has no natural local consequence one way or another, suddenly lands on your balance sheet. One corporation buys up a competitor and loads itself with so much debt that it can be kept afloat only by cutting staff in your locally-profitable-and-efficient corner of the operation. At any moment your livelihood can evaporate, obliterating the value of your assets. Since the future is now permanently opaque, everyone learns to live with a six-month horizon, at the end of which a whole different fiscal jamboree might begin, as arbitrary and ridden by crises and threats as the last.

Your children's teachers, meanwhile, are teaching them that nothing matters except having a nice day, one that must be without insult to their artificial identities and dignities. Your health professionals—too many to count even though you can't seem to get an appointment with any of them—try to ensure all are safe from health and legal hazards you've lived with all your life, and which you thought were to be overcome by common sense and caution. The regulations—as thick and dense as the trees used to be hereabouts, and impossible to penetrate without a lawyer or to get around with self-reliance and enterprise—prevent your kids from investigating the world or physically manipulating their surroundings with anything more complex than soft plastic approximations of the tools by which human beings build skills. They're kept safe and self-involved until they're physical and moral idiots, their range of empathy as narrow as a 17th-century preacher's, and their curiosity comatose or permanently disabled.

That summary of what's behind the things I've seen the past few days buzzes noisily through my head as I walk downtown to meet Paul Strickland at 10:00 in the morning. I've got a list of questions to ask him, along with the slightly malicious intention of reversing our normal conversation pattern: I'm going to ask *my* questions and then deadpan him the way he's done with me in the past.

We're meeting at a place with the impossible-to-remember name of *Javva Mugga Mocha*, a 10-year-old locally based Starbucks wannabe.

I'm early, so I traverse the tiled plaza of the Court House before going in. And of course, Paul's already there, sitting in a corner near the window wearing an Inspector Maigret tartan fedora and a navy windbreaker.

I wave hello, and he leaps to his feet. "Oh, hi, Brian," he says, as if he's surprised I bothered to show up. During our first meetings years ago he was so unsure of himself he called me "Mr. Fawcett." I had to tell him repeatedly to stop before he'd say my first name. Today he's more sure of me, if not of anything else. He helps me get a cup of coffee—it's a hangout of his, I think, but he doesn't say so—and we repair to his corner table. I unpack my new tape recorder while I relate the story of the digital machine—he's already got me doing the talking, I note—and pull out the pad on which I've written my questions. By the time I'm ready, he's looking quite anxious, but he hasn't uttered word.

Behind him is a glass partition, and inside it are the smokers, even here cordoned off from "normal" people. I gesture at the partition, and Paul smiles.

"Yes," he says. "That's been there for a few years now. At first people complained, but they're getting used to it. Would you prefer to go in there so you can smoke?"

"I quit four years ago," I said. "Pregnant wife, and then little daughter. I'm surprised the local safety busybodies didn't realize they were setting up clean-air zones with those partitions."

Paul looks puzzled. "I'm not sure what you mean."

"Pulp mills. The air in there is cleaner than outdoors."

He parses the joke and chuckles politely. "I don't think they care," he says. "Ottawa and the Canadian Medical Association seem to have decided that Canadians shouldn't smoke, and, as usual, they're not very interested in what Prince George thinks."

"So," I say, underlining my first question with my pen. "What are you thinking about these days? What are the big issues in Prince George right now? I mean, in your professional view."

Paul hesitates, uncomfortable about having to express his opinion even though he's agreed to. "I think that having Canfor control most of the forests might turn out to be a problem," he says.

"You mean, because it makes it a one-corporation town?"

"Yes. That could be a problem because they'll respond to an issue in a singular way, and there'll be no serious alternative. So far it hasn't happened, because Peter Bentley is quite sensitive to local issues."

"Bentley is the Canfor CEO?"

"He's the president, I believe. The CEO is a man named David Emerson, recently hired. Bentley has been very active at the university, and has spent a lot of money there. That'll have an influence on the way that place handles forestry-related issues. There may be dangers involved that haven't really shown up yet."

"Who owns Canfor?"

"It's a B.C. company," Paul says, evidently alarmed at the direction in which I'm heading. "But it's a corporation, and . . . I've been on the education beat for a while now, and I'm not on top of what's happening on other beats, so I may not have my facts all straight on this."

"What are the other issues, then?"

"Crime," he says. "Mainly with drugs and young kids. There's a very high suicide rate here, and nobody knows quite how to handle it. I suppose there are teen gangs and drugs in Toronto as well. But here there's the added problem of police instability. The RCMP seems to move its officers in and out of the local detachment before they can learn the situation sufficiently to respond in sensitive ways. There's also a problem with street people vandalizing the downtown storefronts and generally making it unpleasant for pedestrians. And, of course, people blame what they can see. . . ."

When I don't respond, he continues. "There's also a problem with doctors leaving. I believe that made the national news, so you'll know about it. The regional hospital is understaffed in both doctors and nurses. It's been suggested that they burn out from overwork and from a certain lack of support. No one seems to know how to solve the problem."

"That's everywhere with the cutbacks in medicare," I say. "But I guess here it's biting everyone's ass instead of merely being an irritant."

"That's one way of putting it," he concedes. "It does appear to be a special problem in Prince George."

"What about downtown?" I ask. "How are people responding to this latest initiative to bring it back to life?"

This gets a frown. "It's a mixed issue, and people are reacting according to their own interest. Some want it to go ahead, others don't. Even those who support it are reluctant to put up local money. I think they see downtown as a lost cause. And then there's Wal-Mart wanting to come in, and that venture has people on both sides. A lot of people just want the bargains they'll get at Wal-Mart."

"Even if it kills the Northern?"

"That would be a bad thing for the entire area, of course, but politically, the operators of the shopping centres and the big-box stores seem to have more influence. Maybe. It's hard to know . . . Another problem I'm perhaps more familiar with is the problem with population decline. There's been a decline in school enrolment. I think this year, there were 400 fewer students in the district, which is a first. Some of the overall population decline is offset by the fact that empty-nesters aren't leaving any more. They're staying on because it's cheaper to live here than in the Okanagan."

"Having people stay when they retire should be a good thing," I say. "One of the problems Prince George has always had is that people leave after their peak earning years, and take all their capital out of the community. They also deprive the community of an important social dimension."

I'm talking like a sociologist, and it's throwing Paul off his focus. "I think many of them would leave if they could. There haven't been many resources for those people in the past because the city didn't need them. The old people who've traditionally stayed on weren't the kind that go to community drop-ins and play checkers."

"You mean the Coffee Klatch guys?"

"Yes," he says. "They'd have been more typical until recently. I think."

"How's the unemployment? Where does that stand?"

"Oh, yes, that's a concern. Officially it's at about 16 percent, I think."

"What is it really? We both know that people just give up looking for work after a while, and either make their living in the grey economy or go on welfare. It *feels* like it's around 25 percent. Or higher."

"That might be closer to the truth," he says. "But of course I can't confirm it, and no one wants to think about it being at that level.

There are more people on the street than there used to be, but they're hard to count, and they tend to get mixed in with the Native community in a lot of people's minds. So it's a difficult issue to come to grips with. . . ."

He peters out, instinctively not wanting to stick his neck out because he's a good journalist, and comfortable only with facts that can be corroborated. I remind myself that Paul isn't like most people here. He is, in fact, pretty much their contrary. If globalization has robbed locals of their competence and replaced it with phony entrepreneurial zeal and a faith in big corporations that don't give a shit about them, Paul has been robbed of his confidence in his own perceptions by years of having to be more cautious in his judgments than it is sane to be.

"How are things at the paper?" I ask.

"Things have improved," he says, and then grimaces. "They're more settled than they were, anyway. Some good people are in editorial now, and the contractions seem to be over for the time being."

I don't want to torture him over this, because he's famously discreet about his personal life. And anyway, I've been tracking the changes in Canadian newspapers on my own for years. The *Citizen*, once privately owned, has gone through a series of ownership shifts, each one involving a bigger corporation, each one more bottom-lining than the last. Since the late 1960s, the *Citizen* had been part of the Southam chain, which was swallowed in the mid-1990s by Conrad Black's Hollinger chain. But when Black sold his empire to CanWest Global and the Asper family in the summer of 2000, he kept—or CanWest didn't want—the Hollinger daily and weekly papers it held in the B.C. Interior. That's set people to speculating over why, and most of the theories I've heard are goofy: no Easterner like a Winnipeg Easterner; the Aspers figure the B.C. Interior will be turned into American water reservoirs; it's something to do with all the Reform and Canadian Alliance zealots here; or, why buy anything here when most of the trees are gone and the economy is dead. No one has a serious clue why the sale went down as it did, and that creates a small undertow of anxiety: Maybe they know something we don't. . . .

I've gone through a week of recent *Citizen*s since I've been here, and compared with five years ago, the paper *is* a little better. Instead of front-to-back wire stories, there is more local coverage. It does a better job with local sports, entertainment, and street-side issues —who bashed whom last night with a baseball bat, whose car was torched by vandals, and that sort of thing. Issue analysis has declined, probably because the reporting staff is so busy scrambling around covering daily events that there's no time or energy to do in-depth reporting. About a year ago, the paper's bean-counters forced out Ken Bernsohn, who'd long been among the few fair-minded analysts of the forest industry in the province, and the only qualified one in the Prince George area. Serious analysis has been left, by default, to the independent biweekly newspaper, the *Free Press*. Paul doesn't confirm any of this because he can't, except to note that Bernsohn's departure was a loss to the paper, and I don't need him to elaborate on that. Yet, without saying so, he conveys a sense that working for a small daily isn't much fun.

"Have you translated any more poetry?" I ask, naming several South American and Spanish poets he's admired and has translated in the past.

He has, but not much. The job keeps him very busy. He corrects me on the names of the poets he's translated, but he does so gently and without taking offence. Paul's idea of taking offence when you say something he's not comfortable with is to take his eyes off you. He doesn't do that here. I begin to pack up the tape recorder and notebook. "Thanks for this, Paul," I tell him. "You've provided a good primer for me."

He looks pleased. "I wish I had more to tell you," he says. "The premier is coming in on Monday to give a press conference up at the college. We could meet after that if you have the time, and I can fill you in."

"You're covering it?" I ask.

"Oh, no," he says, alarm registering in his face. "That's not my beat. But I'll ask around and find out for you, if there's anything that isn't on the surface."

I agree to call him on Tuesday, pay our bill over his objections, and we leave. "Which way are you headed?" he asks.

"I have to meet an old friend for lunch. He knows the logging business inside out, and he sells real estate."

"You're talking to lots of people, then," he answers, relieved that I won't be focusing on him.

"Oh, sure. I've got a whole list of people. I wanted to see you first so I'd have some context. This has been very useful."

"Are you going to talk to the mayor, or maybe try to interview either the new MLAs or the defeated ones? I think Paul Ramsey is back in town."

I'm not, but it's as much a struggle to explain why not to Paul as it is to anyone else. One of the depressing things I learned while I was working as an urban planner was that the polarities of conventional politics are outright lying and saying as little as possible while occupying the maximum amount of acoustic and visual media space. It's a little-admitted fact that in the public sphere, politicians are rarely asked questions by the mass media to which the answers aren't already agreed upon by both sides. The only exceptions to this are the foul-ups and emergencies that are our only respite from what have become, frankly, "non-disclosive" politics.

I'm not being sentimental by focusing on "ordinary people." Rather, I'd be wasting my time asking politicians questions they can't, won't, or (more commonly at the level of local politics) don't have the means to answer.

"I decided way back," I tell Paul, "to base this book on talking to people who are operating at ground level. People like you or Barry McKinnon or Bill Walsh, whom I'm meeting for lunch. People who have more to lose, I mean, than a few votes if things here keep going wrong. Seems to me you're the ones who're really getting hammered by this mess, not John Backhouse or Lois Boone or Pat Bell and her Wendy's franchises."

"Oh, okay," Paul says, doubtfully. "I guess that's a way of looking at it that isn't seen every day."

We walk together silently up Third Avenue for two blocks. We haven't gone half a block before I'm stopped dead by a closed-curtain storefront with the words "Honarar Konsulat der Bundesrepublik Deutschland" and the German insignia scripted on the door.

"What's this about, Paul? Do you know?"

"It's the German Consulate," he answers, deadpan.

"Be serious."

"Well, it's unofficial," he admits. "It's run by a local man, Egon Schlick I think his name is, who's the honorary consul. He's been here since the 1950s, and he's the president of a German-Canadian association called the Rheingold Club. He says there are 14,000 German-speaking people here, and he does things like translate German documents for German immigrants to Canada seeking to transfer credentials, help with searches for property and persons in Germany, student exchanges. Plus he works with export-minded local firms to make contact with German chambers of commerce. That sort of thing. Do you want to talk to him?"

"No," I answer. "Doesn't look like anyone's home, anyway. But I guess if everyone else is reclaiming their ethnicity, there's no reason why German Canadians shouldn't. I'd be more impressed if everyone just wanted to be competently Canadian."

Paul doesn't blink. At the next corner we shake hands, I turn south toward the Inn of the North and Billy Walsh, and he ambles off toward the newspaper offices with his Inspector Maigret hat and his briefcase. I don't know if he's happy with our conversation, or not. And I don't know if I have the context I need, or not. Context isn't something that remains stable around here, anyway. Like happiness.

33

I've seen Billy Walsh maybe a dozen times since I left town in the mid-1960s. Back then, he was a skinny kid working high-risk industrial jobs, and he lived with so much ill-focused energy that I once rather grandly predicted he'd get himself killed before he was 30. I was wrong.

He's a large man now, with an infectious belly laugh and a stomach to match it. For the past 20 years he's been dressed the same way each time I've seen him, the last time being in 1996: black cowboy boots, blue jeans, blue check shirt, and a navy Eisenhower jacket.

"I like to keep things simple," he explains.

Simple isn't careless. Billy has a tailor sew creases into his blue jeans when he buys them, to make them more formal, and he tosses each pair when the fade grows uneven. The cowboy boots likely cost him $500, and he wears them whether he's driving a Cat or lunching with the mayor. He'd dress the same if he were meeting the Queen. He's deliberate about everything he does, but he remains utterly without pretense. What you see is what you get: a warm, loud-spoken man who knows what he's about.

One of my motives for this lunch is purely personal. For the book I want the earful he'll give me, but for myself, I want to hear him talk. Billy's way of talking is like old, familiar music when you can't pin down the lyrics or play the tune yourself. There's metaphor, there's melody, and with Billy there's an unreproducible rhythm between the elements so uniquely fused in his brain that no one has ever been able to mimic him. When we were teenagers, having Billy in the back seat on a cold winter night was an entertainment all on its own. I used to think rockabilly was listening to Billy Walsh talk. He's older now, and the instrument has mellowed, but it hasn't dimmed in the least.

Billy and I see the world very differently, especially now that we're adults. For me, living has seemed learnable and improvable—and occasionally, something that you can get right. I see adulthood as an intermittent accomplishment rather than a naturally occurring stage on the road to senility, one that is made up of often unrelated story-lines so unpredictable I've stopped trying to control them or predict them.

Billy has lived his life another way. For him, success is a matter of sticking to one's word. Even while we were kids he had a willingness to go the full nine yards on whatever it was he'd given his word on. As an adult, he's the same, whether it's marriage, children, friendship, or business deals. But he isn't willing to pick up the pieces and start over when things don't work out as he thinks they should. He's not afraid of the things in life—marriage is the most important one—that have defeated him. He's very much the contrary: he's cheerfully cynical, been-there-done-that-don't-want-to-go-back matter-of-fact. He gives the impression that he's thought through the big events in his life, and as far as marriage goes, or even domestic relationships with women, he's decided he's better living alone. Why, I'm not sure. I suspect it's because he's not able to make the kinds of compromises that make domestic relationships work. He still likes women, enjoys their company, and is attracted to them. But he now steers clear of them the moment they want anything more than casual and off-the-cuff.

One of my gay friends in Vancouver had a similar attitude toward sex, saying that he decided he just wasn't particularly good at it, and was going to concentrate on the things he *was* good at. That friend was celibate for almost a decade afterward, and he didn't once whine about it. I don't think Billy's been celibate, because he's practical about his physical needs. But those needs come a distant second to his insistence on being who he is. If people can't handle the straight-up, brass-assed Billy Walsh, he moves on.

My first question for him, after we settle across a table in the hotel café and I set up the tape recorder, is about the changes he's seen in forestry since we last talked. He doesn't hesitate, launching into the quickest summary of logging practice I've ever heard—and the most idiosyncratic.

"In the 50s and 60s," he says, "we cut everything that wasn't seed plot down to 12 inches diameter, and herringboned the logs out of the bush, usually around tight corners. Six months later, whatever we left behind fell over and rotted. Then we got clearcutting, which made more sense: cut it all down, then replant. Now, the Greenpeace tree huggers have talked the government into making the loggers cut smaller blocks—50 hectares maximum. That's raised the cost of moving the iron from one block to the next from 25 cents a cubic metre to $1.75 a cubic metre. Stupid."

I ask him what their rationale was for smaller cut blocks, deciding to follow him on his own terms, which revolve around the practicalities of logging rather than the more abstract terms of professional forestry, which tends toward quasi-biblical expressions like "harvest" and "husbandry"—notions that sound asinine around Billy.

He scowls. "Brian, I have no idea. It's just one of the rules of the stupid Forest Practices Code. From a logger's point of view, it doesn't make any sense. Every time you move your machinery, you've got to start all over again, plus you've got to familiarize the people who are working there with the new terrain because they don't know where the traps are: banks or slide paths and so on. And every area you work in has these things, so you've got to discover them every time you move. Whereas if you're in one place, you have time to learn the lay of the land.

"And of course these government guys are all smart enough after the fact. They'll come in after an area has been logged and say, 'This is what was done wrong when you logged this.' Well, the answer to that is that the guy who logged it gets the logging plan slapped onto dash of his truck Thursday afternoon, and he's got to have wood coming out of there Monday, so of course he's going to make some mistakes.

"Loggers aren't stupid people, Brian. They can build you a road up Mount Everest if they have time to plan it and the funds to build it right. The real problem with clearcutting has been that there's no provision for controlling water after a stand is cut, with water bars and things like that—there's no mandate to assay what's been done and either learn from it or make it right. The government has done the right job by getting rid of all the wood and then burning and replanting. But they should do water control, too, and that needs to be done right after logging. Don't leave it for two years, have a big slide, and then blame the loggers. That's got nothing to do with the guys who log. Loggers don't want to make a mess.

"I've got a hunk of dirt that I logged 20 years ago. It's all come back even though it was on a steep slope. There were great big spruce trees on that slope, and I yarded them out, and it's come back wonderfully. Not one drop of mud leaked into the creek.

"But this new Forest Practices Code raised all the costs of logging. You have to move the machinery more—trucking out the logs takes longer because they have to go 3 or 4 more kilometres on temporary roads, and you have to build the roads for them. So, even with the new technology, the costs went significantly higher. Worse than that, we had to pay $50-a-cubic-metre stumpage here while they were paying $15 for the same thing down near Vancouver. That put the mills around here in a corner, and they solved it by putting the boots to the loggers. Everybody who works in the bush up here has had the hell beat out of them by the Code. But not for the right reasons."

I tell him that I don't understand why Prince George should be penalized so the companies operating at the Coast can operate profitably.

Billy throws his hands in the air in frustration. "You tell me," he says.

Then he sees that I really *don't* understand. "Look," he says. "It's called 'water-bedding.' What that means is that the government charges higher stumpage fees up here because we can log cheaper. Even with the Code, our road-building and transport costs are cheaper because it's flatter here. And so there's more profit. So the government saw that as an excuse to tax us to death. We got taxed out of business over the last six years. It's sad.

"And in my business—residential real estate—we're back to 1960 levels in housing starts. Isn't that something to be proud of? Plus, people owe three times the amount of money on mortgages they did in 1981, average. There's been 30 mortgage foreclosures a month, and people are just giving up their property and walking away. And that means divorces, and kids fighting on the street, and all the social pressures.

"Don't get me wrong. I love logging, and I love this place. It's made to grow trees. It's not a farming place. This is tree-growing country. Best one in the world. It rains here, the sun is here, the growth rate is good enough that there's 14 inches between the layers of branches."

Billy stares off into the distance, as if remembering something that's lost.

I prod him with one of my pet questions. "What about soil degradation? If you keep pulling all the carbon out of the ground, aren't you going to have to pay the price? Sooner or later?

Billy stares at me as if I just climbed out of a spaceship. "When you say 'take the carbon out of the ground,' what do you mean?"

I take a deep breath, wondering if I'm about to put my foot in a real soft, mushy one. "Well," I say, "if you take a full generation of trees out of the forest, aren't you removing carbon you have no way of replacing?"

He's not offended. He stops to think about what I've said, takes a mouthful of coffee, swallows. "Soil degradation is just a goddamned term the tree huggers use to describe the damage logging does. But think about it: the regulations say we can't have this machine in there, we can't do that. But then, after we're out of there, the Forest Service sends a Cat in to scarify the whole place, take it right down to the gravel. Does that make sense? Spruce and pine trees don't want topsoil. They can't germinate on anything but bare ground. It's just brush and deciduous that want soil. Nature designed evergreens to come in after glaciers, for Christ's sake."

He's more than a little right: scarification and burning are designed to reproduce the natural regeneration conditions for conifers like pine and spruce, which are the tree species the industry wants to cut and wants to have planted. What he isn't saying is that in an evolving forest, balsam fir, cedar, hemlock, and deciduous species follow a spruce-pine forest that doesn't burn. Those species don't require bare ground, and *can't* seed in it. They need the carbon deposited by the decaying spruce and pine, which even a burned-but-not-cut spruce-pine forest makes available. For a second I think about arguing this with him, and then realize he's not going to be very interested because carbon depletion is an issue for a future he's not going to see and neither is anyone else he knows. Billy is wholly of the here-and-now.

"What I'm saying, Brian," he says, "is that there has to be some give and take here. When you tear something apart, so long as you put it back together in some sort of gentlemanly fashion, that's all that's required. I've been in places that were logged three years ago that you can hardly tell were logged. The carbon and all that stuff hasn't even moved. All they did was saw the tree down, grab it, and get the hell out. And the animals love it. Sure they do. And we've got the technology to put hundreds of thousands of trees a day back into the ground. They also have the chance to put the best trees back, because they can select the cones from the tallest trees. They clip seed cones with helicopters now, did you know that?"

He's on a roll, so I shut up and listen because I've seen him do this before: it might not make linear sense, but it'll be studded with parcels of ground sense.

"There's another thing," he says after a moment. "They haven't done any logging of bug-kill in the parks. They should have done that. If they don't, they're going to have the biggest forest fire in the world one of these days. If we get a hot dry summer around here and the wind goes the wrong way, they'll never get it out.

"The socialists doubled the amount of parks, from 6 percent to 12 percent of the total land area. And they also put little ten-acre parks wherever two rivers come together so it fucks up anyone wanting to do things upstream because, you know, you can't do this and you can't do that because it might pollute their park. Most people will never, ever get to see these parks, or use them. Most people are waiting for taxicabs in the smog somewhere.

Billy's eyes grow bright. I've seen this before, too. He's always put common sense together with his gift for seeing a world that's grander and more efficient and easier than the one he's working with. Some of the possibilities are purely technological, some fiscal. Others are carnal and scatological, and the mix is unpredictable and usually pretty entertaining.

"I was looking at some charts of Hecate Straight the other day," he says. "The water's only 11 to 12 metres deep there, and there's no reason why they can't drill for oil. This is 2001, not 1901. We have the technology to drill those wells and not make a mess. And the mining. Why did they cancel all the mining?"

"There's oil in Hecate Strait?"

He answers this one as if it is something every sensible person knows. "There's lots of oil. There's more oil in Hecate Strait than there is in Alberta."

Then he's off in another direction before I can sort that zinger out (later I'll hear that the new government is lifting a 50-year ban on oil drilling in the Strait). "So you see, when you get the publicity that Greenpeace can generate from that stupid goddamn TV, you can stop all kinds of things that don't need to be stopped. I don't even *have* a TV any more."

I ask him why not, and he laughs.

"Well, I'm sick of watching cooking shows, and all the bullshit. And the news is very biased. It's also very impolite when you go to visit somebody and they've got the TV on. I just melt down. Burn a U-ie. They can go watch their TV without me. I've got a friend who tapes the car races I want to see. I've got Indianapolis and the Grand Prix. That's all I want to look at anyway. *That* isn't bullshit."

He stops to see if I've followed this. I have, sort of. He owns a television set and VCR, so he's objecting to the programmed use of the medium, not its technology. As always, he's consistent. I don't believe there's more oil in Hecate Strait than in Alberta, but he just gave me a clearer picture of what's pissing people off in northern B.C.—and why the political shift to the right has been so extreme—than I'd have gotten from two weeks of interviewing politicians or sociologists.

And he's finished, too. He gestures at my list of questions.

I ask him whether the Canfor's dominance of the local industry will be good or bad for Prince George.

"It's bad," he says.

"How so."

"It's a monopoly, and you know how those work. It's already ruined the supply market for loggers. A few years ago, I could get a million bucks for a quarter section of land with wood on it: 120 cubic metres to the acre. Now you can't get nothing because Canfor won't pay for it and there's nobody else buying. Rustad Brothers used to give the best price in town, and had the most reasonable specs to meet. Now they're gone, and that part of our life is gone with it. If you've got 160 acres of good pine, you'll be able to sell it, but you won't get near what you should."

"There's nobody else buying timber?"

"Well, there's Carrier Lumber, but they've got so much bug-killed wood to log, why would they pay for live stuff? So once again, the guys who are getting killed are the loggers. Big time. Them and the machining companies.

"You see, for the longest time, loggers worked about 1,400 hours a year here. There's 8,800 hours in a year, see. That was the common level of productivity. But I've seen a machine recently that was 18 months old that had 11,000 hours on it. So, that thing was working 24–7. That's what Canfor has done with the loggers. They've now got to work their rigs 8 to 10 months of the year, 20 hours a day, just to keep their noses above water. By doing this, Canfor has eliminated about 60 percent of both the machines and the loggers. Whether that's good or bad, who knows, but it's all to get this wood out of the bush cheaply for Canfor, and in a hurry."

I ask him why he thinks the old government allowed this monopoly to happen, given that they were supposed to be against monopolies.

Billy's face darkens. "I'll tell you what," he says. "I don't know how the socialists can face the people of this town after the way things have gone. They did Prince George no favours. They were arrogant. And I'll tell you something else. They allowed that gambling den here that takes $22 million a year out of this town."

"A casino? Here?"

"Yes. Now, isn't that brilliant? Why don't they legalize prostitution if they're that hungry for money. It all just makes me sick."

This is a surprising turn, but I need more on Canfor.

"Is Canfor Canadian?"

"That's Bentley. Peter Bentley. But those profits aren't coming back here. They're going to Toronto or Vancouver. The old money is gone from here, Brian. It's gone. You see all those big auctions Ritchies are having, you're seeing all that iron leaving here. It's all going stateside. The loggers here buy a new machine every year or two and run the bag off it. After two years they have to dump it. And they have to be getting 95 to 98 percent of the capacity out of it or they can't afford to have it in the first place. And all this crap will be just fine until you have a nice old-fashioned 45-below-ten-feet-of-snow kind of winter for three months, and then it'll all grind to a halt, and when breakup arrives, those loggers will be broke.

"And this value-added thing, they talked about that. But it was just talk. They gave all those guys development grants, and they did nothing. The only one that survived was John Brink. The rest went down the pipe, and $40 million went with it. I could take you through that chopstick factory they built. It's a huge big building—22,000 square feet, with two huge 300,000 horsepower boilers sitting there rusting. It's disgusting."

I ask him what kind of future he sees for Prince George. He stops in mid-tirade, settles back in his chair—and then taxis down a whole new runway.

"If Bill Gates buys the BCR . . ."

"Is he thinking about this?"

"Yes," Bill says firmly. "I have information that he's serious about it. So, if he does buy it, and if he takes it to Alaska, and then takes it underneath the ocean to Russia, three things will happen. There'll be tons of raw wood coming here, and so the mills here will have a permanent wood supply. The second thing that will happen is that they won't double the Trans-Alaska Pipeline, they'll haul crude oil in 100-ton tank cars, 11,000 tons at a time, 110-car trains. The locomotives will run on 10-percent diesel and 90-percent natural gas—just enough fuel oil to lubricate the top end of the engines. And that'll open up a huge North–South trade zone. So, this place will perpetuate itself, then."

He spots my disbelief and stops. "When you go to the northwest corner of this province, there's an area bigger than England that's never been touched. Never been touched. So that'll guarantee wood supply. Once it gets here, it'll go east–west on the CNR, or north–south on Gates' BCR–Burlington Northern–Santa Fe system. Gates is a railroad buff, I don't know whether you knew that. When he travels with his own guys, he's got his own train.

"Gates can make this kind of billion-dollar deal and he'll still have the cash to burn. A computer guy buying hard assets—bricks and mortar! Gates has figured out that it isn't smart to go yahooing to the stock market right now, because you'll come home with no money. If you're smart, go out and buy bricks and mortar. Still not convinced? Look at it this way. We've had to sell out everything here. Now comes the next step. What makes you think those rich dicks in Vancouver and Toronto will be treated any differently? They're no smarter than we are."

His expression becomes wistful. "Anyway," he concludes, "if all this comes together, the forest industry here will go forever. Prince George will go forever."

"But what about the local timber shortfall we've got right now?" I ask. "How are they going to deal with that? By planting deciduous trees and things like that?"

"Deciduous trees do grow back in about 25 years. The future is about wood fibre, not lumber the way we know it now."

"Sure," I say, "but deciduous species require a greater depth of soil to start off with, and you can't plant them up in the subalpine because they won't survive."

Bill stares at me as if I'm a certified idiot. "Well, sure. The pine tree is the only tree in the woods that's like a carrot. It has a taproot, and that gets down into the subsoil for water and nutrients. All the rest have surface roots: spruce, fir, poplar, all that. But the pine tree will grow in the driest part of the world because it can get down to where the water is. The fir will grow in dry areas, but its roots are lateral—12 to 15 metres long. Spruce will also grow in a swamp, and they have big root systems. The tree will dictate where it can grow. That's why there's such a mix here now. If you go to the bush, it isn't all just fir trees. There's a fir, and a balsam, birch, poplar and a spruce, and up on a hill, there'll be a pine."

"Does the replanting they're doing today follow that to any extent?"

"I don't think so. It's mostly softwood—pine and spruce."

I ask him why he thinks the government screws up all the time on forestry.

"I think what happens, Brian, is that the deputy ministers and maybe the environmentalists overpower the practical people. That's my opinion. And then the practical people just get mad and walk away. But they do get overpowered, believe me. Patrick Moore, for instance, went full circle. His grandfather had logged, up at Winter Harbour in the early 1900s. Sure, they dumped diesel fuel in the water to get rid of the mosquitoes, and other things that aren't acceptable today. But to take the wood out is. If you don't, it's going to fall down and rot, or the bugs are going to eat it. So this nonsense about protecting the kermode bear is just stupid. That's just a cinnamon bear —a black bear with a funny coat. And this thing about saving the grizzlies is just another form of gun control. Big Brother just decided they were endangered, on the basis of nothing. We've got bears climbing up our assholes around here. Last year they shot 160 of them within the city limits.

"Nobody likes to ruin nature, okay? That's not in our scope. But I had to walk 220 acres the other day. I didn't take a gun, but normally

I'd take a 30–30 with me so I don't have to run away from some bear that's after my ass. I'm going to turn around and waste him, because if he's chasing me, he's a dangerous bear. Look at that poor lady who was training for the Olympics and got killed by a bear. I don't know what she was doing running around, maybe it was the wrong time of the month."

He pauses to consider that for a split second. "Same as that woman in Banff who was killed by a cougar," he says. "Her sister said she died happy. I'm not so sure. Have you ever watched a cat kill a mouse?

"People do stupid things when they get out in the bush. I blame it on those bloody TV shows. It's all biased, organized so what we get to see is always the poor bird, or the poor grizzly, or whatever. And the bad humans ought to get their asses out of there and leave them be. It's just not fair. It's just not fair, Brian.

"It's the same thing with logging. You don't get your logging plan until the last minute, and you've got to send a buncher in there cutting and a button-topper chucking it out so you can get it on a truck, and you've got to build a goddamn road before you start. So what if it's pissing rain? Loggers can't sit there for three weeks waiting for the perfect conditions. The road should have been built two months in advance. But the forestry companies, and the Forest Service, too, dump everything on you at the last minute."

"Why are they doing that?"

"Because they're assholes. Because nobody there has to answer to anything. You go in to them with a complaint and they'll run you around the mulberry bush until you're dead. It's like any bureaucratic set-up. The system sets up checks and balances so the bureaucrats can cover their asses, not do their jobs properly. I think Tim McVeigh gave some of those jerks a wake-up call. He did it the wrong way, but nonetheless he got the message across that there are wingnuts out there who don't like what's going on and will react. And you can't lock all of them up because there's too many of them."

He closes one eye to think about what he's said. There's something wrong it—on his terms—and he tries to find it.

"They shouldn't have had those kids in the building," he says after a moment's pause. "What were they thinking of? There's a whole lot of things wrong. We survived a decade of Bill Clinton and Janet Reno.

That was not a good deal for Canada. And then Robert Kennedy Jr. comes up here and starts harping about the kermode bear.

"Our government, it seems to me, Brian, has no guts when it comes to the Americans. Not that we can afford to play hardball with them. If we did, they'd just take the place over and leave us kicking horse turds. You go to the Rio Grande River in New Mexico and there's no river going to Mexico any more, thank you very much. That's what the Mexicans get. And now the Americans want our water."

34

The waitress shows up with the lunch we ordered, and I shut off the tape and clear the table of my notebooks. While we eat, Billy fills me in on mutual friends still left in town and on what he's been doing. He's given up his parents' house to his sister and has bought a cabin on Cluculz Lake, close to the one his parents owned while he was growing up; the real estate business is slower than molasses, that kind of thing. It's hard to read what he feels, because he's so cheerful and it's not a mask. This is simply who he is. He'll complain about the government or the corporations, but he doesn't see himself as their victim.

Despite his gloomy depictions of the logging industry, I detect something unexpected: Bill Walsh is a happy man, and as we eat lunch he tells me why. His father, to whom he bears a striking resemblance, died at the age of 50. It turns out that no Walsh male in generations has made it past 50, and Billy is already 56. Sure, he's overweight. But he says he's eating healthier, keeping his drinking in check, and his blood pressure's okay. I believe him. He's headed for 60, and he's probably going to make it.

Billy relates an anecdote that gives me a more specific sense of where his happiness is coming from. About a week before, while he was out at the lake, a boat he'd had tied to his dock turned over in a high wind, and he took his skiff out to fetch the debris. He'd gone out fully clothed and without a lifejacket, had captured most of it, and was leaning out to grab a portable cooler when a gust of wind hit the skiff and nearly overturned it.

"I got the boat back in shape," he says, "turned it right to the wind, and then it hit me: if that little skiff had gone over, I'd have been out there in that water with my boots on, and a jacket, and these heavy jeans, and you know, I damn well wouldn't have made it. So I let the goddamned cooler go. Screw it. Let it go. Never did find the damned thing, either. But you know, here I am. And that's what counts."

We finish lunch, the waitress clears the table and brings some coffee while I reset the tape recorder and notebooks, and we're off again.

I ask him what he thinks this new government is going to do.

He thinks about that for a minute. "Well, I think the Liberals back in Ottawa will begin to recognize what happened here. It's the first time there's been a provincial Liberal government in B.C. since the 1940s. It's really a coalition of everybody, but that's okay. So I would hope they'd try to even things out a little bit. As far as I'm concerned, this is the best province in the world. But it gets the short end of the stick in Ottawa. And with feds having this big bag-load of money, you know that they're going to go and do something stupid with it.

"I had a friend of mine die in front of Vancouver General Hospital last year. He fell off his goddamn house in Chilliwack cleaning the eavestroughs, and they took him from the Chilliwack hospital to Vancouver General Hospital, and he died in front of Vancouver General trying to get admitted. So, have a nice day, what are we doing here?

"Then there's natural gas people. If you're $50 behind in your gas payments, they cut you off. You can't even go and give them shit. They've got the front of their office boarded up. There's a book I read about all this—what would happen with prices going crazy if the government deregulated. It hasn't worked in California, because you can't deregulate a monopoly. And of course not all nuclear power plants are nasty. The environmentalists haven't let them build any new plants in California in the past 15 years, but they don't want people to use batteries, so everything has a cord on it.

"There are no alternatives to sucking energy. We're into the technology part of our lives—the whole country I mean—and we shouldn't be afraid of it. We shouldn't worship it, but we shouldn't be afraid of it. Nothing I like better than technology. I've always used it to the max—turn it up one more notch and see how fast and high it'll go. Down in California, I drove from Beach Boulevard in Orange County to Malibu in one hour, and it's 90 miles. Right through downtown LA at 90 miles an hour. Never got a speeding ticket. Cops would pull right up beside you, and so long as you weren't swerving or laying it on or waving a gun, they just drove on. I got a ticket in Oliver a while back—a little eat-apple town. Well, isn't that brilliant, I go 6 kilometres an hour faster than the limit and they pull me over."

"I've got one more question, and then we can quit, Bill," I say. "It's this: Is life here better than it was 35 years ago?"

His answer is firm and solemn. "No. It isn't."

"Why not?"

"Because right now—today—this afternoon, people are beat up so bad financially that everybody's pissed off. And there's a big dose of Vancouverites here who just want to make money and don't want to know anybody. They just want to make their money and go. Vanderhoof is like Prince George was 30 years ago. People are smiling, they're courteous, they're polite, they're waving at you. Around here it's pretty bad. In my opinion."

I remind him that I've been asking for his opinion and that there's no need to apologize. He isn't finished.

"It's not the same old place," he says. "Years back, you could always get a job here, Brian. Now . . ." He's silent for a moment as he tries to swallow the humiliation. "There are people going hungry."

But just as suddenly, he brightens. "Last summer," he says, "the Union Hall phoned and said they had a seat for me on a loader. They needed me to work on some new retaining walls on the underpass for the new bridge on the Nechako. We built them. I laid every one of them goddamn blocks, eh? And there wasn't one squashed finger, and not one drop of blood. It made me feel good. Old Grandpa Billy can still drive the snot out of a loader with one tire in the air and a hunk of cement dingle-dangle thirteen feet up, and nobody said shit. Just fit her in there, have a nice day. It was like a two-month holiday."

"I heard about it," I say. "Dave Close over at Wendt and Phillips was telling me about it yesterday. He says the story went all around town. Said you'd kept your real estate licence, and that you just wanted to run the loader for the sheer hell of it."

Billy's pleased. "Sure," he says. "I kept my shoe-phone with me, and someone would phone up and I'd say, 'You want to buy a hunk of dirt? Well, wait till 7 o'clock, I've got three more blocks to load.' I worked seven days a week for a month and a half. Made $10,000, paid all my income tax. It was fun."

He mentions a mutual acquaintance, and asks if I had heard what happened to her. I hadn't.

"She gassed herself in the garage of her own home last year," Billy says, shaking his head. "Got into a fight with her husband. He was on coke and all this crap, and then she got into a disagreement with her kids. So one Friday she just went home, opened the garage door, pulled the car inside, and let it run. After that, the husband set out to drink himself to death. Lasted about 10 months. He's gone now, too."

"I'm sorry," I say, trying to picture what she looked like: dark-haired, strong features, young. Much younger than we are today.

"How'd Jack lose China Bob's, Billy? No one seems to want to talk about it."

"It was a combination of things. The town was starting to have tough times, he charged high prices for his sauce, and he paid huge money in rent because his partner was the landlord—one of those deals where the more money Jack took in, the more he paid in rent. And then the landlord had a nephew who'd been run out of Vancouver. So he brought him in and gave him China Bob's to run. Jack's empire went out the window in one day, and now I don't know what he's doing for money.

"I tried to warn him about it. I said, 'Look, you're better off to have nothing than to pretend you have something. When you're dancing with some guy who's got $80 million, you're like a chicken dancing with an elephant. And you'd better watch out, because if he blows a fart, you're dead. It can end in one second.' Jack didn't listen."

If Billy is really unhappy about anything, it's Jack. Part of what brought Jack down, he hints, was Jack himself.

The two men have had a long and complicated relationship. For years, Billy played second fiddle, partly because Jack was bigger and smoother, and seemed faster on the uptake. But along the way Billy grew into his own man, until all Jack had over him was the habit, and the strange kind of moral authority that he carries into all his relationships. Over the years, Billy wised up about a lot of things, and eventually he acquired something that Jack doesn't have: a deep and minable vein of practical wisdom. Jack has ended up with his pride, and with tough times on his neck, that's been hard to maintain.

"If you have to put someone else down to make yourself feel good," Billy explains, suddenly circumspect, "you're brain-dead. This isn't just a theory. As a salesman, I've got no time for that. Don't get me wrong, Brian. I'm not perfect. I like to go out and have a few beers and a nice laugh. But Jack goes too far."

The current bone of contention between them, it turns out, is a dinner at a restaurant that Jack organized and then let Billy pay for, possibly because, with his restaurant gone, he was broke. In Billy's mind, being broke is okay. Just say so, and we'll deal with it. But Jack's pride wouldn't let him.

"He goes to the washroom when the cheque comes, and leaves what must have been a 10 coiler. He was gone about three-quarters of an hour. In the meantime, I've paid the bill—about $200. Well, thanks, Jack."

"I hope the best for Jack," he says. "But I just got tired of all the bullshit and all the criticism. I don't need it. When I was on that loader, he was watching me with a fucking spyglass. He tells me, Oh, old man, you can still do it. And I says, Fucking right. I can get on a dozer and run it right up your ass."

He sighs and lets it go, more sad than angry.

"You know," he says, suddenly wistful, "since I've been living at the lake, there's the nature thing. I like it. There's no fire engines going by the front door, no cop cars. While I was still living in town last November some guy tried to bust in at 2 o'clock in the morning. It just scared the shit out of me. So maybe it's all for the better that I get away for a while.

"Yesterday was the first day of summer. Longest day of the year and the day my daughter was born. I did a whole pile of things yesterday, and then I built a little sundeck. It's got lake on one side, and some bushes on the shore side—there's a huge lawn next to it with a hedge about fifteen feet wide, so you've got to go through this little trail to get there. So now I can sit there, roast my buns, or do whatever the hell I want. It didn't cost anything—just a little bit of wood.

"The thing that I've learned is this: don't leave any stone unturned, and don't leave anybody upset. Like when you're a foreman and you give an operator shit, and then you leave him and don't settle him down, he'll kick the snot out of his machine until you come back. And after he's gone, that machine will have its tongue hanging out and that'll cost you. So you never, ever, leave anyone down."

He looks behind him for the waitress and the cheque. He's said his piece, and he's ready to go. "Brian, I'm not in the ground, and there's lots of water under the bridge. When I got back onto the dirt last week and saw all that stuff floating away down the lake, I thought, Billy, it's just stuff."

We argue over who's going to pay the bill, until I convince him that he's given me good information on the cheap and that the least I can do is buy him lunch. We walk outside together. Down the street I spot the old Ford pickup he's been driving for about 20 years. It's painted gold and with the lake pipes and cab visor, it's hard to miss.

"How's the old beast running?" I ask when we get to the truck.

He gives the hood a slap. "Oh, you know how it goes. If it has tits or wheels on it, it's going to give you trouble. But this baby's been better than most. Hop in, I'll give you a ride wherever you're going."

I tell him I've got to go pick up a rental car, so sure. He knows where the rental agency is, and asks me some questions about what kind of car I've rented. He isn't just making conversation, either. It's technical, so he's interested.

On the drive over—it isn't far—he asks if I'd like to have dinner with Jack and his current girlfriend while I'm here. I would, and we settle on Monday night.

"Call me Monday afternoon and I'll tell you where we're eating, and what time."

35

About 9:30 that night, the phone rings. Joy answers, listens for a moment, rolls her eyes, and hands the receiver to me. It's Ken Bernsohn, whom I've been trying to reach since I arrived. Bernsohn is a man who enjoys a good talk, but only if it's on his terms: he's the teacher, you're the student. Okay by me, and I begin to pop the questions I've been asking the others, along with a few I haven't bothered with: *Is the emergence of Canfor as the primary forest corporation operating in the area—making Prince George a one-corporation town for the first time since the Grand Trunk Railway came through—a problem? Will the announced cut of pine beetle–infested forests around Tweedsmuir Park go forward? Why are trainloads of raw logs still leaving town? What was wrong with the Forest Practices Code? Is carbon deficit going to be a problem if clearcutting continues? Why isn't there more secondary manufacturing?*

Ken Bernsohn has different goals than most people. He says that his major goal in life is to keep himself moderately amused until he croaks, and that he'd have to cheer up to be called a cynic. Part of this is pragmatism. "If everyone had the same value systems, he tells me, millions of people would be after my wife, only a handful of diseases would get research done on them, there would be one television station and one movie company." That's why he doesn't try to convince people about anything.

It makes him a pain in the ass to talk with: you learn things, but they aren't always what you want to know. He doesn't provide clips, sound bites, or simple answers. He discusses questions and issues the way a rabbi offers discourse on the Torah, always beginning with the premise that we live in a world where there are neither easy questions nor simple answers—and that both asker and answerer have to extract the truth without belittling the complexities.

Bernsohn freely admits he does know something about forestry, and he doesn't bother to position me or himself as pro-logging or pro-environment. Despite his irritation at having to answer some questions twice because the telephone line is whizzing and crackling, he's thoroughly prepared to give up what he knows if I can get to it.

Canfor, he tells me, *is* a problem, but the evolution it reflects is probably inevitable, and the owner-operators are at least provincially owned and reasonably accessible—pretty much what the others have told me, in other words. But Bernsohn has fine-grain stuff to add. The big cheese, Peter Bentley, has a sense of humour and recognizes that he has some local responsibilities, even if he exercises them by employing the Microsoft method of creating dependent and grateful charities. The CEO, David Emerson, is new to the lumber industry, but is a Grande Prairie–raised kid who was responsible for rebuilding Vancouver International Airport during the 1990s—no small accomplishment. More often than not, Bernsohn goes on, the operators of a corporation are better than the corporation itself, and struggle to be human within a restricting mission just like the rest of us have to struggle in our own lives.

The beetle infestation around Ootsa Lake and Tweedsmuir Park, which he points out is the product of excessive zeal in fire suppression over the past 40 years, will go forward, but he isn't sure how far it will go. He suggests that it might be a better alternative than the massive forest fire that is the only other possibility if nothing is done, and opines, as did Billy Walsh earlier in the day, that such a fire could be the sort of superfire that might burn for years. This possibility loops him into a long anecdote about the gigantic forest fire in Borneo a few years ago. He concludes by citing German social forester Berthold Siebert's explanation: "Forestry is a symbol of man's impatience with nature."

I laugh at this, and don't object to the incorrect gender pronoun because it happens to be accurate. Bernsohn doesn't think it's funny, cautioning me to remember that around here, theory is one thing, practice is always another. He goes on to point out that the forest industry has learned a few things since the Bowron was cut, but stops short of saying there won't be another industrial riot like the one that happened in the Bowron River valley.

He admits that sawlogs are still leaving the area, and then launches into a discussion of the rapid growth of the middle classes in India, and the pressures this has put on Japanese markets for recycled paper.

I suspect he's merely entertaining himself with this, spinning out his own blithe narrative because he senses an audience that will indulge him and can follow without utterly losing the trail. When I rein him in after a few minutes, he gives up the straight goods. Fewer logs are leaving the area than used to, and while God isn't in his heaven, at least he's headed in the right direction, and all is basically right with the world on this particular issue.

"Look," he says at one point. "You assume that exporting logs is bad. Under some circumstances, that's true. Today, when local mills are more willing to make what people want to buy it *is* true. But in the late 1970s when a Japanese buyer came to B.C. and said, 'This is what we want,' no one would make it anywhere in the province. Then a few years later, when times were tougher, a few mills agreed to try. In some years some mills have gotten triple the American lumber market price for Japanese spec wood. Demand goes up and down, but the Japanese have always been willing to pay more than Chicago's Hines Lumber, the biggest wholesaler in the Midwest."

The very mention of the Forest Practices Code fills him with pedagogic exuberance. He treats me first to the Forest Service's simplification: *Don't Squish the Fish/Don't Hurt the Dirt/Don't Goose the Moose/Don't Leak in the Creek.* "That's not a bad summary," he adds.

He acknowledges the common sense of the Code, but admits, when I remind him of what the road to hell is paved with, that there are limitations to its common sense. His primary objection to the Code is the rigidity of its application, and that it allowed the companies—or The Company—to squeeze the loggers for their profits when lumber prices drop. In this he's once again in sync with Bill Walsh, but he adds nuance to what Billy told me. I think Bernsohn likes the Code, but he also knows it's not working. It has become process- rather than goal-oriented.

I expect ridicule from him when I raise the issue of carbon depletion. Instead, I get a ranging discourse that starts with several plausible definitions, then moves on to an examination of the definitions in terms of different locations around the globe: Oregon, Scandinavia, New England, northern B.C. He admits that you can't remove biomass indefinitely, but says the depletion scenarios and timelines differ widely, and that data is incomplete. "Local soil depletion Armageddon," he says, "might not happen until the year 2270, and who knows what we'll be able to make things from then?"

I counter that by reminding him that asking the future to solve today's problems is an old and evil habit around here, and ultimately, that it is bad faith masking itself as risk-taking because the risk-takers are the future generations who aren't party to our calculations. He answers that he's not evading the question, just trying to put it into a perspective that isn't wholly abstract and moral. Carbon depletion in northern B.C. will become a problem eventually, he agrees, but there are other problems more likely to do us in before carbon depletion reaches critical proportions.

I wonder aloud that if salvage cuts the size of the one on Bowron keep being opened up, carbon depletion might be on us a lot sooner than the 23rd century.

"A little sooner, maybe," he says, not taking the bait. "But not significantly so."

I turn to the lack of secondary industry in Prince George, confident that this issue, at least, is straightforward. He comes back with the most obtuse response he's given me yet. "It isn't," he says, "a question of 'what's the product.' The real question is 'who's doing your marketing.' Did you know that all the wood tabletops currently being sold by Ikea are made in Prince George?"

I didn't know that, and I say so, adding that I thought the only secondary industry that had come out of all those promotions and schemes over the past few decades was the finger-joint mill built by John Brink in the mid-1980s.

Bernsohn declares the Brink mill the most glittery success, and we agree that the locally famous chopstick factory, reputedly set up by the Korean Mafia to launder money and quickly abandoned when it became clear to everyone it was a shuck, was the most damaging failure. Then he tells me that several of Canfor's mills are now producing a much wider variety of products than they did even a decade ago —things like tabletops and specialty mouldings. He also thinks that these diversification trends are likely to continue, simply because they're more profitable than producing spaghetti wood products, and aren't likely to be covered by U.S. trade sanctions.

He launches into an anecdote about helicoptering a single Sitka spruce log out of the bush for eventual use in producing guitar bodies, naming an astronomical figure for the value of this single log. This, he says, is the way to make more with less. He also tells me that the Sitka spruce are then taken to Oregon, Washington, and Alaska for the cutting and drying that will turn it into Steinway pianos.

When I ask him if one of the reasons for the lack of secondary industrial development is corporate culture itself, he balks.

"England," he says, "has coal and iron—and good table manners. France has no natural advantages aside from wine, but it makes good food, and dictates fashion and elegance in leather goods. Places where things are common never, ever realize how good those things are. The United States has one natural advantage over the rest of the world: it's the best place on the planet to grow wheat. Yet it dominates the world's music, film, video, and computer software, and it runs the financial markets. None of these things can be used in a garden or to keep people warm. They're selling ideas.

"Prince George," he adds, "has too many resources to really take advantage of what we have."

I point out that a corporation exists to extract maximum profits with minimal capital outlay and minimum risk of missing the market. This, I say, is as true in New York City's financial district as in Prince George. In Prince George, the corporations seem to want to keep cutting spaghetti lumber because the market is in and the technologies are developed.

Bernsohn agrees, but only after attaching three riders. 1) Some corporations are better than others; 2) Lumber markets are notoriously volatile today; 3) NAFTA's jerking around with softwood duties has created a climate where diversification is more readily accepted by producers because value-added products are more likely to elude whatever countervailing duties are being placed on our wood.

"You're saying that Canfor is a better landlord to the forests than Noranda and Fletcher Challenge would be because its headquarters are in B.C. and not offshore or back east?"

"Yes," he says. "And Peter Bentley of Canfor is easier to deal with than Adam Zimmerman at Noranda was, for the simple reason that he's closer. But personally, I always found Adam honest and even candid when I had to talk to him."

A few months later, I sent Bernsohn an e-mail about the 19-percent U.S. softwood lumber tax imposed by the Bush administration just after I left town. I asked him the following questions:

> What basis does the Bush administration have for slapping import duties on our softwood lumber? It's clear they did it because they're being bullied by their own lumber interests to elevate the profits American producers make by making Canadian construction wood more expensive. But they've consistently based their argument for import duties on the notion that B.C. stumpage rates constitute a de facto subsidy. How can they be saying that when our own producers are squealing almost as loudly that the stumpage rates are too high, so high, in fact, that they're making it unprofitable to operate? And how can the new B.C. government cut the stumpage fees when the Americans are saying the fees are already far too low? Are operations in B.C. that much more efficient than those in the U.S.? Are they basing their claims on the "average" B.C. rate, and not accounting for the water-bedding that gives the northern producers much higher stumpage fees? Do you have any figures on the input/output ratio of stumpage fees in the Northern Interior—related government spending that got everyone so fried last year?

Two hours later, I got this answer back:

> Let us go back to 1776. That's when Adam Smith wrote, in *The Wealth of Nations*, that "People of the same trade seldom meet together, even for merriment and diversion, but the conversation ends in a conspiracy against the public, or in some contrivance to raise prices."
> Competition from Canada, Russia, Austria, or anywhere else means lower prices for lumber produced in the U.S.A., so

American producers don't like it. Further, our system is different from theirs. Theirs is crooked, only in different ways, as Walter J. Mead pointed out in *Competition and Oligopsony in the Douglas Fir Lumber Industry*, published by the University of California Press back in 1966. Companies in the U.S. regularly revalue their timber lands depending on whether they want their company values to go up or down. Our system, in contrast, is crooked. Until the early 1990s companies were paying Cdn$1.36 a cubic metre for raw materials, less than restaurants pay for food, oil companies pay for crude oil, or any other industry you care to name pays for raw materials. But the present stumpage fees are based on a bunch of assumptions which are false, known to be false, and just plain wrong. This makes us no better or worse than the Americans, just different.

Americans tend to believe that "Different is Bad." So because our system is different they feel free to attack anything in it, and that's what they're doing now. Meanwhile, if American firms attack us at a cost of $30 million U.S., and we're kept out of their market, they obviously feel they can make more than the $30 million cost on the deal. Attacking Canada is more cost-effective than rebuilding a sawmill. There's now a scandal in the U.S. Forest Service over subsidized auctions that are selling timber for less than it's worth. The U.S. Forest Service office in Portland, Oregon, has, over the years, been very helpful answering questions honestly. I recommend them way over the office in Madison, Wisconsin, which suffers from boosterism.

You asked if our mills are more modern and efficient than theirs. On the whole, yes. But we have some real loser modern mills (poorly designed, workers hate the owners, etc.) and they have some very cost-effective old mills in Mississippi where wages are terrible and unions are virtually non-existent.

You asked about water-bedding and other baloney. Don't bother. I've talked with John Ragusta, the chief American lawyer for their producers. He is out to get his clients the best possible deal. Period. He doesn't care about anything other than that and he won't care even if you sign him up for spam from Obscure Religions.org. His attitude has made him a millionaire.

Now for the news. The new B.C. government is going to dump a huge amount of stuff the government has been paying for onto the companies. My sources, high in government, tell me, "Business wanted less government. They're going to get it . . . in spades." The announcements haven't been made yet, because Victoria is still working on the spin.

You asked about inputs and outputs. Don't go there. Try instead: have companies been making money? The answer is some companies, on some products. L&M Lumber in Vanderhoof makes the boards used in millions of box springs a year. You sleep on L&M. They're doing okay, although normal lumber sales are down. Another local company's executive told me that "the key isn't making lumber. It is selling it. Our relations with our customers are the real value in our business, not the mill equipment." That company is in the black. Is Canfor making money on lumber? No way.

I hope I'm being clear. If not, I'll give you the exact truth from one of the 10 best books ever written on investing: *Popular Delusions and the Madness of Crowds*, written by Charles MacKay in 1841. He wrote that "No group is more intelligent than its least intelligent member." Based on this principle, we can be assured that on each side of the border there's at least one lumber executive who is hidden in a closet, drooling.

36

On Saturday the fine weather of the past several days fades, and when I grope my way up to Barry and Joy's kitchen from my dungeon Sunday morning, the sky is industrial steel with sulphur-yellow shadings. By the time Barry and I stumble outside a half-hour later to wait for Kent Sedgwick's arrival, it is spitting rain, the air torpid and chilly at the same time and stinking of sulphides.

Rain rattles off the windshield of Kent's '91 Chevy pickup as we climb the hill above the Fraser, east of the city. Over Kent's left shoulder I can see the white puffs from the pulp mills drifting southwest across the city—proof of the Williston Lake wind that didn't exist 35 years ago, when what little wind the city got moved with the jet stream, west to east.

Barry sits between Kent and me holding an empty Thermos we're planning to fill with coffee at the service centre at the top of the hill. In the back, protected by a fibreglass canopy, are Kent's two middle-aged but excited white Labs, both female. They were pups when I saw them in 1993, but are old enough now that one is overweight and arthritic.

With the dogs are two picnic coolers, packed with enough food for several days. Barry's explanation when I asked about all the food was terse: "Kent likes to eat when he gets outdoors."

"Isn't he bringing his own food?"

"Sure. But watching him eat always makes me hungry, too."

After our coffee's bought and we're back on Highway 16 heading east, the rain becomes the heavy, steady downpour I remember from my Forest Service days, but as soon as we cross the bridge over the Bowron River and turn onto the bumpy forestry road that runs south from the highway, it tapers off. Before we've gone a mile, it has stopped. If I believed in omens, this would be one. Trouble is, I don't have any sense of what it's supposed to foreshadow. A lifetime of overcast? Or the clouds of blackflies and mosquitoes we'll get whenever we stop.

A couple of kilometres down the road, and well before we're into the clearcut proper, I spot a sign at the edge of the main road announcing a "Decommissioned" road. I ask Kent to stop.

"Oh," he says, "the Forest Service has been decommissioning skid- and haul-roads for four or five years now."

The idea, he explains, is to make it difficult for hunters to get too far up the passable roads because this is where, drunk and disorderly, they start a lot of forest fires, get into drunken fights, and occasionally shoot one another—always by accident, of course. Kent backs up the truck, pulls it into the decommissioned road, and I get out. I have to walk less than 100 metres up this one to discover that the decommissioning is accomplished by removing one or two of the 30-centimetre culverts that criss-cross these roads at regular intervals. It means that the only way to travel up a decommissioned road is on foot or in a high-bed four-by-four. This method of decommissioning might sound like a good idea in principle, but in actuality, there's a flaw. It's the drunkest and the craziest of the hunters who tend to be the ones who own the high-bed four-by-fours. From the tire marks on the far side of the removed culvert, it didn't stop them here.

On the far side of the second excavated culvert, I discover a truck plate. The licence tag is only a few months out of date, so I deduce that it came off last fall during hunting season. Judging from the bullet holes in the culvert and the dents in an abandoned water tanker nearby, the owner was too drunk to look for the licence, or too engrossed in shooting up the place to care.

While I'm examining the plate and the bullet holes, the bugs discover me, and I have to retreat to the truck in a hurry for the can of bug spray I've brought. Barry, who has been sitting in the front seat of the truck drinking coffee, is laughing. I spray each wrist 360 degrees, douse the back of my neck, and run the spray nozzle up and down the fronts and backs of my legs. Then I spray the palms of my hand long enough for the aerosol to pool, and rub my face, making sure my eyes sting because it's the best way of ensuring the bugs won't crawl behind my glasses to bite my eyelids.

Barry climbs out of the truck while I'm doing this, stands close to me to keep the bugs at bay, but doesn't take the spray can when I offer it. Within seconds a blackfly takes a chunk from his unprotected neck, and he scrambles back into the truck, swearing. Kent is busy with the dogs. They bounce out of the back the moment he drops the tailgate, run around wildly until the bugs discover them, and leap back in, satisfied for the moment. The bugs don't seem to bother Kent.

Back out on the main forestry road, we don't get half a kilometre before Kent's truck starts to make a deafening racket. For a moment he keeps his hands on the wheel, hoping whatever it is hasn't happened, because of course it could be much worse than just a broken muffler. But soon he pulls over, and he and I crawl under the truck to inspect. The pipe in front of the resonator has snapped just back of the cab, but the clamps have kept the system intact, so we're mechanically sound. We agree that it's better this than the flex pipe that comes out of the engine, but there's no way to do a temporary patch, and we'll just have to live with the noise.

I can see that Kent's instinct is to turn around and return the way we've come. That's more alarming to me than the threat that we'll asphyxiate on the exhaust fumes, because it would mean another trip later in the week. I've got things I can't *not* do in here.

"I can't smell any exhaust," I say cheerfully.

"Just drive faster," Barry says. "The fumes will blow out the back better. And hit a few of those potholes, too. That'll shake the carbon monoxide out of the nooks and crannies."

Kent agrees to continue, a little reluctantly. I slide open the side windows in the canopy so the dogs will get fresh air, and on we drive. Kent distracts himself by looking for the carcass of a moose he'd seen along this same stretch of road late last fall, and even though I know damned well a winter-kill carcass will be scavenged to nothing within a month, I go along because it gets us down the road. Within a few kilometres, we've gotten used to the truck's throaty roar, and things go back to a noisier version of normal.

We don't find the carcass, and there's little else we can see except roadside gravel and underbrush. The regenerating forest now crowds the margins of the road with 3- to 6-metre trees. This transforms the clearcut, visually at least, into bush again: the condition of not being able to see the forest for its trees. I consider the accuracy of that homily along with the ubiquitous piles of bear scat at the edges of the road-bed. Just before we enter the main clearcut, there's a recently cut tract, probably only a few months old. It looks to be 20 to 30 hectares in size, and it reminds me of how barren it once looked all through here.

At one of the four stops we make before we reach the river, we drive off-road to an abandoned log landing. Almost 20 years have passed since this area was logged, 15 since it was burned for replanting, and the degree of regeneration is pretty good. The gravel exposed by the landing is nearly covered by a thin layer of silt-like topsoil that is mostly itself covered in pale olive drab moss. Surrounding the land-ing are 3- to 5-metre lodgepole pines, their foliage a rich kelly green, and dotting the surface of the landing are tiny spruce, some no more than a few centimetres tall. Coniferous seed is tough. These ones must have sat dormant for a decade waiting for the right conditions to germinate.

Some garbage left by camp-ing hunters is strewn around the landing, but a series of shallow holes tell us that at least these ones tried to bury it.

"You know what the new *Forests Act* calls these things?" Kent says.

"You mean log landings?"

"Yeah," he says. "Now they're called 'borrow pits.' Isn't social democracy great?"

A few kilometres south we come to Haggen Creek and stop for an early lunch, driving 200 metres down a slippery side road to its junction with the Bowron River—one of the parks Billy Walsh was complaining about. Though there's been heavy rain, the two streams are reasonably clear, which means that topsoil isn't being washed away any more. For the first time, I realize that I'm feeling reasonably normal while I'm inside the clearcut, and I can't quite decide why. The silence and desolation around me felt like a physical weight. Kent and Barry seem to think it's quite okay being here now, too. They break open the coolers and each wolfs down mountains of food, while the dogs run around merrily despite the spitting rain and the clouds of hovering bugs. I pick out a few rocks and try to throw them across the river, just to see if I can still do it. They plunk into the water a metre or two from the far bank.

"High water." Barry shrugs.

Though he's agreed to traverse the entire clearcut for me, Kent seems to be intent on highballing it through and out in a hurry. I have to use the excuse of needing photographs to force a few stops. I duti-fully snap the photos, changing the camera lenses to buy time, but I'm really using the photo ops to sniff the air, renew my sense of the place. It's as easy to take in the character and structure of a forest by smell as by sight. A stand of spruce-balsam smells different from a pine-dominant stand. Spruce trees have a faintly sweet aroma; pine has a more acrid, almost dusty perfume that's unaffected by wet weather. There are other markers, too. A stand of mature spruce after a windstorm is nearly as perfumed as the rarer cedar stands because the trees bleed pitch from the micro-cracks the wind inflicts. It's less pleasant to the nose than cut cedar, and most of it quickly dissipates as the sap hardens. By contrast, a clearcut has almost no scent at all a year after the trees are removed. And after a regeneration burn, all you can smell is the charcoal.

Either by sight or scent, the clearcut I came to see has ceased to exist. In its place is a young forest. There are few vistas where I can test this visually, and I get Kent to stop the truck whenever I think I can have one. Where I'm able to see for any distance, it is apparent that the desolation has dissipated except up toward the alpine, where the mismanaged slash burns have left a collar of white snags. It's only because I remember where to look and how that I can detect what I found here a decade ago. The best vista is from a hillside prospect just after we cross from the east bank of the Bowron River to the west and head up into what was once the crossroads at the epicentre. There, I recognize a spot where the replanting was done in different years using different species: on one side, a stand of taller, bright-green lodgepole pines crowds against a plot of smaller spruce with foliage a shade darker. From my bag I pull out a photograph Don White took five years ago, and compare it to what's there now   and then forget to snap a parallel photo.

A committed environmentalist would no doubt see all this differently. Most of the replanting has been done with one species—likely whatever the suppliers happen to deliver to them that week, and the trees went into the ground without much regard for the suitability of the soil or terrain. There's been no serious attempt to provide bio-diversity, which the industry tends to equate with underbrush and competitive non-commercial species whether they admit it or not. To them, these are farms for trees, and they're not about to deliberately introduce weeds or even mix together the commercial species to confuse the next harvest. Those sorts of battles are for the reclamation of future clearcuts, and will require an entirely different imagination—on both sides—to resolve. That said, this clearcut is looking pretty good.

Even in the old-growth forests I've been in up here, I've had trouble feeling the presence of the giant Gaia mushroom that environmentalists believe unifies and nurtures the Great Forest—itself a concept I have trouble with. Northern boreal forests are vast and remarkable, but they don't ever make you feel like they're upper-case "Great." My instinct is that the Gaia Mushroom Theory is one of those tweedy sit-in-your-faculty-office notions that serves the thinker better than the subject, in the same way that the upper-case Free Market System is the self-serving invention of suit-wearing MBAs sunk deep in leather executive chairs at the top of high-rise office towers. The Free Market System doesn't feel free to the people in its gritty depths driving the forklifts and packing the boxes of widgets from one conveyor belt to the next, and the Great Forest doesn't feel great or unified if you're working inside it with a horde of blackflies up your nose.

This doesn't mean wrongs weren't done here in the Bowron River valley. They were. But the recovery point has passed in this rough-scrabble landscape. Any settling of accounts—and a settling of accounts remains necessary for a raft of good reasons—will have to be played out on a different stage. It ought to be settled between  the corporations who took away all the profits from logging this valley, and the governments who permitted too great a share of the harvest to be enjoyed too far from the community that has had to live with the consequences. If there's anything to be frightened about here, it is that we have no instruments to settle such accounts, and no will to see them settled. We have, instead, grids of righteous belief to blind us to every point of view but our own and those of our ideological allies.

So, despite some damaged or permanently lost biodiversity, the Bowron is once again a living forest. There are birds here, and more insects than I can use. There's moose pellets and bear scat everywhere I look, and grouse flutter as foolishly through the underbrush as they ever did, which is itself alive with plant species that give professional foresters indigestion to think about. The Bowron River valley is going to survive this assault. The soil cover is thinner, the river has more silt in the water than it did when I tried to canoe it in the 1960s, and salmon are rare, if there's any left at all. The regeneration doesn't mean this forest will survive another clearcut, but the valley is healing.

37

In spite of my photograph-taking delays—and several other flimsy excuses I think up for stopping—we're on the far western edge of the clearcut before I'm ready to leave. I spot several tracts where I think they've used herbicides to hold down the underbrush, and another where it seems possible that sheep have been grazing. But stopping to look takes little time, and I can't say with certainty that my theories are correct because I haven't brought rain gear and thus can't get very far into the bushes without getting soaked from head to toe. The truth is that there's very little to look at once we're away from the river. On the west side the vistas are more closed than on the east, and after a few hours, one 5-metre pine tree looks pretty much the same as the next, even to an ex-cruiser like me. With the intermittent rain, penetrating the new growth is a too-soggy proposition to think about, and getting far up the decaying haul-roads in a truck with a damaged muffler and no four-wheel drive isn't practical. We're all chilled, and I'm wet from bushwhacking along the edges. It's too early for a shot of whisky, which we haven't brought anyway; and all three of us are too old and way too clean-living to stop for a smoke.

So it isn't very long after lunch when we cross the west boundary of the clearcut, rumbling down into the Willow River watershed near the south edge of Narrow Lake where Barry and I camped in

1990 with our sons. Kent is still fretting about his broken muffler, but there's no hint that the fumes are getting at us or the dogs, and it's easy for Barry and me to talk him into stopping at the Narrow Lake forestry campsite. The dogs need a run, he agrees. I glance at my watch: it's just after 1:00 p.m.

On the way in, the Narrow Lake campsite is as I remember: the road is bumpy and ill-maintained, the bed as much run-off boulders as gravel, the ruts axle-breaking deep. But the campsite has changed for the better. A half-dozen camper trucks, several with boats and trailers, are visible in the camping bays. The campers are mostly couples, middle-aged, and their vehicles aren't new or flashy—there's not a motorhome on the site.

As we're getting out of the truck a 20-year-old Ford 150 pulling a 4-metre skiff on a rickety trailer bumps past. The driver is a large strong-jawed man about 60, probably a millwright or a railroader near retirement. His wife is overweight, red-haired, and has a bottle of beer in one hand and a cigarette in the other. She ignores us, but he gives us a nod as they pass, not quite friendly—the acknowledgement customary in the backwoods. It translates as "You're out here, too."

As we walk down to the lake, I'm struck by how clean the camp is. There's no strewn garbage anywhere, no broken glass, no recently hacked-up trees, no fishing line in the bushes. By each camping bay is a neat stack of firewood, some of it birch but mostly spruce, and next to that, a 45-gallon barrel for garbage.

Barry sees this too. "The only thing missing are the 'No Smoking' signs," he says.

The lake level is high, but what little shoreline between the lake and the trees it hasn't taken is clear of debris. Kent's two white Labs are already in the water, barking at us to throw sticks to them. At the water's edge is a potbellied fisherman with a casting rod, and two scruffy toddlers, the older of which might be five. The fisherman has a cigarette dangling from his lips, and a half-full bottle of Kokanee parked by his right boot.

Kent tries to coax the dogs out of the water, but they're not going for it, so he apologizes to the fisherman. "I hope my dogs aren't scaring off the fish," he says.

The fisherman turns to us without ceasing to reel. He's younger than I first thought, no older than his late twenties. He's also pissed to the eyeballs. "Oh, s'no problem," he says, gazing blearily at the dogs as if he's just noticed they're there. "I'm fishing far enough out so they won't be in the way. Wanna beer? There's a case over in the bushes."

We each shake our heads, no, and in answer, he flicks the rod upward and back over his head, and I hear something whistle between us and the toddlers. A silver lure snakes within a few centimetres of the ground, no more than a metre from the toddlers, and is gone as the fisherman extends his arm. We watch the lure sail over the water, 20, 30, perhaps 40 metres before it plunks into the lake.

"Not many fuckin' fish this morning," the fisherman says to no one in particular, then zeroes in on Kent. "Changed my fuckin' lure twice already, but nothing. Good last night, though. Caught a couple of 2 pounders in the first 10 minutes."

I pick up a short stick and toss it out for the dogs. They both swim for it, but the skinnier one easily gets there first. The other waits, treading water, and grabs the stick on the way in, and they trot out together, tails wagging.

"Try a bigger stick," Kent says. "They'll do the same thing. It's all teamwork for them."

Barry finds a bigger stick, throws it out past them, and they drop the small stick and splash back into the lake. These are dogs that would do this until they dropped, even at their age. Maybe that's why the fisherman decides that there's no fish to be had or that the dogs really are scaring them off. He reels in his line, clips the hook deftly to the eye closest to the reel, walks over to the bushes, drains the beer he's been careful not to knock over, and drops the empty into the half-hidden case. Or tries to. One of the toddlers gets tangled up in his legs and he falls ass-over-teakettle into the bushes.

He crawls out, red-faced and cursing, but the toddlers have wisely retreated up the road to look for their mother. The fisherman disengages the rod from the underbrush, lifts the beer case out, and squares his shoulders. He gives us a watery-eyed grin and staggers up the road after them.

Kent takes this as our cue to get moving, and calls the dogs out, explaining that the older one's arthritis can't take water this cold for too long. The dogs do what he asks, only a little reluctantly, with the stick still in their jaws.

Ten kilometres up the road we catch up to the camper and boat that had been leaving as we arrived. The driver is tooling along the middle of the gravel road at about 40 kilometres per hour, in no hurry, maybe because the boat is bouncing around precariously atop its trailer, and he wants to stay where he is until the road is wide and flat enough that he can pull over to let us pass. Kent flicks his high beams at him to let him know we're there, but all he does is pick it up another 5 kilometres per hour. We follow him for several kilometres that way, likewise in no great hurry, just far enough back to avoid the gravel spew.

Barry, who's sitting between Kent and me, begins to doze off, which makes me wonder if we're getting some exhaust in the cab after all. I roll down the window a few centimetres, then check the dogs, who seem quite happy pacing around the box, occasionally sticking their snouts near the canopy opening. As I turn back, I see a burly arm appear from the driver's side of the camper. It releases something, which flies up and back, shattering on the gravel by the side of the road. It's a beer bottle. As if to confirm this, a moment later the arm appears again, and a second bottle sails into the bushes.

Kent, on a reflex, lays on the horn. "Jesus H. Christ," he says. "That jackass just tossed his empties out the window."

I know what Kent's thinking: People who use the bush don't do that any more. Or shouldn't. Maybe if you're a 20-year-old, and oblivious to everything but your dick. This guy damned well ought to know better.

Barry's eyes open. "What's happening?" he asks.

"That jerk in the camper just smashed an empty beer bottle on the road," I explain.

"Take down his licence plate and we'll report him. Or run him off the road or something."

The driver of the camper decides Kent's horn blast means we want past, and he slows a little and moves to the edge of the road. As we go by, Kent shakes his finger at him. He doesn't respond except to shrug, but his wife gives us her middle finger: screw you. Barry pulls a scrap of paper from the glove compartment and scribbles the licence number on it, then puts the paper back into the glove compartment and slams it shut. By the time we reach town we've decided that it's useless to turn him in.

An hour later I remember I had my cell phone in my pocket, and mention to Barry that we should have called the cops to report the litterer as a drunk driver. He was tossing beer bottles out the window, so he must have been drinking them. At very least, the police would have given him a hard time, and if he actually was drunk, an impaired charge would be better punishment than a citation for littering.

"Yeah," Barry agrees. "We should have done that. But we didn't think of it."

I've got the rest of the afternoon free, so I use a little of it to drink some near-beer with Barry, and the rest to move across town to John and Vivien's place. It isn't my part of town, but at least I'll see the sun come up, and it'll be quiet. I'm here to work, I remind myself.

One of the neighbours is working on a boat in the adjoining driveway when I get there, and he eyeballs me while I find the key and go over, in my head, the instructions for turning off the alarm. Before I put the key in the lock I wave to him, and he smiles and goes back to what he's doing. I open the door, flip open the alarm box right beside it, punch in the code. It's nerve-racking, but not very difficult. The red light stays on longer than I'm comfortable about, but then the green light illuminates, and I'm okay.

The house, tidy without being excessively so, smells of camping equipment, an odd melange of woodsmoke, canvas, and mosquito dope. Otherwise the place is unremarkable. It has the feel of a dwelling whose occupants prefer to be elsewhere and so spend as little on upkeep and interior decorating as they can. That's accurate enough. John prefers his farm on the Buckhorn, and Viv prefers any of the thousands of places across the planet she hasn't yet visited. I park my bags in what I decide is the guest room, which is furnished similarly to the master bedroom but is smaller. Both rooms contain beds, tall bookcases filled with books, and sawdust-board dressers. In the basement, each of them has a spacious office, with computers and wide desks, and floor-to-ceiling bookcases. But except for a few pictures of family members and themselves at younger ages, the offices are curiously impersonal for people who each led complicated lives before they collided with each other. I guess that makes sense: they work and live here during the winter months, and dream of being elsewhere.

I set up my laptop on the kitchen table, plug it in, and boot up. Then I make myself a cup of herbal tea and sit down to work for a few hours.

The sun awakens me the next morning at 4 a.m., even though the guest room windows face west. I get out of bed, dress, and sit on the front porch for an hour listening to almost nothing at all while the sky slowly brightens. A pair of robins are singing in the bushes next door, and further off, I hear chickadees and crows. The overcast isn't quite as heavy as it was yesterday, but still promises more rain. The only other sounds are the transport trucks jake-braking just before they reach the Nechako Bridge, then racketing up the highway on the far side.

38

The Simon Fraser Inn, the city's first modern hotel, didn't make it to the 21st century. It was swallowed by a succession of hotel chains and is now a Day's Inn, redecorated in that corporation's Spartan pastels over new stucco. The coffee garden has also been reconfigured and renamed "Ruby's." I'm sitting in a side booth to see what's left of the Coffee Klatch, and at 9:30 in the morning it isn't looking very promising. There's a single Klatcher at their nest of adjoining tables, an ex-mill-owner in his eighties whose name eludes me, dozing with his chin slumped on his chest.

I order breakfast and settle in with my notes, content to wait this one out. Sure enough, one by one the Klatchers begin to trickle in.

By the time a half dozen have collected, they're as boisterous as schoolboys, cantankerously baiting one another and the waitress, who evidently knows and likes them. Just as they used to, they soon take over the café. It's easier today than a few years ago because the place is as deserted as the rest of downtown Prince George was when I drove here.

When these men were my age, to make a run into this downtown was to wade neck-deep through opportunity and good fortune. Now, for them as for everyone else, there's a palpable sense that the axe is about to fall. For most, the axe-holder is a bank employee with a foreclosure notice. For the Klatchers, the axe is liable to be in the hands of the Grim Reaper.

By 10:30 a dozen Klatchers have arrived, including Harold Moffat. He looks older, but alert and healthy. He's still the group's alpha male, plunking himself into a chair mid-table and proceeding to rag on the others with his strong, slightly nasal voice. Yesterday in the clearcut, Barry mentioned that Harold still goes to work every day, even though he's given up control of the store to his son Ted. Ted has set him up with an office on the ground floor, in plain sight of one of the main cash registers. He's doing what I think he always liked best in the hardware business: answering customers' questions, finding things that no one else in the store can find, and taking orders for what he doesn't have in stock. Now that I think about it, that's why my father always spoke of Moffat with respect even though the two men probably didn't get along. My father understood how important hand to hand service was in a small business, and that the moment you say "I can't get you that," someone else will, and you and your business are toast. Harold Moffat was the embodiment of that principle in Prince George, and if Barry's story about his new office is accurate, he'll continue to be until the day he drops. Not a bad way to go out.

At 10:45 Wally West ambles in, and the hubbub peaks. It's my cue, too, since I've finished my breakfast and have my notes in order. I cover the cheque, slip a two-dollar coin under the edge of my coffee cup in case I have to come back in a few days, wander over to the Klatchers, and tap Wally on the shoulder. He turns, blinks, and the lights go on.

"Ah. Brian, isn't it? You must be here inspecting the family assets."

I don't correct him. He's earned the right to think whatever he likes, and not be bothered by children or writers needing to assert their irrelevant identities.

"Your Dad was through here a month or so back, you know? With Ron's son, Jason, wasn't it? I think he was"—he pauses to grimace—"looking for a housekeeper. I'm sorry about your mother."

"So am I," I answer. "But she was 90, and prepared to go—she got more years than she expected. . . ."

I cut the spiel short because Wally's body language tells me he'd prefer to move on: these are men who know enough about people dying that they don't enjoy talking about it. There's a moment of awkward silence, and then he turns to the assembled Klatchers, who by this time are staring at me curiously, and begins the introductions.

Harold Moffat's head snaps up. "Hartley's boy, right? The one who lives back east?"

"Yes," I answer. There's no malice in his expression.

"Your old man was in town here a few weeks back. He was supposed to come down and say hello, but he didn't show up."

"I'm surprised by that," I say, even though I'm not. As it happens, I'd heard the story about him being invited and at the last moment refusing to go. Jason, who told me the story, was puzzled by his grandfather's reluctance, but generously decided that it was his poor hearing—which makes him increasingly at a loss in groups—that was the cause.

Moffat grins, and there's a flash of the old malicious light in his eyes. "I think," he says with a showman's pause, "it was because the last time he came down here, we nicked him for the bill. He always was a cheapskate."

The Klatchers who've been paying attention find this accurate and thoroughly amusing, and so do I.

"That sounds about right," I admit. "But I think he's been having a lot of trouble with coffee recently. Never had much of a stomach for it, and his system is getting a little delicate now that he's in his nineties."

Moffat peers at me, not quite willing to be serious, but cautiously curious. "You write books, don't you?"

I resist an impulse to answer with "Yes, sir," and nod my head instead.

"Good for you," he says, and turns back to his conversation partner across the table.

I shake hands with a few of the Klatchers near me, some of whom still have no idea who I am and ask me to repeat my name. Moffat looks up, and I lean over to him and extend my hand. "Nice seeing you again, sir," I say.

He takes the handshake but doesn't answer. The slight smile on his face confirms that he heard the "sir," and that he understood it wasn't the usual insolence.

39

I leave my rental car parked on the street and walk to the public library, a block away through the rain to the new Civic Centre complex. About five years old now, it is a pastiche of almost every popular architectural cliché going, with faux steel-pipe buttressing, a clock tower not tall enough to be seen outside the complex square, and several prominent Native totem poles, even though the local Carriers weren't carvers of wood. It has the ergonomics of a strip mall, and the only reason it doesn't resemble one is that there are no franchise logos visible.

In its defence, it is what you get when you try to duplicate Walt Disney World on a restricted budget, and have to pay lip service to militant Native Indians, the disabled, and other people you don't understand and want to prevent from clogging up the place with their protests. It is also what you get if you believe your city is for people who aren't there: tourists, conventioneers, a future influx of the elderly.

The Prince George Public Library sits immediately behind the Civic Centre on dozens of thick concrete stilts. It has a wholly clashing style of architecture, but since the library was built first, it is whoever approved the Civic Centre's design that's to blame for the mishmash. Despite the symbolically goofy gesture of elevating itself above the goings-on of the city (the ground level is used for parking), the library is airy, light-filled, and functional once you're inside. For a summer morning, even a rainy one, it is also surprisingly busy. The open areas are full of patrons coming and going, and what I can see of the stacks shows them filled with people who seem to know what they're looking for.

I ask a smiling middle-aged woman to show me the newspaper microfiche section, and she takes me over, explains the set-up, and when I ask about photocopies, quickly shows me that as well. She doesn't seem to want a library card or compensatory ID, she merely wants to be helpful. The 1990 microfiche seems to be at the dry cleaners or otherwise occupied, but within five minutes, I'm pouring through 1993 and 1996 newspapers. What I'm looking for is context: what was happening locally and globally while I was wandering around the clearcut on the Bowron.

The weather at midsummer in 1993, according to the *Prince George Citizen*, was much as it was a few days ago: clear skies, 20 degrees, and about to cloud over and misbehave. Kim Campbell was the Prime Minister of Canada; B.C. had recently embarked on its second social democratic government; and Canfor president and then CEO Peter Bentley had just been in town trying to raise support for letting the forest companies "manage" the forests: code for letting the corporations have permanent tenure over the forests and letting them cut whatever they think they need. Since such a changeover was unlikely to be popular under any government, Bentley was making a pre-emptive strike against the inevitable reductions in the annual allowable cut that was bound to be considered by a government that got itself elected by promising to be more sensitive to environmental issues and to the general viability of the longer-term economy.

That same week the local RCMP detachment was looking for a 28-year-old Native Indian involved in a murder, and the latest version of downtown revitalization was coming unglued over recent property tax hikes, which the downtown merchants were unwilling to pay because they were also being asked to shoulder most of the burden for revitalization. Revitalization, 1993-style, appears to have consisted of returning Third Avenue and George Street to four lanes of traffic and dismantling the other "improvements" made in the 1970s.

After a half-hour trying to make sense of 1993, my eyes begin to sting, and I break off—able to do so without losing my access to the machine because no one else seems interested in the past—or at least, the past as interpreted by the microfiched *Citizen*. To my right, I spot a room that houses about a dozen computers, each running a 19-inch monitor—apparently, state of the art. All of the machines are being used by young Net surfers. Half of them are Native, young, large, healthy, and mesomorphic: things have changed.

Then I stroll out into the rotunda and see something that makes me ask myself if things really have changed. Climbing the open staircase are two familiar-looking men. They're middle-aged, or at least look that age, both under five foot eight, and both skinny as rails. They're talking to one another, slowly and with exaggerated deliberateness, as if the other is speaking a strange, hard-to-comprehend language. They're mounting the stairs in the same cartoonish slo-mo, as if each footfall has to be consciously planned and executed.

They're also Native Indians, these two, and 30 years ago they'd have been frogmarched out of any public building in the city. But today, no one is paying the slightest attention to them, and they don't seem self-conscious about being where they are. So, things *have* changed. I watch them reach the level I'm on, commune silently as the other people in the library move past them as if in another dimension of time. Then, with the same, somehow indeterminately slow but confident deliberateness, they begin the journey up to the next floor. As they mount the stairs, I try to figure out why they seem so familiar.

I return to the archive, literally scratching my head, and begin to go through the newspapers for the second week of September 1996: September 12th was sunny and 18 degrees, but the night temperatures are dropping close to freezing, and rain is predicted. Among the stories I stumble across is the watershed announcement that the NDP government plans to rob the $800-million Forest Renewal Fund of as much as $400 million—thus setting the course that led to the party's political eradication from the B.C. Interior. Deeper in the same paper are the beginnings of a controversy over hunting bears that declares the binary battle that still rages between conservationists and hunters. British Columbia, it states, has between 120,000 and 160,000 black bears, and 10,000 to 13,000 grizzlies. Hunters want to keep their right to shoot bears at the current rates: 3,000 black bears annually, and 300 grizzlies. Conservationists are petitioning to have any sort of bear-hunting made illegal, citing falling grizzly populations but ignoring the fact that the current black bear population is at an all-time high, and that the bears are a dangerous nuisance at every garbage dump in the northern half of the province. The problem with the sensible solution—which is to ban grizzly hunting and allow the black bear hunt to continue—is that it doesn't satisfy the emotional-ized agendas of either side. The conservationist want every bear to live in splendour—provided with pillows and bedsheets by the govern-ment—even though this will mean that garbage dumps will crowd with nuisance bears and children in isolated communities will be justi-fiably afraid to play outdoors. On the other side, the hunters fervently believe their testicles will shrivel up and fall off if they lose the right to massacre the only predator on the continent that isn't afraid of them.

What else? Another of the endless debates about the "appropri-ateness" of Mr. PeeGee is going nowhere; Prince George reports the highest per capita rate of drivers zapped by photo radar; a prominent local Sikh suggests that turbans are an acceptable substitute for motorcycle crash helmets: ". . . the turban protects quite a bit from falls," he says. The silly season in northern B.C. extended well into September that year, I guess.

While I'm pulling the 1996 reel off the machine, there is a tap on my shoulder. It's Bev Christensen. As it happens, I'd seen her just a few weeks ago, in Toronto, where she was visiting family and, I think, taking a break from Prince George. I took her for late breakfast at the Senator, the restaurant I figured could most closely approximate the hearty Prince George–style breakfast I assumed she'd be pining for. But Bev was enjoying big-city pleasures. She ate fruit and yogurt while I picked her brain about what's been going on in the city politically since the provincial election. For her, politics now means the School Board, of which she's been an elected member since she retired from the *Citizen* in the early 1990s. Since the School District over which the board presides is the largest and most complicated in the province, it tends to be nearer the centre of local political issues than in most cities. The change of provincial government has cost it three of its sitting members, one of whom is now the Liberal member for one of the local ridings and, reputedly, a major player in the new government.

Bev likes the newly elected board members, but she isn't unreservedly enthusiastic. "They'll be an improvement mainly because they'll *be there*," she says. "A board with three members who were never at meetings was barely able to function."

I ask her what the big issues facing the board are, given the current economic woes and a shrinking school enrolment.

Her answer is swift and firm. "Funding for special needs."

"You mean ESL, adult literacy?"

"No," she says. "The biggest problem in northern B.C. is with FAS children, and the learning and social disabilities involved."

It takes me a minute to unravel the FAS abbreviation as "Fetal Alcohol Syndrome," and I miss part of the explanatory spiel she's doubtless repeated several hundred times. What I do hear is that it has been a problem here for decades, but that only within the past two has anyone recognized what it was they were dealing with, particularly within the Native Indian population.

"White people around here just thought Indians were like that," she concludes.

The moment she says it I know precisely what "like that" means. It's those two men I watched climbing the stairs a few minutes ago, the ones who are probably just now on their way back down the staircase, happily out of the rain for a few hours, but permanently lost in a fog they did not create, one that is not natural to any member of the human species but which they can never escape.

40

Outside the library, the rain has stopped and the skies are lightening. To the west, the cloud is even breaking into patches of open blue. I was planning to drive up to UNBC and crash the premier's news conference, but since I've never had much stomach for that sort of aggression, I was dreading it. And anyway, now I have a better option. I'll drive out to the Huble Homestead.

I don't have a pressing reason to go except that I like it there, and I'm curious to know if I got the wildflower species I saw in 1993 correct. There'd been a graphics chart in the then-new building being used as a gatehouse, and I'd written down the names of the plants, lost the notes, and later had to reconstruct them with an ancient guide to northern plants I've had since childhood—and some half-educated guesses. Another thing I'm reconsidering was what I recorded about the road in to the farm eight years ago. I described it as running along a depression that made it impossible to see the trees at the edges of the fields. It was, I wrote, like being on the prairies. Was that accurate?

A snippet of last night's conversation with Barry is making me question these sorts of "facts," along with my powers of recollection in general. He mentioned, as we were sitting around the fire, that he and Joy had left town partway through my visit in 1993. His mother had died, and they'd left in a rush for Calgary to attend the funeral. I'd remained in the house alone to take care of the dog. That meant that a walk I'd written about, with the two of us circling the block where hockey player Brian Spenser's father had been shot to death by the police, was a memory clip from some earlier visit, and that Barry hadn't been present at a subsequent lunch with John Harris at Other Art. While I had Barry making witty remarks in a Prince George café, he was in Calgary burying his mother.

In 1993, the death of one's mother wasn't something that registered on me: my own parents, though elderly, were still hale and healthy, and I still believed, as people do long after they cease to be children, that parents are immortal. In 2001, with my mother six months gone, finding that I'd totally forgotten the death of Barry's mother is disturbing. Are all historical accounts constructed the way mine was? I've already spoken to the fate of objectivity in this world: snowballs in hell. But this was simple recollection, not ideology. What other things have I missed?

These questions makes the drive out to the Huble Homestead not quite the casual event it might have been. It becomes a test of what I'm here to see and write about, and how I'm doing it. I begin the drive as I usually do, recreating the landscapes I grew up in and checking them against the present. For the first few kilometres of the highway the disjunction is almost total: nearly every metre of it is now urbanized, and what little had been developed 40 to 50 years ago has, except for a single ramshackle motel, been redeveloped, sometimes several times: hills have been levelled, swamps filled, and trees cleared, often for kilometres on each side of the highway. As an exercise, I force myself to reverse the order of my perception: I look at what is here on this day in June 2001, consciously record the details, and only then allow the past in. In 2001, it is a 10-kilometre strip mall, backgrounded by some well-constructed suburban homes. In, say, 1961, it was a patchwork of decaying homesteads, half-finished shacks, gyppo mills, abandoned cars, and a few near-to-the-building-code homes handbuilt by immigrant families without the money to buy land in town. Then I ask myself which is the better version, and am slightly surprised by the answer: 2001. The relative aesthetics are a wash, but today's homes are more livable, the services improved, the risk of disease (mainly from poorly constructed or non-existent sewage disposal systems) much reduced.

At the Chief Lake turnoff, the sight of a taxidermist shop that has been in the same log shack for 50 years ends the exercise and gives me back the world I grew up with. The highway turns east here toward Salmon River. Little has been altered save for the few homesteader shacks replaced by permanent homes and prefabs. The landscape is broad and relatively flat, sloping gently eastward into the river valley, much of it productive farmland. Geologically, the area is unusual: the soil is deep, and where the drainage is adequate, the tree cover is heavily deciduous—poplar and birch. Under the topsoil is some clay, but there are deposits of coarse sand instead of the usual gravel and glacial moraine, a gift from the vast lake that covered the Prince George area after the last glaciation. The Salmon River has since carved its serpentine way across it, joining the Fraser a few kilometres to the south. There is another feature to the landscape that I haven't understood until now. While the glacial lake ebbed and waxed, it was no more than an underwater ridge. Today that ridge separates the flow of water to the Arctic and Pacific oceans.

Once across the Salmon River the terrain rises sharply up onto the ridge. The highway, here and there, likely runs along the crest of the Divide, crossing it for good just before the turnoff to the Huble Homestead. Which I have trouble finding, of course, because I'm really looking for it to be just beyond the crest of every rise. After the third or fourth of those, I drive several hundred metres past the turnoff before the sign registers.

I'm wrong about the road in to the Homestead. It doesn't run along a depression. Trees are visible at all points along the margins of the field, and I stop the car in the middle of the deserted road to try to figure out why I got it so wrong eight years ago. It's nothing very complicated: the fields cover an upland plateau, and no hills break the horizon's stable plane. That elongates the sky, and with the overcast by now broken up into ribbles of fluffy cloud, it *feels* like I can see forever. That's what I'd recorded.

The Homestead is closer to the way I recall it. The draws and ditches at its edges are filled with masses of wild lupens, ox-eye daisies, Indian paintbrushes, the fields flat and, where they haven't had a mower taken to them or been grazed, covered in tall grass. Close by the road, several parcels are now enclosed by period fences made of small logs, designed to keep livestock in and wild beasties out. The breeze is softer here than it was in the prairie above, and the wind soughs quietly through the grass, rippling the strands without quite disordering them. Several new buildings have been constructed, the centrepiece among them a recreation of the original store that stood at the west side of the fields, 150 metres from the main house, and close to the starting point of the Giscome Portage. I have my cameras with me, and I snap several photographs of the site so I'll have it right for next time, then walk down toward the river before looking through the buildings.

The Fraser River is a remarkable organism, milky brown, eddied, with the audible rumble I remarked on in 1993. In the distances it takes on the silver-grey of the overcast, with wisps of low cloud overhanging its banks. I sit down on a wooden bench to take it in, and am instantly assailed by three ravens. Each asserts its rights to something inside a fenced and covered duck pen that contains several scrawny domestic birds. The ravens think I'm a competitor. Whatever it is they're after—probably a small pile of food pellets meant for the ducks—they're not going to get it. But they natter away at me, and at one another, as if it were life and death.

The river is at or close to high water, and is higher than in 1993. The river seems to fill the countryside, and the tree-lined banks in the distance merge with its eddies. Where I am, the currents nibble at the banks less than a metre below the path that runs along its edge. Beaver have been around recently, too. They've chewed through a thick cottonwood, with only a small flat-top at the top of the cone where the Homestead staff must have chainsawed the fallen trunk for the river to drag away. Another tree, this one snapped by wind 3 metres up, hangs in the current, quivering. Out in the river more snags drift along, each one shifting, disap-pearing, resurfacing, and spinning about as the currents grab and release their remaining branches. There are fewer sawlogs in the river than a few years ago—signs of improved forestry practice—but they're evidently still making no attempt to salvage breakup wash-down. The pulp mills could process these trees, I suppose, but they don't seem interested in anything that doesn't arrive on a government approved–and-subsidized platter with a thank you note or a dire threat attached.

I shoo away the ravens, this time standing up and waving my arms at them, but they're not intimidated. I leave the ducks to them and walk along the riverbank path until it turns inland. This was the beginning of the pack trail that led past the store and onto the Portage. An ancient freight barge is decaying in the grass by the edge of the trail, too far gone to be restored. It's slightly more than 2 metres across the gunnels, 6 or 7 metres long, and though the timbers are grey and rotting, the galvanized sheeting on what seems to be a motor housing is still surprisingly clear of rust. It must have been sitting there for at least 75 years.

All around it, and along the path up to the store, the tall grasses are infested with a small-leafed plant with tiny racemes of deep blue florets. I pick several of the racemes and press them into my notebook with the fragrant sprig of wild rose I picked on the hillside on the way down. I'll check them later in the plant manual Barry picked up at Costco.

Four staff members in period costumes, two of them women and all in their early twenties, are slouched around the store when I enter. They look up expectantly: what am I doing here? I explain, in general terms, that I'm a writer working on a book about northern B.C., and could they, um, help me to identify a plant I just found? I pull the notebook from my camera bag, remove the tiny blue flowers, and place them carefully on a piece of white paper already on the counter. I push the paper toward one of the young women.

She looks startled. "Oh, geez, we've all just started a few days ago," she says. "I'm not from northern B.C., anyway, so I don't know this sort of stuff. The manager might."

"Sure," I say. "Is she around?"

"She's upstairs. I'll get her."

She clumps up a set of rough wooden stairs in a pair of heavy hiking boots that clash with her period costume.

While she's gone, I take in the store. The only false note is the window glass, which has panes far too large to be authentic. When the original store was built, everything came in by river barge, and glass in 1x2-metre sheets wouldn't have made it.

A dark-haired woman not much older than the others arrives in tow a moment later, the same plant manual Barry bought under her arm, and "time-wasting crazy tourists" written on her face. We sift through the manual together, and she gets interested despite herself. So do the others. Together we agree that my specimens have to be bird's-eye speedwell, locally rare but present. The manager is puzzled by how much of it is on the site, actually, and speculates that it might have been brought here deliberately as a decorative plant when the Portage and store were going concerns.

"I've tracked all over the area around here," she says, "but right here is where I've seen the most of it. It really didn't hit me until just now."

The others seem to take their cue from her, and warm up. They start asking me questions about what I'm here to write about, and what other places I'll be visiting. They don't listen to my answers, which are deflective, anyway. They've decided I'm some sort of eccentric botanist, and that's good enough.

I buy a framed drawing of the store for $18 and a half-dozen postcards, a buck each, and they warm up still more. I ask about the graphics of local plant species I'd seen here in 1993, but none of them recalls seeing them. One of the young guys offers to walk me over to the gatehouse when I go and see if they're up in the rafters.

I say my goodbyes to the others, thank them for their help, and the young man and I head over to the main house and the gate. I stop to take some photographs of the store, and as I'm snapping the photos, he gives me the short form of his life story. He's a History major at the University of Victoria, grew up on Vancouver Island, and is very interested in pioneer history in B.C.

"This should be a great job for that. A lot of the local history here is uncollected, or not archived."

He nods, less interested in that line of conversation than in showing me the summer kitchen at the main house. Would I like a tour before I go?

"I've seen it," I say. "Anything been added lately?"

He doesn't know. I don't burden him with my theory about the summer kitchen being set where it is to keep the trappers and Native Indians out of the house—and to preserve assets in case of a fire. Nice kid, but he still thinks the past was filled with dumb people, old-fashioned equipment, and not enough entertainment opportunities.

"It's interesting out here," he admits after we've searched the gatehouse unsuccessfully. "But Prince George is kind of strange."

"You'll get used to it," I tell him. "By the end of the season, you'll probably like it. It's a good place to be young and healthy."

On the way back to town, I slow down at the bottom of the hill on the east bank of the Salmon River, and pull onto the road that, in

1990, led down to the river. This time, the road peters out within a few metres, blocked by a massive tangle of uprooted trees, most of them cottonwood. The park that had been a litter-festooned dumping ground a decade ago has been obliterated by floods, probably the result of upstream logging, judging from the size and mass of the debris. Its only inhabitants now are ravens, because they're the only ones who can get to it.

Well, this was a place that needed a scouring, and got it. Even the shards of broken beer bottles that lined the river bottom will lose their capacity to injure swimmers as the river gravel wears away their sharp edges. That everything good I want to recall about this place has also been obliterated therefore doesn't quite constitute tragedy. Along with the free access went the garbage, washed downstream, and by now it's probably glitzing the bottom of the Fraser on its way to Vancouver. The better part of it is that there's now no way for the human barbarians to get to the river to deposit the next load of abuse and carelessness.

But wait. On the far bank, there is a blue panel truck with its rear doors open. A man in a blue jacket is standing behind it, gazing into the back. I sit down on one of the logs, pretend to fiddle with my camera, and watch him. He stands motionless for a moment, then turns and gazes across the river at me—until I look up, at which point he busies himself with some activity that's impossible to determine at this distance. It looks suspiciously like he's polishing turds, which is what you do when you're waiting for someone to bugger off so you can dump something you shouldn't, or take something that isn't yours.

The vandalism at Salmon River hasn't ended, apparently. It isn't just crazy teenagers doing their thing, either. It never was. Human stupidity is cultivated, not inherited.

41

The phone rings inside John and Viv's house while I'm renegotiating the alarm system. It makes for an interesting moment or two—if I get distracted and screw up the code, chances are I'll be arrested for trespassing. Since my hosts are farther away than the moon in modern communications terms and haven't left behind any notes that explain that I'm caretaking, getting myself out of it might be tricky. I steady myself, remembering that I've got 20 seconds to punch in the correct sequence, and, since John doesn't have a messaging device on the phone, as many rings of the phone as the caller's patience gives me. I take a breath, enter the code, walk the five steps to the phone, and pick up the receiver. It's Billy Walsh, reminding me that we're having dinner with Jack Butcher and his girlfriend tonight. He names the restaurant, gives me the directions, and we hang up.

The restaurant, named Moxie's, is the town's newest, an upscale franchise furnished in dark wood, earth-tone brocades, and ceramic tile. Within seconds, the decor disappears below my radar, except for an inescapable sense of its being ersatz plush, its rich mahogany photographed onto a veneer no more than a few millimetres thick.

"I'm looking for two elderly fat guys," I say to the waitress.

She grins at me. "Oh, right. You're the skinny Santa," she says, giving me a once-over that lets me know my skinniness is strictly relative. "They're right down there."

She points to a window booth where I see Jack waving at me. The Santa gag sounds like Jack's sense of humour, but Billy's loud laughter carries far enough to bring several more tables in on the joke. I slip into the spacious booth next to Billy, and he introduces me to Maxine, Jack's girlfriend. She's small, carefully groomed, and has a heavy Newfoundland accent.

It's a good thing the booth is spacious. Billy must be closing in on 280 pounds, and Jack, from the look of him, at least 250. I'm over 200 for the first time in my life. Yet as I look around me, I realize how lame my joke to the waitress at the door was. Asking for the fat guys could have gotten me to two-thirds of the booths in the restaurant.

We talk and we drink. I have a glass of red wine, Jack and Billy have a couple of pints of beer each. They've already been here for an hour, which means they've already put away at least two pints each. Moxie's isn't quite an old-style Surf & Turf franchise, but the dish is on the menu. Billy and I do turf—eight-ounce strip loins—while Jack and Maxine hit the surf—fat prawns on a bed of linguine. We easily snuff two bottles of Chilean red with our meal.

During dinner I find myself warming to Maxine, and not just because she's holding up her end of the drinking. She's the sort of plain-spoken woman who doesn't hide her opinions but doesn't think they're anything special, either. She also knows how to spin a decent story. Some of her anecdotes—and Jack's—reveal her as a woman with a temper, and God help its target when it fires. Nice to have her with us, because most of the other conversation is in code and it is illuminating to watch her translate. Billy is making oblique references every two or three sentences that suggest Jack has insulted him and ought to be making restitution, but he won't quite come out and say so. Jack's responses to this are just as cryptic. He denies the legitimacy of Billy's insult, but he doesn't do it openly enough to instigate a confrontation. There's a lot of water under the bridge with these two, but there's still lots upriver. Neither of them wants to lose a long and valued friendship.

The code between Jack and me is still more obscure. It's ancient, but no longer very serious. We use it to continue the same guarded conversation we've been having for nearly 40 years. When we were teenagers Jack hadn't much appreciated my flippant attitude or smart mouth, particularly when it involved matters of family. This led to a few painful lectures from him, along with a couple of fist fights that I quickly lost. Jack pushed me around, but I understood even then that his intentions were good. So it felt like parental disapproval, which meant I only had to be respectful in his presence. In my mid-twenties, I wrote a story about one of the fights—in which I'd landed a couple of solid rights that hadn't put Jack on his backside the way I'd expected. Jack read the story, laughed hard at it, and he and I haven't seen each other since without him mentioning it.

"How's the teeth doing?" he asks.

At first I think he's commiserating about being middle-aged and having grown up with Prince George's fluoridation-free water. Then I realize he's referring to the story, which early on features the line *"Jack owns my teeth."* That'd been my way of acknowledging that he could have punched them down my throat, but had let me go. He's still asking me to acknowledge that ownership here.

"They're fine," I answer. "What's left of them. How're yours?"

We talk about that for a while—dental woes, not fist fighting—and about my improved attitude. As the evening moves along I find myself refereeing between Billy and Jack—and once I cotton to how important it is to both of them, trying to patch the rift between them. The offence has been particularly painful to Billy, more than he let on at lunch a few days ago. Billy is like his father that way, not very quick to anger, but hard to talk down once an insult registers. I talk to them about the old days, using Don White as the lubricant between them, relating my worry that he'll stop talking at some point, I mean, to anyone, and noting how lucky he's been to have had his wife Georgina, whose ability—and will—to maintain old friendships is often the only adhesive to the past Don has. I talk elliptically, careful not to let them see I'm deliberately filling the gulf between them with talk about the importance of friendship and goodwill. Finally, after an hour or so, Billy begins to relax, giving his anger up to the sweetness that's more native to him. Maybe he'll forgive Jack for being who he is, and maybe not. For tonight, though, once he lets it go, it's gone.

And so the evening sweetens. The three of us chatter on about what it's like to be men in our fifties, not very candidly because Maxine is present, and, of course, we keep drinking. After dinner I switch to coffee and iced water, but they're back to beer and then on to Irish Coffee, and suddenly it's 10:00 p.m. and time to move on. I'd cheerfully pack it in, but they're not having any of that. "Moving on" turns out to be a trip in the front seat of Billy's pickup down to a bar 10 or 12 blocks away, where we continue to drink at roughly the same pace established at dinner: me less, them more. It isn't quite the way we used to drink, but they're closer to their old pace than I am to mine.

Nearly everybody who survives growing up in Prince George has developed a sixth sense about when the people around them are about to go off the rails. In the old days, I blew out the back door when that sensor kicked in, or, if I'd seen the potential mayhem far enough in advance, I found excuses not to show up in the first place. Tonight, while we're waiting for the bill to arrive, Jack and I rejig the storyline on one of those long-gone occasions. It involved my having stepped back from a late-night car trip to Quesnel with Jack and a mutual friend named Elroy Moe after the three of us found ourselves with a couple of cases of cold beer and the keys to someone else's near-new Mustang hardtop. I begged off; they went to Quesnel and flipped the Mustang six times just outside the Quesnel city limits. Elroy, who'd been driving, suffered a broken neck and spent more than a year in traction. Jack, in the passenger seat, fell out of the car after the first flip, but somehow walked away with no more than a few scratches. I'd have been in the back without a seat belt. . . .

"Yeah," Jack says, grinning at me as he comes to the same conclusion we've come to before, "I kind of don't think you'd be sitting here right now if you hadn't slipped out the back door on that caper."

"You were a smart boy that way," Billy says. "Not like me. You remember the time I went out with you guys and ended up with that shotgun stuck in my ear?"

It really isn't a question, because he knows we remember. It was the incident that'd convinced me Billy wouldn't survive to see 30. "That was White's fault," Jack says. "He had the bright idea to steal all the beer in the house."

"The only reason I wasn't where you were," I say to Billy, "was that Don ordered me to help him carry the beer."

"That's your story," Jack says. "More like you were probably hanging on his ass because you were too snooty to talk to anyone. Or were afraid someone would smack you if he wasn't there to protect you. But you're right about Billy always liking to yap too much for his own good."

"Probably true," Billy agrees. "That's why I ended up as a dirt salesman."

It's time to go. My head isn't spinning, but I'm over the legal limit and I'll have to concentrate if I'm to get the rental car safely back to John's place. Billy and Jack don't seem drunk, but some simple addition of the volume they've been putting away says otherwise.

As the four of us are crowding into the front seat of Billy's pickup, it comes to me that I'm in the situation I always managed to avoid when we were younger. My sixth sense, whatever it once did for me, hasn't protected me tonight. We're out of control in a beyond-the-warrantee pickup truck with a too-big motor, the drunkest among us is at the wheel, and I don't have the slightest clue about what'll happen next, except that this time, I'm in for the ride.

Billy gives me a hint about what's next when he jams the key into the ignition, cranks up the old V-8 loud enough that several people in the parking lot turn their heads, and starts on about what good shape the old baby is in and how fast she'll still go. We get out of the parking lot and onto the street without ramming anyone, but at the first intersection Billy pulls a left turn that has the truck's back wheels spewing gravel as it fishtails off and then back onto the pavement, and has Maxine gasping for breath as the G-forces push Billy's bulk against Jack's, and onto her.

Billy floors the pickup, hooting, the revs climb with a throaty roar, and I try to push my foot through the floorboards, remembering *exactly* why I never rode the distance with these guys. For a split second, I see the humour. I left Prince George because I didn't want to die this way, out of control in a stupid automobile, and now I'm going to die that way anyhow.

Then I recognize that it's more interesting than funny. Jack and Billy are risking their lives the way they did 35 years ago, and judging from how comfortable they are with the script, as they've done in the intervening years hundreds of times. They're risking their lives because, well, that's what you do if you stay where you start: you remain inside the continuum of normality you had when you were 18 or 20 years old. Here, they're taking the kind of risks that have been normal all their lives. Because I left, I haven't had to face those risks—when my hormones let up on me a little, I stopped taking them. It's been years since I've felt the urge to piss on a fire hydrant this way.

So, in the midst of my terror, I feel a wave of tenderness and awe for Billy and Jack. *What a hard life these men have had! And what courage they've wasted with these goofy games.* For a moment I feel cheated by my own good luck, but just for a moment. Then I wise up. I was too fragile to have survived their lives.

And while I'm thinking these thoughts, the moment is over. Billy brakes at a stop sign, and when he swings right the second time, there's no spewing gravel and no neck-snapping acceleration. There's just a rusty pickup truck with about 900 pounds of middle-aged meat squeezed together on the bench seat, close to 800 of it clinging to the achy bones of three men who didn't weigh half this much the last time they were in a pickup truck together. Billy's talking about sacking out on Jack's couch, sensibly not willing to drive the 80 kilometres home to the lake. I'm thankful the years have robbed him of his old stamina.

"I'd do it," he says, "but you know, I'd fall asleep and drive off the road. Life's too short to die that way."

So, I'm going to survive, then. All I have to do is get my own car home. And if Billy can make it to Jack's place in his condition, I can make it to John and Viv's. And I do.

42

Around 10:00 the next morning I meet Frank Peebles in a small coffee house on Fourth Avenue, decorated in deep blues and greens with blond wooden furniture, and smelling of coffee and cinnamon. It feels like Seattle, not northern B.C.

Frank isn't very Seattle. He's in his late twenties, tall, dark, and sharp-eyed. He tells me he was born in Burns Lake, which is about 200 kilometres west, then grew up on a cattle ranch at nearby—and beautiful—François Lake. I ask him if he's an ex-student of Barry's. He isn't, but wishes he was. He moved to Prince George after he finished university in Victoria, to work at the then-starting-up *Free Press*. That was in 1994.

"I'm one of the two originals left," he says proudly.

"What made you come back to this part of the country?"

"I wanted to work as a journalist. No one else wanted to come here, so I did."

He's glad he came back, and sees the *Free Press*—and himself with it—as an important part of the non-corporate community in Prince George. He tells me his paper, with its twice-weekly publication, has become the true local paper, the one people go to if they want to know what's going on in their community. He's probably right about this. At very least, the *Free Press* is the reason for the still larger-circulation *Citizen*'s improved local coverage in the past five years.

"What can you tell me about how Prince George is doing, generally."

He laughs. "It's at the bottom of a hole right now. It's as if all the forces that make up the world economy have converged here to screw us, because we're too dependent on the forest industry. First off, lumber happens to be the industry the Americans are using to rattle a bunch of other resource concessions out of the federal government, so they're slamming us with excise taxes and quotas, claiming that our forestry stumpage rates give us an unfair advantage. Then the environmentalists from Europe decided it was easier to attack us than the Brazilians for irresponsible forestry practices, so they're pressuring their governments not to buy our products. And then there are all the corporations eating each other, so you can't tell who's responsible for what or who's really running things. In the middle of that, the provincial government starts cheating on the Forest Renewal Plans, and using the north as its cash cow."

"And your local politicians aren't helping."

"It's too big for them. Nobody can even get the attention of the big players in this game, let alone talk them into acting fairly. But, you know, things will get better, mainly because they can't get worse. We've got the beginnings of a serious tourism industry here, and if there's a concerted effort, this could be a major money-maker in, say, the next five years. And now, finally, people are getting serious about secondary manufacturing."

"I thought the only success Prince George has had with that is John Brink's finger-joint mill."

Oh, that's just reman," Frank answers.

"What's 'reman'?"

"Remanufacturing. Brink trades his allowable cut for Canfor's bad spaghetti, so the net gain is really pretty minimal, particularly when it comes to jobs. I'm talking about actual manufacturing, more labour-intensive stuff."

I tell him, truthfully, that I don't quite understand the distinction.

"See that chair you're sitting on. That table? Why would that come from anywhere else?"

"Because there's no hardwood around here?"

"Sure there is. Birch. It's a fine wood. Until recently it was treated like junk. And there's lots of other things that can be done with softwood."

We wrangle this one for a few minutes but don't get anywhere. I begin to see that Frank's optimism is based more on the lack of alternatives—that is, things can't get any worse—and in his faith in the fundamental resourcefulness of people than on anything substantial.

"If Prince George doesn't develop some secondary industries, it's going to die," he says. "Or be an insignificant little town forever." The way he says it tells me he thinks the latter fate might be worse.

I move on to some questions about downtown renewal.

"That'll go ahead," he says. "Part of it, anyway. They'll take down the stupid canopies, redo the sidewalks, help the landlords clean up the storefronts. But we need some reason for people to be down here, and that costs money and involves risk. The private sector won't do it. Government has to."

"What about the idea of bringing some of the big-box stores downtown?"

"The big-boxes don't want to be squeezed into some corner of the downtown, so they won't come. I don't think that's right, anyway. They're better up out on the highways. We need some major public facilities, like a casino, or a new baseball stadium. The point is that the City has to stop moving public facilities out to the middle of nowhere like it's done for the last 35 years, and start moving them back in."

I leave the casino issue alone because something tells me Frank won't want to defend it very vigorously. "Where would they put a baseball stadium?"

"Well, not 30 kilometres out of town, like they're talking about at the moment. Why not a really good one, down at the end of the Queensway Industrial Park, say."

I mention that there was one down there until 1949 or so, and that it was torn down for the Malkins warehouse on First Avenue. "It was a beautiful place, with an all-wood grandstand and wooden fences in the outfield. I think the grandstand held about 1,000 people."

"I wish I could have seen that," he says. "I wonder if there are pictures of it in Wally West's archive? There used to a lot of great things here—the ski-jump behind City Hall, and the other one out on Cranbrook Hill."

"They had access to a lot of cheap wood in those days," I say.

Frank ignores my half-baked joke. "What bothers me," he says, "is that they're all gone now because the City kept shuffling everything like that out of town. Now, why would anybody want to be down here after 7:00 p.m. unless they're dead drunk or broke?"

"Do you think housing should be built downtown?"

Frank thinks so, but he's skeptical about how to do it, saying that it would need to be the sort of quality apartments that professional people would want to live in.

"Not the three-storey walk-ups we've got. The old money's on the North Nechako, what's left of it, but the new professionals want to be downtown like in any other city. I think old people would want to live down here, too, if there was the right kind of housing for them. But it needs better lighting, better policing."

"What about the street people, and all the violence?"

"There's definitely got to be better policing. That's already on the way. And the Native peoples need their treaties settled, so they can start to take care of their own."

Frank is in favour of settling the local Native land claims, and he thinks it ought to be done generously.

"The one thing we can be certain about is that the Native bands aren't going to be investing in the Peruvian rain forest or flying off to live in Hawaii. They're going to keep their money local, which is something no one else has ever done."

I ask him about the effect of having one corporation running the forest industry here.

"It's just the way things are." He shrugs. "And to tell the truth, I don't think it'll be any worse than it was before. We're kind of lucky, actually. If we're going to be a one-industry town, we're probably better off under Peter Bentley's thumb. Canfor's an evil empire, sure, and it doesn't take its stewardship of the forests seriously enough because its shareholders come first. But Canfor isn't as bad as the gas companies and a lot of others. If they'd set aside a percentage of the annual allowable cut for secondary manufacturing, we'd be fine, and it may be easier to get Canfor to do it than six or seven squabbling foreign-owned corporations."

He looks doubtful about the last remark, but I suspect a few of the things he's said have made him uncomfortable. It's as if I'm making him listen to a lot of contradictory ideas that have accumulated over a few years of working in an environment where contradictions are the everyday fare. He can sense the water getting deeper and more murky, and we're on the record. It's time to let him off the hook.

I have just one more question, anyway: "Do you think that the Northern Hardware will survive Wal-Mart?"

"That's one I really worry about," Frank admits. "They're an institution, and I'm a sucker for institutions. I mean, Harold Moffat's responsible for most of what's wrong with downtown, if you look at it carefully. I still have respect for Moffat going to work every day, but he made a mess of this town."

When I ask why he thinks that happened, I get a self-doubting frown.

"It's hard to say. Lack of education, I guess. Those old guys were just as wrong 30 years ago as they are now. And it'll cost $70 million to really make things right here again. In a way, we're lucky they've lost most of their power. Sometimes"—here he takes a moment to consider what he wants—or ought—to say—"I just don't know. It's like the will to say 'I'm responsible for myself' has disappeared around here. I guess it's because the world just seems too big not to give in to. I mean, *I* feel that way sometimes. It's like an 800-pound gorilla is sitting right on top of Prince George, and it doesn't seem interested in getting off. So it's hard."

We talk for another half-hour, and it's payback time: he's interviewing me for the *Free Press* before I realize it. I don't really want to talk about what I'm writing, or the way I'm going about it, but I'm tired, and my curiosity is more or less spent. Still, I leave the coffee house feeling cheerful. Frank is the kind of civic-minded guy Prince

George needs. And from what he's said, there are more like him around than I thought.

In the afternoon, I sit down with Barry on his porch and ask the same questions I put to Frank. Our companions throughout the taping are a half-dozen noisy crows and some starlings. The crows are high in the elm branches, shouting at one another over some piece of carrion they've discovered—or an unattended nest of young starlings.

I start at the beginning: "What do you think is going to happen in the next five years?"

Barry seems puzzled by the question. "To me?" he asks. "I'm heading out, I think. It isn't that I want to retire. But I'd like to be somewhere where I get out as much as I put in, and that isn't happening here any more. I guess I'm tired. I joke about wanting to live part of the year in Tumbler Ridge and the other in New York City, but I'm serious. That way I'd have the good things about the north, and the rest of the time I'd be in the culture of a great city."

"Why have you given up on Prince George?"

"I haven't," he says, and pauses to think that over. "I think the town has given up. There was a lot of fun to this place when I first got here. You'd go downtown, do your shopping, maybe stop for a beer about 4 p.m. with a bunch of people you knew. Everybody knew I was different, but that didn't matter. I used to go down there and put up posters for poetry readings, and nobody bothered me.

"Now it feels dirty and threatening. A couple of days ago I was downtown, and two Native guys—they were drunk or drugged on I-don't-know-what—were walking behind me, talking about how they were going to mug me. I ducked into a hotel because I could see they were serious, and if they'd gone after me, no one would have done a damned thing to stop them.

"I didn't feel like I was part of the town when I first moved here, but I tried to create a habitat—'cultural work,' I called it—to make it more livable. That seemed like a worthwhile thing to do. But I got into more and more trouble for it, and now I feel like I could slip out the side door and no one but a few people would know or care. That's demoralizing. I guess I feel like I've paid my dues, and I'm just fading away because nobody here gives a shit about cultural work unless it's good for tourism.

"So, I'm more pessimistic than I used to be. If you live here you need to be both negative and positive at the same time. If you're not negative, you don't spot the crap coming at you until it's too late, and if you're not optimistic, you miss all the good things about living here. In a way, the town, which for me really means the downtown, hasn't changed physically since I got here 30 years ago. But back then, we could do everything down there, shop, hang out. The buildings are more run-down now, some of the same street people and businesses are still there. What's gone is the sense of it being a frontier you can make something out of. The only time I go downtown now is to look for books in the thrift stores, or maybe to get something at the Northern Hardware.

"About the lumber industry—and I don't know anything about this—but the more I think about it, I can't see why we've never developed secondary industry. We can't manufacture spaghetti forever. But every time someone tries something else, it turns to shit, like with the chopstick factory, or the Silicon Valley North nonsense. The shysters got all the money, and they took it and ran. Failure has come to be expected, and there's a cynicism here there never was before.

"There's a line from the American poet Charles Olson, about how people don't change, they only stand more revealed. I think that's true for cities like Prince George. This is still a transportation and service hub, but the cynicism has made it feel like it's nothing more than an auction hub for worn-out machinery. And I guess it's harder to have a sense of community when all the shops are franchises you can find anywhere, and the employees are minimum-wage kids and the profits go to Vancouver or Toronto or Christ-knows-where-else."

Barry sighs. One of the crows flits down from the elms to perch on the fence, still shrieking, but now at us. From its point of view, *we're* the problem. Maybe he's been appointed by the others to drive us away.

I wave my arms at the crow, and change the subject slightly. "What sorts of positive changes have you seen lately?" I ask. "Or, better, what are the positive influences on the town?"

Barry brightens at this, at least for a moment. "Well, there's education," he says. "The college is a good influence, on balance, and so is the university. But you know, I've had about 6,000 students come through my classes, and for most of them education was a ticket out. I mean, when the economy goes down, people here go back to school. But not to make their lives better. They do it so they can get out.

"So about the future, I don't know. Everybody wants another mega-project or a cataclysm to create changes, but I don't see any cataclysms coming, and the mega-projects never work. So things just seem to get worse, gradually, because the town has lost that ability to do anything for itself.

"I think some people still come here with a lot of idealism, particularly the professionals, because you don't come here to do that kind of work unless you have an urge to make things better. But it gets kicked out of them. I'm disappointed that so many professionals— biologists, chemists, college teachers, and so on—come up here and then ultimately don't do a thing to make things better. Their idealism wears out pretty quickly and they hunker down and build things they can sell-out with and go elsewhere. I mean, you're always stepping in dogshit around here, and I guess it breaks people more quickly than it used to."

"What about the Native peoples?"

"Well, there's two Native cultures now. There's a whole new generation of well-educated Native people, who're confident and aggressive about their rights, and they're grabbing every opportunity the system gives them. That's great. But a high percentage of the street people are also Native, and a lot of them are like those two guys who were talking about mugging me the other day. Those people are more confident too, but confidence without education just means violence. They've got better self-esteem, and that gives them the sort of freedom to act along with the educated ones. So it's like everything. Some things get better, but somehow they get worse at the same time."

Barry looks away from me out into the street, frowning. I ask him if he wants to say anything else. He doesn't.

As we sit, a starling dive-bombs the crow that's been yammering away at us, and the crow gives up his perch and flies off. A moment later the other crows lift off, and as soon as quiet reigns on the street, from somewhere in the elms, we hear the sweet carolling of robins. But, of course, they're not robins at all. They're the starlings, happy that they've driven off the crows.

"Words fail me," Barry says, breaking in. There's a slightly surprising bitterness in his voice, and he turns away from me and gets to his feet. But a split second later, I hear him chuckling. "Shut the stupid tape recorder off," he says. As he turns back toward me, a grin is spreading across his face. "This is hopeless."

The moment he says it, I recognize that I'm done. This is it: the way things are. Or, as close as I can get. About the business of cutting down trees, I have a less-clear idea of what should be done in the forests than when I began this book 11 years ago. People *are* going to cut down trees in the northern boreal forest, and for the time being, clearcutting seems like the best way of doing it. But they've got to do a better job of cleaning up afterward, and they're still not doing either the cut or the cleanup as if they believe there's going to be a future. It's precisely over this point that I've changed my mind, and not just about forestry. I've always wanted the future to resemble the past. That's foolish, because it never does. What's coming to these forests is inherently unpredictable, and only a fool would try to predict what it will be.

Prince George is slightly different. I can't foresee its future because the same rule applies, but I can see what is here today. Life in the north isn't going to end, but in the next few decades it is sure as hell going to get harder and uglier. When people get around to looking for someone and something to blame, the forestry corporations will either be gone, or will have changed names and share structure so many times that no one will recognize them as the culprits. This doesn't mean we should stop cutting down trees. That's as crazy as the belief inside the forestry industry that it is possible to keep raising the harvest levels forever. There are no simple answers here. That's the way things are.

As Barry and Frank Peebles both said, there's got to be some public will to make things better, and it isn't there. Part of turning things around might be to get citizens to recognize that big corporations like Wal-Mart aren't going to act in the interests of the people of northern B.C. any more than Canfor will. Corporations are designed to make profits for their shareholders. That isn't negotiable. But there has to be a stronger local will than is here today if the corporations are to be given a rule book that makes them return equivalent value for what they're taking.

I don't believe, in other words, that Bill Gates is going to save Prince George. Tourism isn't going to save it either. It's a long way north here, and tourists aren't going to want to come for knocked-down forests, polluted rivers and lakes, and the lower echelon of consumer franchises they can find at home. And they're not going to come for the weather.

Prince George in the year 2001 is in deep trouble, like hundreds—or thousands—of other hinterland communities across North America. Maybe Frank Peebles has it right when he says that the town is at the bottom of a cycle, and things will get better. But maybe he's not right, and things will keep on deteriorating. Sure, the town is at or near the bottom of a boom–bust cycle that has always been more extreme in the forest industry than in most other resource-based economies. And it's true that the town is being screwed in a special way by all the wealth-sucking forces of globalization. But, finally, what's killing the place isn't any single one of those things. The true poison is the town's inability to recognize and protect its own interests.

The clearcut I originally came back here to write about is healing. It is no longer visible from outer space, even though no one out there has confirmed this one way or another. The astronauts are too busy flying commercial missions or making public relations appearances in classrooms and shopping malls to care about a bunch of skinny spruce and pine trees in a valley where no one has any reason to go until the next generation of trees is ready for cutting. So as the trees grow larger, the story, for me, gets smaller, more specific, and less personal. It is about where people go, where people stay, and how they succeed or don't. And beneath their feet is the question of what it might mean to stand one's ground in the here and now.

On the day I leave, the news from the new premier's press conference is settling in: another big salvage cut is coming, this time to the west, around Ootsa Lake. The premier announces that a political panel (a pale-yellow ribbon panel, so to speak) is being appointed to come up with a politically palatable announcement of the cut. Most of the local officials are already giddy about it. They're already talking about views from outer space—LandSat photos have recognized the dead and dying trees the corporations will be sent in to "salvage." The mayor of Vanderhoof, a small town 100 kilometres west of Prince

George, is the only politician who doesn't instantly lose his mind at the news. This time, he says, we need to find some way to ensure that the local communities get some value for the trees that are taken out.

Nobody listens.

One more thing. A few months after the rainy morning when I left Prince George, I received an e-mail from Kent Sedgwick.

"You may not believe this," he wrote, "but I think I know how the Millar Addition got its elm trees. Planting was started on Elm Street sometime in the early 1960s after a $300 donation from a couple who lived on the street. After that, the City just kept on planting them. My aerial photos confirm this. In the 1959 photos, the area is virtually treeless. In 1963, there are definitely some trees along the streets. Now, you can't see the streets at all."